Atrocity Without Punishment

The Cultural Lives of Law
Edited by Austin Sarat

Atrocity Without Punishment

A Political Theory of Leniency in Mexico's War on Drugs

Juan Espíndola

Stanford University Press

Stanford, California

Stanford University Press
Stanford, California

Library of Congress Cataloging-in-Publication Data
Names: Espíndola Mata, Juan, author.
Title: Atrocity without punishment : a political theory of leniency in Mexico's war on drugs / Juan Espíndola.
Other titles: Cultural lives of law.
Description: Stanford, California : Stanford University Press, 2026. | Series: The cultural lives of law | Includes bibliographical references and index.
Identifiers: LCCN 2025027511 (print) | LCCN 2025027512 (ebook) | ISBN 9781503644281 (cloth) | ISBN 9781503644922 (paperback) | ISBN 9781503644939 (ebook)
Subjects: LCSH: Punishment—Mexico. | Punishment—Moral and ethical aspects—Mexico. | Drugs—Law and legislation—Mexico. | Drug control—Mexico. | Drug traffic—Government policy—Mexico. | Criminal justice, Administration of—Mexico.
Classification: LCC KGF5467 .E87 2026 (print) | LCC KGF5467 (ebook) | DDC 364.60972—dcundefined
LC record available at https://lccn.loc.gov/2025027511
LC ebook record available at https://lccn.loc.gov/2025027512

Cover design: Daniel Benneworth-Gray
Cover art: Cottonbro Studio

The authorized representative in the EU for product safety and compliance is: Mare Nostrum Group B.V. | Mauritskade 21D | 1091 GC Amsterdam | The Netherlands | Email address: gpsr@mare-nostrum.co.uk | KVK chamber of commerce number: 96249943

Contents

INTRODUCTION In Defense of Principled Leniency   1

ONE Bargaining with Criminals   17
Trading Penal Benefits for Forensic Truth

TWO The Limits of Penal Benefits   47
On the Use and Abuse of Collaborators

THREE Punishment without Legitimacy   67
Exploitation, Domination, and Communication

FOUR Punishing "Crimes of Infirmity"   97

FIVE Forgetting the Forgotten?   133
When the State Shows (or Feigns) Compassion

CONCLUSION Morality and Leniency in Times of Atrocity   153
A Fool's Errand?

Acknowledgments   159
Notes   161
References   181
Index   203

Atrocity Without Punishment

In Defense of Principled Leniency

Uncaging a Hawk?

This book makes a case for the lenient treatment of perpetrators of "drug crimes"—offenses loosely connected to the often-atrocious actions of organizations that produce, transport, and sell drugs in Mexico. The example of *halcones* (hawks), who are embedded in this criminal ecosystem, serves as an entry point into the book's core ideas. In essence, *halcones* are lookouts and informants.[1] Criminal organizations need both a well-defined territory—over which they exercise a monopoly of resource extraction—and a "filter" to distinguish between insiders and outsiders. This in turn requires permanent surveillance, which *halcones* provide. They are tasked with monitoring the circulation of people and vehicles within a given organization's "territory," and with reporting the presence of state security forces or any other suspicious events. Collectively, *halcones* form a powerful system of human surveillance. As Natalia Mendoza observes in Sonora, the territorial control of criminal organizations would not be possible without the combination of flexibility, discretion, and precision of this surveillance mechanism. *Halcones*, Mendoza concludes, "carry out everyday work of social recognition."[2] Their harm—even lethal—must not be downplayed. Despite their seemingly peripheral position, *halcones* function as vital cogs in the machinery of atrocity: their surveillance enables extortion, obstructs justice, and strengthens these organizations' stranglehold on communities.

The state's response to *halconeo* has been unequivocally punitive. A recent proposal sought to make *halconeo* a federal crime for which offenders could receive a sentence of up to twelve years in prison. Local penal codes in more than twenty states can be even harsher, imposing penalties of up to fifteen years in prison. As an example, the Penal Code of Tamaulipas, a northern state of Mexico, declares that,

> a sanction of seven to fifteen years in prison and a fine . . . will be imposed on those who stalk, monitor, alert, report or carry out espionage, on activities, operations, location or, in general, with respect to the work carried out by the elements of the armed forces, or public security institutions or the prosecution and punishment of crime. . . . The penalties referred to in the preceding paragraph shall be increased by one-half more when: a) The crime is committed by public servants or former public servants of the armed forces, public security and criminal prosecution institutions, in which case dismissal from office or commission and disqualification from holding another for up to ten years will also be imposed; or b) Children, adolescents or those who lack the capacity to understand the meaning of the act are used to commit the crime.[3]

Regardless of whether local authorities enforce this provision, there remains the key question whether such punitive laws are themselves ethically acceptable. This book suggests they may not be. Rather than imposing criminal punishment, there are good *ethical* reasons for extending leniency to *halcones*.

For one, this excessively punitive response overlooks the fact that many *halcones* have diminished moral responsibility for their actions. Adverse socioeconomic backgrounds might make becoming an informant a legitimate response to the lack of other job opportunities. If we assume that *halcones* perform their roles as a means of subsistence, and if we interpret *halconeo*—somewhat benignly—as a malum prohibitum crime (wrong simply because it is prohibited, not because it is malum in se, wrong in itself, as murder or kidnapping would be), then *halcones* may not bear full moral culpability for their work.[4] Admittedly, not all *halcones* are in a dire situation that leaves them no other choice, but many are. Even if lacking reasons to cooperate, *halcones* have no choice but to partake in this activity. In the most extreme cases, they might be directly forced to become informants, as in the case of the forcible recruitment of immigrants from Central America.[5] It is also quite common for *halcones* to be recruited under duress in contexts of state complicity with criminal organizations. In such cases, in which the allegiances of public officials are unclear, the consequences of *not* cooperating with criminal organizations might be fatal. Public officials might themselves become *halcones*, whether for economic gain or, in most cases, out of well-founded fear of criminal organizations, whose power may outmatch that of the state. In addition to these attenuating circumstances, it is unclear that *halcones* condone the goals and methods of the criminal organizations wreaking havoc on the country. For *halcones*, the scale of their contribution to wrongdoing may also be hard to grasp (do they buttress the social domination of these organizations, making it more oppressive? Do they instead contribute to making such domination more tolerable by allowing organizations to "administer" violence less indiscriminately?).[6] For all these reasons, *halcones* may have diminished moral responsibility.

As informants, *halcones* traffic in the raw material that is information, and collecting it is the crux of their work. In times of atrocity, such information is critical for authorities, who need intelligence to combat exceptionally well-resourced criminal organizations. Most importantly, this information is also critical for victims who, in the context of widespread disappearances, may desperately seek to discover the whereabouts of their relatives. Under these circumstances, it may be reasonable for authorities to extend lenient treatment to *halcones* on the condition that they share some of this information.

Suppose that we prosecute and incarcerate *halcones*. By belonging to the lower strata of criminal organizations, they will likely have very few financial resources available and no alternative lifeline if they are cast out or abandoned by the organization. If they are incarcerated in a state-level penitentiary, where exploitation and domination run rampant, they will experience what can be described as cruel and unusual punishment, even if granted the lightest possible sentence for *halconeo*. If they happen to encounter members of a rival organization while incarcerated, their very lives will be on the line.

More basically, we might argue that the state must not punish *halcones* too rigorously because, by virtue of the conditions of exclusion or discrimination many of them have experienced, they deserve compassionate treatment instead.

All these considerations raise the question whether *principled* leniency—or punishment that is mitigated for the right reasons—is a more appropriate response than harsh punishment. Once again, there is no indication at present that most *halcones* are, in fact, prosecuted, let alone imprisoned. This, however, is not because the criminal justice system deliberately refrains from doing so for ethical reasons. Rather, it lacks the means to enforce the prohibition. This is not principled but rather *arbitrary* leniency—the reflection of a broken and ineffective criminal justice system. By contrast, this book seeks to show that, even in times of atrocity, withholding punishment may be the right thing to do. Rejecting abstract normative frameworks, here I construct a political theory of punishment situated in the Mexican context of state fragility, corruption, and widespread structural violence. It is in this context that I argue for leniency, for practical and especially for *ethical* reasons.

Principled Leniency and the "War on Drugs"

The more extraordinary and widespread crime is in a given society, the more urgent the perceived need to severely punish criminal offenders. This powerful perception is often countered by the argument that punitive strategies are ineffective at combating crime. But what if it is not just their effectiveness that should be questioned, but also, and more importantly, their morality? Focusing on the recent spate of drug-related violence in Mexico, this book advances a counterintuitive proposal: the need for leniency. Leniency is necessary as a practical response to the crisis of mass murder and incarceration and as a way to reconsider the ethical foundations of criminal justice. The Mexican case should not be seen as a deviant exception but rather as part of a broader global failure to address rising violence through current strategies. Leniency might sometimes be the ethical response to atrocity.

In the last two decades, drug trafficking and the state's counterreaction unleashed an endless cycle of violence in Mexico. The resulting human toll is catastrophic. The number of homicides now exceeds one hundred thousand. Disappearances, human trafficking, and internal displacement have also surged massively. One of the state's responses to this escalation of violence has been the harsher and more expansive use of the criminal justice system, especially incarceration, by broadening the definition of criminal offenses, imposing more severe sentences, and even adopting measures that stand in tension with or openly violate due process. Mandatory pretrial detention of those accused of drug-related crimes is the most revealing example. In fact, a separate penal regime has been devised for members of "organized crime," one that strips large portions of the citizenry of their individual rights. The punitive turn has predominantly affected the least well-off. Meanwhile, those with economic or political power often escape prosecution, maintaining a legacy of impunity.

Mexico's criminal justice system is blatantly unjust. That has been clear for decades. This opinion is shared with criminal justice systems in other nations, particularly the United States, where mass incarceration creates egregious injustice for minorities. Angela Y. Davis has spent decades making this point, with philosophers like Thomas Shelby, Erin Kelly, and many others building on her ideas. In Mexico, many assume a clear path forward: systemic overhaul to protect the innocent, along with greater legal accountability and dissuasion in an environment that has radically cheapened the cost of deadly crimes. This book takes no issue with this rather uncontroversial claim. It both unpacks and further elaborates on the implications of this assumed diagnosis. And yet, egregious though they are, the imprisonment of the innocent and the impunity of the guilty are not the book's main focus. Instead, its main interest is in offenders whose criminal culpability is beyond doubt: those who did commit a criminal offense and are therefore thought to deserve the sanction stipulated in the penal code. Along with the *halcones*, mules and *sicarios* (hitmen) are prime examples of such individuals. The book does not seek to be another examination of a criminal system widely known to be dysfunctional. Rather, it seeks to provoke deeper questioning of that system's ethical underpinnings and of its social and political side effects.

The book advances what I call *principled leniency*: the idea that there are nonarbitrary reasons for imposing lenient legal punishment on certain perpetrators (from reducing sanctions to eliminating them altogether), and that this is in fact a morally permissible, even obligatory, way to hold perpetrators accountable. I argue that, given the characteristics of the political and criminal justice systems, prevailing background injustice in Mexican society, and the massive scale of the violence unfolding across large regions of the territory, punishing many criminal offenders *leniently* is the morally correct thing to do. While conceding that some perpetrators have committed serious offenses for which they must be punished, the book nonetheless puts forward powerful moral reasons for imposing lenient sentences or, in some cases, refraining from punishing them altogether.

The book, then, engages with some ethical reasons that justify leniency. These reasons—at the heart of political and legal theory—range from mitigating excuses and appeals to compassion, to considerations related to the state's lack of legitimacy to impose punishment as well as to the benefits of "bargaining" with members of criminal organizations to exchange penal benefits for their cooperation in criminal investigations. Thus, the book problematizes the relationship between punishment and core political values such as legitimacy and justice. Moreover, the book shows that in the political and social environment prevailing in Mexico, those confronting violence and its detrimental consequences must grapple with and ultimately accept moral compromises that contradict the ethical principles holding in ordinary circumstances.

At this point, readers familiar with the landscape of the criminal justice system in Mexico might object to the idea of lenient punishment. They might claim that, given the system's high impunity rates, a book advocating for leniency is untimely, ill-conceived, and even reprehensible. A response to these concerns is implied or developed at greater length in the coming chapters, but it is worth taking stock of them in a concise manner from the outset.

Consider first the following objection: why worry about or articulate a case for principled leniency when the overriding concern must be the criminal justice system's tendency to cast an overly expansive net that ensnares the innocent? This is not a problem that can be resolved through leniency, the objection would continue, and focusing on it circumvents the more radical and urgent need to overhaul or even abolish that system. Several responses can be offered to address this criticism. Even if the problem of false positives (that is, innocent citizens are incarcerated) were to be solved, the question remains of how the guilty ought to be treated, which is a central concern of this book. Moreover, advocating for leniency does not conflict with—and in fact necessitates—a profound systemic reform. While prison abolitionists may dismiss leniency as a timid half measure, given their stance that incarceration inherently fails to reduce crime and disproportionately targets marginalized groups, abolitionism itself remains a contested and divisive position. Principled leniency, by contrast, offers a middle path between abolitionist demands and the status quo.

A more critical objection to this project is that since overall rates of impunity for crimes, including homicide and forced disappearance, are staggeringly high—consistently above or around 90%—entertaining the idea of principled leniency is out of touch with the reality of violence in Mexico and is deeply insensitive to its human toll. If anything, we need more, not less punishment. Surely, so the objection would go, we need a reform to the criminal justice system, but in the current circumstances leniency can only aggravate impunity and violence more generally.

There are several ways to respond to this unease. First, we should take due note of the fact that the most reprehensible aspect of impunity in Mexico is not its sheer volume, although that is of course a problem, but that those who most benefit from it tend to be powerful perpetrators who leverage their economic and political resources or simply brute force to avoid prosecution. Impunity rates could be brought down—to less than 60%, imagine—but if these resourceful wrongdoers (who oftentimes commit the most egregious offenses) remain among those who go unprosecuted and unpunished, the problem in its most fundamental aspect would be left uncorrected. The point of developing a case for principled leniency is precisely to discern between the cases where impunity must not be tolerated and those where it might.

Second, while certainly impunity rates in Mexico are inexcusably high, addressing the problem requires better, not more, punishment. Exploring all the ways in which the criminal justice system can be improved is of course beyond the scope of this book. However, part of the strategy for improvement, given the budgetary and other kinds of constraints (for example, legal, of staff and expertise), rests *not* on pursuing *all* perpetrators, but only those who most deserve it or whose prosecution and imprisonment would yield the best results in terms of deterrence, to allude to the two classic justifications of punishment, briefly discussed in chapter 3. Thus, confronting impunity to some extent requires, rather than being opposed to, principled leniency.

Third, any plausible defense of penal institutions and practices rests on the assumption that they perform as intended, at least generally. But numerous analyses have made it abundantly clear that in Mexico a chasm exists between the aims and the effects of punishment. While the existence of this chasm does not necessarily mean that we should get rid of punishment—it is sometimes better to maintain a dysfunctional institution than to have none—it means that its imposition must be conditional on circumstances. According to this logic, for punishment to be appropriate it is not enough to establish that an offender has committed a crime warranting a sanction stipulated in the penal code. There might be good reasons, given the dysfunctionality just alluded to, to refrain from meting out the full force of punishment. Thus, a case-by-case analysis is needed to show that punishment is indeed adequate. This kind of reflection is consistent with the notion of principled leniency.

Finally, we can turn the impunity objection on its head. Since impunity is already widespread and curbing it seems implausible for the time being, why not use it productively? That is, why not reflect on those circumstances in which it might be more advisable—and ethical—to forgo punishment, if we thereby serve a higher purpose. This is in fact the gist of chapter 1. Such rationale is compatible with continuing to reform the criminal justice system, including its investigative capacities, so that someday thinking of leniency does indeed turn out to be objectionable more generally.

Book Overview

Chapter 1 provides the book's first justification for principled leniency: "negotiating" the severity of perpetrators' criminal sentences can encourage them to disclose valuable information, leading to more effective law enforcement and to clarity as to the whereabouts of victims who have been forcibly disappeared. The chapter notes that this course of action presents a trade-off or dilemma. A choice must be made between fulfilling the ends of criminal justice and those of what I shall call forensic truth. When proposing the "bargain," authorities mete out a less severe punishment to perpetrators than would otherwise be their due. Such bargaining is even more controversial as it happens in a nation with extraordinarily high levels of impunity—a phenomenon that is in part responsible for criminal violence in the first place. The main argument of the chapter is that authorities would be justified in following this course of action; obtaining information about victims' whereabouts outweighs whatever benefit, if any in the Mexican context, that might be gained from imprisoning perpetrators. Deterrence and the repudiation of crime are less valuable than helping relatives find disappeared loved ones. Crucially, information on loved ones' whereabouts can help them to overcome "ambiguous loss," the inability of grievers to mourn and receive proper closure in such contexts of uncertainty. The benefits of punitivism, if any, pale compared to these palpable gains.

Chapter 2 continues the discussion about perpetrators who collaborate with public authorities to examine the risks of turning the practice into a durable and widespread feature of the criminal justice system. While bargaining with wrongdoers and showing leniency in their sentencing can serve a just cause, we must resist generalizing the practice—as has occurred in the United States and other criminal justice systems with so-called plea bargains—because in Mexico such bargains might end up harming collaborators and, in some cases, the citizenry as well. In a constitutional democracy with low levels of corruption, strong security and justice institutions, and moderate level of socioeconomic deprivation, social and political conditions might be sufficient to protect perpetrators who collaborate with the criminal justice system, as well as to immunize the civilian population from any collateral damage arising from such collaboration. But extending such protections is more challenging in Mexico, by virtue of the persistence of authoritarian enclaves within formally democratic institutions, the corruption and lack of accountability of public officials, the weakness of security and public institutions, rampant violence, and the precarious socioeconomic conditions prevailing in many regions of the country. The failure to provide such protections is exemplified in the chapter by the reliance of Mexican authorities and the US Drug Enforcement Agency (DEA) on informants—a practice that often exploits collaborators and wreaks social havoc while failing to deliver justice. The chapter also examines the counterargument that authorities' more aggressive use of collaborators is justified—even if it puts collaborators' lives or safety at risk—because they enabled crime and should share its burden. The chapter's response to this argument is that putting wrongdoers in harm's way is an objectionable manner of confronting wrongdoing in all but exceptional cases. The chapter's analysis ultimately challenges the presumption that plea bargains can be safely normalized in fragile states.

Chapter 3 shifts gears from the benefits of attenuating or suspending punishment to the wrongs of *not* doing so. It argues that state punishment in Mexico must be lenient given the penitentiary system's inability to achieve its professed goals and its role in enabling the wrongful exploitation and domination of inmates at the hands of custodians or other inmates. Leniency, in other words, is a corrective to the objectionable wrongs of imprisonment. The chapter examines the two dominant justifications for punishment. First, for instrumental theories punishment is valuable insofar as it contributes to a further goal, usually crime deterrence, by incapacitating the perpetrators or by setting an example for other potential offenders. For retributive theories, by contrast, the most defensible argument is that punishment is intrinsically good because it imposes on offenders the treatment they deserve and expresses repudiation of their wrongdoing. Assuming for the sake of argument that these perceived values of instrumentalism and retributivism indeed hold elsewhere, the chapter shows that in Mexico they are severely compromised. The inability of prisons to control inmates or prison life in general calls into question the efficacy of prisons as crime deterrents. The state lacks *full* control of prisons and will be unable to regain it any time soon. The opposite is, in fact, true: prisons are criminogenic spaces rather than tools for disincentivizing crime. With respect to retributivism, the illegitimacy of the Mexican criminal justice system calls into question its standing to repudiate wrongdoing and its ability to communicate a *credible* message of repudiation. Putting aside their failure to achieve the ends of punishment, prisons in Mexico are also objectionable for placing the incarcerated in conditions ripe for exploitation and wrongful domination. To be sure, it might be countered that, while imprisoning offenders under conditions of indignity is definitely wrong, leaving them scot-free would be even worse, because it would place other members of society at risk. And yet such an argument must still reckon with the objection that imprisonment under such conditions turns the state into a wrongdoer, an unacceptable method for combating crime.

Chapter 4 elaborates on a classical, albeit still relevant and compelling thesis: some socioeconomic circumstances foster criminal behavior, and where such circumstances prevail, they lessen the moral culpability of wrongdoers. While the thesis is commonplace within political discourse and even academic debates in Mexico, it frequently lacks rigorous examination. The chapter addresses this deficit by drawing on legal and political theory, distilling a conceptual and normative framework tailored to engage with the intricacies of mitigated responsibility. The framework demarcates and delves into fundamental concepts such as excuses, justifications, duress, provocation, "rotten social backgrounds," and toxic cultural environments. Based on this framework, the chapter evaluates the conventional trajectories that lead countless individuals to partake in drug-trafficking-related violence. Coerced recruitment is the paradigmatic and least controversial case, but there are other subtler and more diffuse forms of influence, such as manipulative propaganda in contexts with weak social (that is, communal and familial) controls. While controversial and difficult to identify, such forms of manipulation, which include gendered social norms, are critical to recruitment. In recent times, such manipulative influences operate through novel and powerful channels of communication, such as social media. Consequently, the chapter briefly delves into the normalization of drug trafficking and its attendant violence on digital platforms, which have also served as conduits for recruitment in drug trafficking organizations.

Finally, chapter 5 examines another rationale for principled leniency: compassion for offenders. Compassion denotes the view that there is something about the life of the accused that should elicit an empathic response on the part of society, rendering rigorous punishment unjust. The chapter explores a particular instance—the 2020 amnesty—in which the Mexican state invoked compassion as a rationale for refraining from punishing drug offenders who belong to Indigenous groups on account of the legacy of discrimination they have endured. The chapter contends that while appearing to be, at first glance, a plausible case of principled leniency, the amnesty is in fact an example of *un*principled leniency, of feigned compassion. This is because several other policies enforced by the very same state that enacted the amnesty support or leave untouched practices that fly in the face of compassion. The amnesty is then a smokescreen that contributes to maintaining the punitive inertias of the state. In addition to developing this claim, the chapter briefly traces the historical shift in rationales for amnesties in Mexico, from the pragmatic approaches of the nineteenth century—when amnesties served as bargaining chips for public authorities to quell political unrest—to the twentieth century, where some amnesties begin to be framed as an alleged act of compassion toward offenders.

A Note on Method

This book engages in empirically oriented political theory. It harnesses the conceptual and normative tools of political theory, broadly conceived, to evaluate punishment and leniency in contemporary Mexico. In so doing, it advances a set of ethical claims about what is appropriate or objectionable, but it does so on the understanding that such prescriptions cannot be divorced from the empirical realities to which they belong. Many normative theories of punishment are premised on an idealized version of the institution of punishment or of the societies in which punishment is imposed.

A case like that of Mexico, and potentially others from the Global South, furnishes insights to call these theories into question.

Recent scholarship is increasingly interested in developing normative theory along the lines just described. For example, Lisa Herzog and Bernardo Zacka develop what they call an "ethnographic sensibility" in political theory. This is an approach to normative theorizing that starts with the assumption that the observer must be committed to interpreting social practices and meaning before she can offer any prescription for what actors ought to do.[7] Herzog and Zacka envision several tasks for political theory with an ethnographic sensibility. This brand of political theory need not conduct *original* ethnographic research, but it must be informed by secondary empirical sources and should help us understand the moral demands individuals encounter in their particular social contexts or roles (an epistemic task) as well as the obstacles they face while trying to address these demands (a diagnostic task). It should also help us understand the kinds of values individuals seek to honor in specific circumstances, whether these are values they ought to have (a valuational task), and whether these values can be advanced through the prevailing political and social practices and institutions (an evaluative task). Finally, an ethnographic sensibility can help us contest taken-for-granted social ontologies, that is, assumptions about human nature or the nature of specific social institutions (an ontological task).

This book undertakes all these tasks. On the epistemic and diagnostic fronts, it seeks to unveil the obstacles that offenders confront as they try to resist the pull of drug trafficking and criminal organizations. Are the obstacles such that they diminish the culpability of offenders for joining these groups? On the valuational front, some of the book's chapters try to understand how victims of violence prioritize different values when confronted with difficult choices. Are they willing to reject some of the criminal justice system's goals if they believe doing so could tangibly alleviate their pain? More specifically, are relatives or those close to victims of enforced disappearance prepared to accept, or even to demand, that the state refrain from punishing perpetrators in exchange for revealing the whereabouts of the disappeared? On the evaluative front, the analysis casts light on the ability of criminal justice institutions to navigate conflicting demands. Can these institutions adapt to this proposal—penal benefits—and other relatively innovative proposals and accrue the required expertise and resources to enforce them? If this is not the case, should they nonetheless carry them out imperfectly? In the ontological dimension, the book calls into question assumptions about what kind of institutions prisons are and the goals they pursue. Based on the reality of Mexican prisons—and not on what they ought to be—is it morally permissible to task them with punishing offenders? All these considerations must shape normative assessments of the merits of principled leniency.

While its main goal is to develop ethical arguments based on empirical secondary sources, the book also relies on examinations of primary sources: media (recent sources but also some that are several decades old), relevant legal frameworks, and some semistructured interviews with operatives of the criminal justice system in Mexico.

The book will be of interest to scholars interested in Mexico and Latin America, criminal justice, punishment, and "punitive populism," as well as empirically oriented political theory. It will also be of interest to nonacademic audiences, such as human rights practitioners, the general public, and especially students, since the book is written in a simple style and reviews essential philosophical and political debates relating to both punishment and Mexican history.

Some Caveats about Criminal Violence in Mexico

Academic and public discussions about the criminal violence now unfolding in Mexico are teeming with references to "cartels," "organized crime," or even "drug trafficking," as if these were transparent and uncontroversial categories. The overarching narrative attached to these categories is that criminal violence is the work of highly sophisticated organizations called cartels that, in their aggressive search to expand their markets and control more territory, produce most of the violence in the country. While this narrative and these categories capture some important truths, and while they may apply more to some organizations or regions than others, they oftentimes simplify the richness of social reality and even characterize it incorrectly.[8] For example, such terms obscure parallel social processes that contribute to criminal violence as well as the widespread participation of ordinary people, especially from the lower strata of society, in such violence. We should also be leery of labels that are often circulated with the hidden purpose of delineating an "enemy" against whom extreme measures appear to be justified.

In light of this simplification, and since throughout the text I will sometimes refer, for simplicity's sake, to "criminal organizations," "drug-trafficking violence," or to "drug crimes," let me make a few basic caveats about the challenges of conceptualizing the criminal violence associated with drug trafficking in Mexico.

To begin with, drug trafficking is a multifaceted phenomenon. Very basically, it involves the illicit *cultivation* of plant-based drugs, which occurs in rural areas far from urban centers, as well as the *production* of synthetic drugs, which occurs in both rural and urban areas. Then there are issues such as drug *dealing* and *consumption*, complex processes that overlap in different ways with cultivation and production. Criminal organizations are also involved in a wide range of other activities, from mining to gasoline theft, human and arms trafficking, extortion and street vending, that go beyond the commercialization of narcotics. Indeed, the wealth these organizations accrued in the 1990s served as a stepping stone to diversifying their activities, their power resting "on the armed privatization of public space, the ransom of public liberties, and the forcible appropriation of public goods."[9] Each of these processes and combinations produce a wide array of circumstances and actors.

There is no common root, or even a common time frame, to trace the origins of violence across the entire country. Consider the case of homicidal violence alone. The scholarly debate includes a few explanatory approaches, competing in some regards and complementary in others.[10] For some, the main engine of homicidal violence were the turf wars that began toward the end of Vicente Fox's administration (2000–2006). As the drug business became ever more profitable, criminal organizations resorted to violence to capture new markets and distribution routes. Government strategies during Felipe Calderón's (2006–12) administration, such as kingpin strategies and heavily militarized operations, attempted to curb trafficking, and while they had transitory victories, they also triggered a violent response from criminal organizations, upsetting fragile equilibria among them and displacing established organizations. This in turn generated a spate of disputes among organizations. In some cases, particularly with respect to kingpin strategies, decapitating criminal organizations brought competition over succession and interorganization violence in tandem. In parallel, the government adopted military warfare tactics against drug-related criminal organizations, which drastically increased the lethality of its interventions. Furthermore, in the wake of the transition to democracy, cooperation between local and central governments became increasingly fraught, as different parties controlled different levels of government. This was in contrast to the prior arrangement, where the reigning Partido Revolucionario Institucional (PRI) had a close grip on all levels of governance. This resulted in an inability or a reluctance to cooperate in law enforcement and security tasks.

There are also external forces: changes within international drug markets, such as shifting cocaine prices; the enforcement of US counternarcotic policies abroad (Plan Colombia), as a result of which criminal organizations relocated from Colombia or created new routes for trafficking; and even the lifting of the ban on the sale of assault weapons in the United States in 2004, which allowed criminal organizations to dramatically increase their weapons capacity. All these dynamics unfolded against a backdrop of security institutions on the brink of, or in, total collapse and, more generally, of weak statehood, which meant criminal rackets could "capture" institutions and officials in all branches of government. And then there was the socioeconomic backdrop of poverty, unemployment, and abandonment of schooling that created a reserve army to feed the lower ranks of criminal organizations.

To add further complexity to this explanatory framework, we should bear in mind that the manifestations of the constantly and rapidly evolving criminal violence that has engulfed the country in the last few decades are multiple. They include confrontation among members of criminal groups or between the army and criminal groups; carefully planned exterminations of alleged rivals within communities or even within prisons; abduction of migrants headed toward the United States; extrajudicial killings by the military; and political assassinations of journalists and public officials, including police personnel, customs officers, and so on. Some forms of violence were more prevalent two decades ago than they are today, and others have seen an unprecedented increase in just the last five years (for example, political assassinations). These are only instances of homicidal violence. Ever evolving instances of disappearance and forced internal displacement supplement this catalog of internecine violence.

The landscape of violence in Mexico, then, is highly complex, and within the limited scope of this book, I cannot provide a comprehensive explanation of its sources and dynamics. Likewise, this book does not aim to offer a history of drug trafficking in Mexico. It will therefore avoid delving into highly detailed accounts of local trafficking histories, such as meticulously tracing the genealogy or evolution of specific organizations. Nor is this book a history of prisons in Mexico or a set of policy recommendations. Rather, it is an attempt—nothing more, but also nothing less—to delineate the public morality of principled leniency.

ONE

Bargaining with Criminals

Trading Penal Benefits for Forensic Truth

This chapter begins the discussion on principled leniency by exploring the reduction of criminal sentences for perpetrators who collaborate with authorities to clarify the whereabouts of thousands of Mexicans who have been forcibly disappeared in drug-trafficking violence. Disappearances in Mexico have reached alarming levels.[1] An official report revealed that between 1960 and the last day of 2019, there had been a total of 61,637 missing persons. Of those, 60,053 had disappeared since 2006, that is, almost 97.5%. According to the most recent estimate, subject to acrimonious controversy, more than 111,000 people have disappeared. Close to 6,000 clandestine graves have been discovered across the entire country.[2] Almost three thousand bodies, hundreds of skulls, skeletons, and skeletal remains have been found. Worse yet, only 1,738 of the victims have been fully identified.[3] The state itself has compounded the problem of the disappeared. Between 2006 and 2012, public authorities violated the law by sending around 24,000 bodies to mass graves without first identifying them.[4] Meanwhile, the criminal justice system has been captured by organized crime, paralyzed or overwhelmed by the magnitude of the problem and by its own negligence, incompetence, and complicity.

In view of the unprecedented number of disappeared bodies[5] as well as the inefficacy of many operators of the criminal justice system, the cooperation of perpetrators to obtain information about victims' whereabouts—in forced detention centers or, more often and more tragically, in clandestine graves—is critical. In most cases, however, such cooperation would be self-incriminating for the perpetrators and is unlikely to be given voluntarily. Therefore, authorities must encourage cooperation by offering incentives, such as reduced sentences. By doing so, authorities are forced to choose between two conflicting courses of action. On the one hand, they may choose to punish the perpetrators proportionally and with the severity that their often-atrocious crimes deserve. In doing so, however, it is highly unlikely that they will obtain information conducive to clarifying disappearances. On the other hand, the authorities may choose to reduce punishment and thus obtain information that sheds light on disappearances. In this case, however, it would fail to mete out the appropriate and morally just punishment for the crime. This is the dilemma of the disappeared:[6] the predicament of choosing between proportionate punishment and what I shall call, following Iosif Kovras, "forensic truth." Such truth provides a degree of clarification that may or may not lead to a broader and more ambitious level of truth-telling in which light is shed on the root cause of atrocities and perpetrators are brought to trial.[7] The chapter argues that, consistently with principled leniency, when faced with such a predicament the state must favor a sentence reduction agreement, privileging finding missing persons over proportional punishment.

The chapter is structured as follows. The first section of the chapter provides a brief overview of the situation of the disappeared in Mexico. The second section provides an outline of the challenges that arise in the search for disappeared individuals. The third discusses Mexican law's tepid acceptance and limited experience with sentence reduction measures in exchange for assistance locating missing persons. The fourth section develops an ethical rationale for such mechanisms.

The Machinery of Disappearances

The government response to disappearances has been, from the outset, delayed and incompetent. Even the very act of counting the disappeared has been plagued by inefficacies. It was only in the last phase of Felipe Calderón's term (2006–12) that the government began to seriously address the issue of counting (let alone searching for) missing persons. Only as recently as 2017 the government created the National Registry of Data on Missing and Disappeared Persons (*Registro Nacional de datos de personas extraviadas o desaparecidas*), to bring some rigor to the search and identification processes. Beyond the inherent uncertainty when counting the disappeared, the Registry raised many concerns, such as the fact that the figures failed to distinguish between the categories of missing persons and include people who disappeared for noncriminal reasons.[8] More recently, the government stepped up its efforts to locate and identify missing persons, creating a government agency (the National Search Commission) tasked with this goal. Despite early promising results during President Andrés Manuel López Obrador's term, the overall success was disappointing. In a tragic turn of events, after years of attempts to make the tally more accurate, President López Obrador's administration concluded with him rejecting official data from his own government. He claimed the records overcounted the number of disappeared persons, which was then used as part of a smear campaign against his leadership. He therefore instructed officials to "purge" the database. The head of the National Search Commission—whom López Obrador himself had appointed—resigned in protest.

How do societies immersed in extreme violence deal with the problem of the disappeared? How do they locate the graves, identify the remains, and hand them over to relatives so that the relatives may have the opportunity to initiate a mourning that has been wrongly delayed? The process—difficult even in those places that have fully committed to it—is fraught with obstacles, which have been present in Mexico as well.[9]

The first challenge is institutional failure—the limited ability of institutions to cope with and deliver on the demands of the relatives of the disappeared to find their whereabouts. In Mexico, this is the function, among others, of forensic bureaucracies, such as the Forensic Medical Services, or SEMEFOS, which have utterly failed in their mission. Forensic bureaucracies across the nation are often overwhelmed due to limited resources and capabilities, resulting in institutional paralysis. Jalisco, a state in western Mexico that has been plagued by drug-related violence, is a case in point. The increase in violence led the state government to rent two refrigerated trucks to store the excessive number of bodies arriving at local morgues. In 2018, one of the trucks was found in the middle of the municipality of Tlajomulco, near Guadalajara, the state capital. Unable to move the truck following a series of bureaucratic errors, forensic officials had decided to abandon it—with 238 dead bodies inside. The truck was soon discovered by the traces of blood on its exterior and by the stench it emitted.[10]

The most recent efforts to improve the situation have all failed. At the start of López Obrador's administration, search collectives pushed for the creation of the Forensic Identification Mechanism (Mecanismo de Identificación Forense). Designed to operate with a degree of technical and managerial autonomy, it was tasked with conducting forensic examinations to identify bodies held by prosecutors' offices. However, its legal foundation was weak, and its operations were sluggish—while its dissolution was swift and decisive. After five years, the mechanism has been abandoned, left without coordinators, and yielding meager results. In its place, the National Center for Human Identification (Centro Nacional de Identificación Humana) was established to facilitate mass identification of bodies using automated comparisons of genetic profiles and fingerprints from unidentified corpses with those of missing persons. But this, too, proved a failure; by mid-2024, it had managed only about twenty identifications, adding yet another case of underfunding and neglect to the record. In the end, neither institution was more than a powerless, inconvenient, and precarious auxiliary to entrenched and corrupt prosecutors' offices, which remained unwilling to cooperate.

Another challenge for addressing the problem of disappearances is building a strong movement of relatives of the disappeared, one that is independent from other civil society actors, upholds a strictly humanitarian orientation (that is, it is to some degree depoliticized in the sense of postponing the demand for immediate public accountability). In the Mexican case, the victims are already beginning to meet this challenge. In recent years we have witnessed the emergence of associations and organizations of victims and relatives of disappeared persons that have come together to promote self-organized search strategies (with the formation of regional search brigades, supported and accompanied by NGOs and other sectors of civil society) and institutional reforms such as the Law of Disappearance and the creation of the National Search Commission (both promoted by the National Movement for Our Disappeared).[11]

The types of violence leading to disappearances can of course vary, creating a variety of challenges when it comes to tracking the location of the disappeared. In situations of extreme violence in other regions of the world, violence has been perpetrated by the military as a counterinsurgency method. In such cases, violence is used for a short period of time. In others, the logic of violence is very different; its perpetrators are paramilitary or criminal groups whose goal is to sow terror as a method of social control by targeting civilians over an extended period of time. At first, it would seem as if the process of gathering forensic evidence is more challenging in instances where paramilitary or criminal logic prevails; there are multiple perpetrators, many operating clandestinely. By contrast, within authoritarian systems the challenges diminish over time. If there is only one party responsible for the violence (the military) then, as elites change, military leadership could eventually contribute to the forensic truth process. Conversely, it may be the case that forensic truth emerges more easily in contexts of paramilitary or criminal violence. This is because, where military hierarchies may suppress the truth by discouraging or even punishing autonomous behavior from soldiers, members of criminal organizations operate without the burden of such hierarchical structures. This makes them more likely to accept "incentives" to cooperate with the authorities to find bodies.[12] At any rate, the point is that each case raises different challenges.

The search for the disappeared in Mexico encounters both types of challenge because disappearances can be traced to both military and police violence and violence linked to criminal organizations, or even a combination of both. Criminal organizations perpetrate the bulk of disappearances, with a wide variety of motivations. The case of San Fernando, Tamaulipas, sheds light on some of them. At least two massacres and disappearances of undocumented immigrants in transit to the United States took place there in 2010 and 2011, with close to three hundred victims if we add together both cases. The kidnappings, assassinations, and clandestine burials, attributed to the Zetas, are believed to have had three motivations: the victims resisted being recruited; they were mistaken for new recruits of the Gulf Cartel, the rival organization; or their relatives did not pay ransom.[13] These motivations—penalizing those who resist recruitment or are affiliated, however loosely, with rival groups, and ransom—are replicated in other regions of the country and are often compounded by other aims: castigating business owners—from street vendors to corporations—who refuse to pay the "fees" the organizations impose, or punishing political representatives or candidates, public officials (policemen, custom agents, judges), and even innocent civilians who fail to fall in line. The disappeared might also be collateral damage in confrontations between criminal groups or between these groups and public security forces. While criminal groups are responsible for most disappearances, there is evidence from different parts of the country that both the army and other public authorities (local, state, or federal police) are actively involved as well. In Nuevo León, for example, almost half of the disappearances can be traced, according to information provided by family members or witnesses, to military checkpoints, searches, arrests, arbitrary detentions, and interrogations, all of which reveals the involvement of authorities.[14]

There are other challenges in the search for the disappeared: the intimidation of *madres buscadoras* by criminal groups;[15] the fact that the remains of victims can be disposed of in ways that pose almost insurmountable obstacles for their retrieval (they may be burned and pulverized in sugarcane mills, incinerated in clandestine or army crematoria, dissolved in acid and stored in plastic barrels, dispersed and thrown into a river . . .); and the widespread complicity or forced cooperation of civilians—as when the operator of a backhoe is forced to excavate and cover clandestine mass graves,[16] and more generally when individuals turn a blind eye to the illegal inhumations taking place in their surroundings. Such collaboration enables the stealth and enormity of the machinery of disappearances.[17]

Given the magnitude of the problem and the level as well as the nature of the challenge of searching for the missing, the cooperation of the perpetrators cannot be dispensed with. This is why human rights organizations and the families of the disappeared themselves have actively promoted penal benefits as another tool to cope with the crisis.[18]

"We don't want justice." Penal Benefits for Criminals, and Victims

Penal benefits are widely supported by many searching families in Mexico and are in fact part of their broader strategy to obtain cooperation from, and even engage with, criminal groups in order to receive useful information about the whereabouts of their missing relatives. There are several documented instances where families of victims have reached out to criminals or where criminals themselves, seeking to reap some benefit, have provided information in anonymous calls, emails, and even, in one instance at least, in the alms box at a local church. The largest mass grave in Latin America, an area in Veracruz called Colinas de Santa Fe, was discovered when a group of *madres buscadoras* (searching mothers, as they have come to be known) received a map from what appeared to be members of a criminal organizations. These individuals irrupted into a gathering of *madres buscadoras* and handed the crowd fliers with a handwritten map containing the location of several clandestine graves.[19]

Thus, *madres buscadoras* have opened an informal and precarious line of communication with criminal groups through social or traditional media. Addressing their petitions directly to "los jefes de los carteles" (cartel bosses), *madres buscadoras*, many of whom have since been assassinated or threatened simply for searching, have pleaded for truces or requested "permission" to conduct an unobstructed search for their disappeared. In petitioning criminal groups, searching mothers repeat, as they always do, what has become one of their slogans: "We don't want justice, all we want is to find them and give them a proper burial." As a mother inured by atrocity puts it, "What we ask is that, when they kill them, they leave them in a visible place where we can find them. . . . In Ciudad Obregón the day before yesterday, they left some dead people lying there, so we believe that it is a response to our request." The appearance of a response has also been visible on *narcomantas* (literally "narcoblankets": a banner or sheet with poorly drawn letters carrying a message to other groups or public authorities) ordinarily used by criminal organizations to send threatening messages to rival groups or authorities, or to intimidate civil society. In this case they have been used to signal a truce. Such communiqués have also appeared in carefully choreographed messages circulating on social media, as in one case where members of a criminal organization appeared online, heavily armed and with their faces covered, to declare that they "accepted" the truce out of concern for the welfare of the country. A few mothers even claim that they have been contacted by spokespersons of alleged criminal groups.[20]

The first petition of this kind was signed by a group of searching mothers from the state of Tamaulipas in 2021 and was addressed to the leader of Los Ciclones del Cartel del Golfo. The mothers claim that, in response, the criminal organization allowed them to excavate an extermination field in the region of La Bartolina, from which they extracted half a ton of charred bones. To date, mothers claim they have asked nine criminal organizations to allow their work and to halt the threats against them.

Penal benefits are far from being a recent invention in Mexico.[21] They date back to the Federal Law against Organized Crime (1996) and, inspired in US models, were coupled with protection programs for witnesses who provided information to dismantle criminal networks and initiate criminal proceedings against their leaders. The crisis of the disappeared has generated renewed interest in penal benefits. Thus, President López Obrador offered a reward to anyone who "broke the pact of silence" to provide information on the enforced disappearance of the forty-three students from the teachers college of Ayotzinapa in the state of Guerrero, on September of 2014, a case that enthralled the entire nation.[22]

In reality, the "offer" of penal benefits for useful information predates his administration. The General Law of Enforced Disappearance of Persons (2017), which distinguishes between the crime of enforced disappeared, involving state actors, and disappearance by individuals, grants prosecutors the authority to extend benefits to offenders who have been prosecuted and sentenced if they provide information in connection to the specific crime (with specific victims) for which they were or are being charged. The problem with this provision, however, is its narrow applicability. Insofar as it vests prosecutors alone with the authority to bargain, it excludes the government commissions tasked with the search for the disappeared from participating in the negotiations. And, since it only benefits offenders who face criminal charges or have been charged, it leaves out those who are not detained or facing prosecution, the majority in the context of wide impunity that prevails in Mexico. Furthermore, because it restricts benefits to the crimes for which the offender is charged, it forecloses the possibility that offenders might share information about other disappearances. Beyond these limitations, the background criminal law framework in which the law is embedded is antithetical to the kind of cooperation that penal benefits seek to elicit. To name just one instance of this constrictive background, public officials are under an obligation to denounce crime, an obligation that prevents them from offering confidentiality to criminal organizations or at least limits their ability to do so.[23]

It is difficult to document how useful penal benefits can be in the search for missing persons because information about criminal investigations is not always publicly accessible. Until very recently, reduced sentences had rarely been used to uncover the whereabouts of the disappeared.[24] However, consider the case of Gildardo N., who in all likelihood participated in the forced disappearance of the Ayotzinapa students. Public outcry led Enrique Peña

Nieto's administration to appoint special prosecutor Jesús Murillo Karam to investigate the disappearance of the students. His investigation produced the (in)famous "verdad histórica" (*historical truth*),[25] as Murillo Karam's version of the events came to be known in public opinion. According to this version, the criminal organization Guerreros Unidos and a few rogue members of the local police forces abducted and killed the students, mistaking them for members of a rival group. They later incinerated their bodies in a municipal dumpster in Cocula and dispersed their remains in a single location, near the San Juan River. The narrative was convenient for authorities as it exculpated state actors, including the military, and dispensed with the need to trace the remains of the students (irretrievably lost in the waters of the river), which might tell a different story when examined forensically.

Gildardo N. was apprehended during the investigation of the *verdad histórica* as one of the perpetrators of the massacre. However, he was later released when a judge held that the evidence authorities presented against him, while incriminating, had been illegally obtained.[26] He was later recruited as a *testigo colaborador*, the legal term of art to describe offenders who collaborate with authorities. According to many media reports, the information he now shared as "testigo Juan," which in part amended his prior declaration, steered the investigation in a different, potentially more promising direction, and away from the impasse to which it had been (according to some deliberately) directed. Against the findings of Peña Nieto's team, Juan's testimony reveals the complicity of security forces at all levels (municipal, state, and federal, as well as members of the army). Furthermore, while the witness confirmed that all students had been killed on the orders of "El Güero Mugres," a kingpin from the Guerreros Unidos criminal organization, his testimony revealed that the students had been split into groups and taken to different locations across the state. The bodies of some had been dissolved in acid, others incinerated in different locations, including several private crematoria and Coacoyula, an abandoned mine. Only when the massacre gained media attention were the remains of the students taken to the Cocula dumpster.[27]

To be sure, Juan's testimony raises concerns on several counts, all addressed in the scholarly literature on collaborators: their tendency to lie, exaggerate, and exonerate themselves from the crime while in turn implicating adversaries.[28] Notwithstanding these sources of concern, what is critical about Juan's testimony is that it allowed investigators to follow the trail of the students. This testimony contributed to locating fragments of bones belonging to two of the students, Christian Rodríguez and Jhosivani Guerrero, in the Barranca de la Carnicería, a location that had been absent from the investigation connected to the *verdad histórica*.[29]

Beyond this high-profile case, and notwithstanding that the social movement of the families of the disappeared is not homogeneous, full of diverse and sometimes conflicting goals and demands, there are numerous instances where relatives of the disappeared are inclined to forgo accountability, that is, punishment for perpetrators, on the condition that they provide useful information about the whereabouts of their missing loved ones. These are some of their testimonies:

- A *madre buscadora* from Guanajuato: "When we already have a guilty person, a possibility must be opened by the law, so that in some way if he has already been sentenced and condemned, his sentence confirmed, then perhaps some benefit could be given to the accused on condition that they tell us what happened to our relatives."[30]

- A father from Baja California: "The sentence of those accused can be reduced so that they can tell us where our children are. An example: a criminal told us the location of graves, and all he asked in return was to be transferred to a prison in Nayarit. There are prisoners who want to talk about the missing in exchange for soap, cornflakes or chocolates. This . . . can be legislated."[31]

- A father from Coahuila: "Have a heart. We do not want justice, we only look for our disappeared."[32]

- A mother from Sonora: "I'm not looking for justice, just for a mother to know where to tuck her son in for the last time."[33]

- The banner of a *madre buscadora*, on behalf of her search brigade: "To the cartels I ask for mercy: do not kill or threaten *madres buscadoras*. . . . We will not stop because we are looking for the reason for our life. We don't want justice or jail, just to protect those we give birth to, and a place to pray to them." (Note that the use of a banner is a deliberate attempt to address criminal organization by adopting the very same vehicle of communication they oftentimes employ, the *narcomanta*.)

The question I now turn to address is whether penal benefits are morally defensible. The fact that these demands are articulated and advocated by victims gives them prima facie credence but does not entirely justify them or make them unassailable. Victims do not always uphold ethical vindications. Lynchings are oftentimes conducted by victims with legitimate grievances and expectations for accountability of actual perpetrators that the state leaves unaddressed. However, neither unattended grievances nor frustrated accountability expectations render lynchings admissible. I do not mean to suggest, of course, that angry mobs seeking to lynch a criminal and the families of the disappeared advocating for penal benefits are analogous. In fact, I argue that, unlike lynchings, penal benefits are morally permissible. Yet a normative account is needed to defend this claim. I elaborate such an account in the following section, which clarifies why the dilemma of the disappeared must be resolved by selecting penal benefits over criminal punishment.

Peace (of Mind) or Justice? The Dilemma of the Disappeared and the Priority of Forensic Truth

The case of Cyprus illustrates the dilemma many nations face when using reduced sentences or partial immunity to search for disappeared persons. Following the civil war that pitted Greek and Turkish ethnic groups against each other, Cyprus created the Committee for Missing Persons (CMP) under the joint sponsorship of both ethnic communities. Although decades late, the committee was successful in exhuming and identifying victims of the conflict. It was successful largely because it offered immunity and confidentiality to low-level perpetrators who cooperated in the search for missing persons, a decision that was criticized for creating an "immoral" trade-off between forensic truth and immunity for perpetrators. The reason for its success, in more detail, is as follows:

> If a family decides to initiate a process of legal accountability, this will immediately affect the progress of the CMP. Eyewitnesses will be reluctant to provide incriminatory evidence that may lead to their own prosecution, the process of exhumations will stop and thousands of families desperately looking for the remains of their loved ones will be forced to keep waiting. So far, this has not happened because of a subtle but robust sense of solidarity and respect for the need of families to bury their dead. An implicit hierarchy of priorities has been

established, whereby all relatives seem to prioritize the need of other families to get the remains back over their own right to [criminal] justice.[34]

This "implicit hierarchy of priorities" where the "the need of families to bury their dead" takes precedence over full-blown legal accountability (that is, unmitigated punishment) must be made explicit and defended to show that the trade-off is not "immoral." This is what I set out to do in this section. Let me restate and elaborate the problem and its resolution: there are two principles in tension. The proportionate punishment principle maintains that the state must punish all those who commit a crime proportionally to the crime in question.[35] In turn, the forensic principle establishes that every person has the right to know the whereabouts of her missing loved ones, and the right to receive their remains if they are deceased. This right complements the duty of the state to embark on a search and carry out a comprehensive investigation regarding the disappearance, and to employ all necessary means in doing so. I argue that the forensic principle holds lexical priority over the proportionate punishment principle. By lexical priority I simply mean that the principle or goal in question is situated on top of a hierarchical relationship, that because it sits on top of the hierarchy it must be pursued with priority, and that the goals on the bottom may be pursued only once this priority goal has been achieved and only so long as doing so does not compromise pursuit of the hierarchically preceding goal.

By proposing reduced punishment only so long as perpetrators share information that is conducive to finding the disappeared, these circumscribed penal rewards reflect the priority of the forensic over the proportional punishment principle. They do not simply assert one principle at the expense of the other but bring the two into a hierarchical relationship. To clarify this point, consider why, unlike penal benefits, a conditional amnesty may go a step too far in embodying the proper relationship between the two principles. Amnesties entail the forbearance of punishment altogether. This means that the condemnatory message of punishment (of the wrongdoing and of self-attributed superiority of their perpetrators) is sacrificed entirely. This is not what happens with penal benefits. These benefits are an instance of what Colleen Murphy calls "principled compromises," in which the competing values of different measures or policies are recognized and respected, without sacrificing any of them. Instead of a crude trade-off, such compromises establish a minimum threshold for abiding by the values embraced. Above and beyond this threshold, compromises are tolerated and inevitable. There will be *partial* sacrifices of the values in question here.[36] Thus, reduced sentences retain the condemnatory import of punishment, even if condemnation is less strongly conveyed given its lack of proportionality, while at the same time accommodating the values enshrined in the forensic principle. By contrast, amnesties sacrifice the expressive value of punishment in its entirety. Therefore, amnesty does not embody a compromise between the principles in conflict.

With this clarification in mind, let us begin the analysis. The choice between forensic truth and proportional punishment can be evaluated based on instrumental (means to an end) and noninstrumental (good in themselves) reasons. I will show that, for either set of reasons, considerations in favor of the forensic principle are more compelling, at least under the circumstances prevailing in Mexico, which are not circumstances of ordinary criminality.[37]

Consider the proportionate punishment principle first. This principle is usually defended on instrumental grounds that have been broadly explored in the philosophical literature on the justification of punishment. I will discuss them at greater length in chapter 3. For now, suffice it to say that instrumentalist theories of punishment maintain that it is only justifiable to punish a person insofar as punishment serves a higher purpose, such as preventing crime, or other goals, such as the rehabilitation of the criminal.[38] In this vein, proportionality is an important part of the argument for punishment as preventive. If a serious crime, such as the disappearance of persons, is not met with a severe sentence, then the dissuasive function of the punishment is weakened. Lack of proportionality in punishment may then contribute to perpetuating disappearances.

These considerations in support of proportionate punishment are not easily extrapolated to contexts of massive violence like Mexico. Deterrence-based justifications for proportionate punishment are particularly robust in the presence of a minimally competent and just state and where crime is sporadic, plainly attributable to a single or limited number of individuals, and is inflicted on one or a small number of victims. The kind of violence unfolding in Mexico is different, as are the willingness and the ability of the state to cope with the violence. The dynamics of victimization in these scenarios are much more complex than in ordinary circumstances. They oftentimes arise from actions carried out or tolerated by political/criminal organizations or the state itself (and sometimes by the two in conjunction, forming macro-criminal networks) where direct perpetrators are weak links in the chain of complicity. In such a context, and especially with the state "captured" in this way, punishment of a few perpetrators alone is unlikely to abate crime unless such punishment is extensive (that is, broad), reaching all perpetrators.[39] As a result, the deterrent effect of proportional punishment loses *some* of its force.

The Ayotzinapa case is a paradigmatic example in this regard. In this case, it is unlikely that the arrest of characters such as El Chereje, a low-ranking member of Guerreros Unidos and, according to the attorney general's investigation, one of the principal culprits in the disappearance of the students, would have any deterrent effect if the criminal networks that facilitated the crimes remain intact. As documented in the National Human Rights Commission's report on the investigation into the forced disappearance of the Ayotzinapa students under the Enrique Peña Nieto administration, the authorities failed to recognize a "primary instigator" who made crucial decisions regarding the fate of the students. That instigator, El Patrón, would be "a subject with a high-level management and organizational capacity to carry out illicit activities."[40] As long as El Patrón, himself is not held accountable, the arrest and punishment of low-ranking perpetrators will not prevent the perpetration of similar crimes in the future. In other cases of forced disappearance, like Ayotzinapa in their outcomes for victims but which have not and will not receive the same degree of public attention or state investigative resources, cooperation by the perpetrators may be the only means to determine the whereabouts of the disappeared.

It could be countered that punishment might still have deterrent effects in scenarios of macrocriminality as long as it is not imposed narrowly. Given the diminished capacity of the state to impart criminal justice, it is unclear whether the state is capable of imposing punishment of the requisite breadth without flouting due process. To compensate for its limited resources, the state may choose to impose punishment strategically. It could, for instance, target specific perpetrators, perhaps those with greater responsibility, to provide exemplary punishment, a strategy that might yield a deterrent effect. Many nations emerging from conflict and with weak criminal justice systems do indeed conduct their prosecutorial efforts in this manner. Having to choose in their retributive efforts between breadth and accuracy, that is, between punishing the highest possible number of wrongdoers with a low level of accuracy (that is, confidence in their culpability) and the highest accuracy possible with a low number of convicted perpetrators, postconflict societies tend to choose the latter.[41] But note that this strategy of prosecutorial selectivity already implies relaxation of the proportionate punishment principle in two regards. First, by definition the strategy rejects the principle of proportionate punishment with respect to cases that are *not* selected for prosecution. Such selectivity may be harnessed in support of the forensic principle if those selected for exemplary punishment come from the group of perpetrators *without* information that can lead authorities to the disappeared. Second, to be an effective deterrent, selective punishment must be accompanied by complementary measures, such as a robust truth commission that contextualizes and gives meaning to selective punishment (for example, by informing the public of the gravity of the crimes committed by those who are chosen for prosecution).

We shall now turn to discussing the forensic principle and its defense from the instrumental perspective. The arguments in favor are weightier than those that support the proportional punishment principle. The unhindered search that the forensic principle enables will, in the best-case scenario, result in finding the victims alive and able to give testimony to the authorities. In cases where perpetrators have murdered their victims, the recovery of bodies may contribute to preventing further killing given the potentially incriminating evidence that may be found in clandestine graves, at least in contexts in which violence is ongoing. Moreover, finding victims alive or in clandestine graves can reveal the modus operandi employed by perpetrators. In fact, this evidence may lead to the punishment of perpetrators who are *not* collaborating with the justice system, resulting in *partial* compliance with the proportionate punishment principle. Another instrumental argument supporting the forensic principle relates to the financial sphere. Most of the disappeared are men who usually sustained a household. Under the circumstances, their dependents may be left in legal limbo with no access to the missing person's inheritance or pension, since the death of the right-holder cannot be certified; locating the disappeared is therefore of the utmost importance to their relatives.

In sum, based on instrumentalist considerations, this brief comparison shows the greater importance of the forensic principle compared to the proportionate punishment principle. Part of the dissuasive potential of the proportionate punishment principle would appear to be lost or diminished in the Mexican context. Even if this were not the case, however, *partial* departures from the principle—reducing the severity of some convictions—would not severely compromise its aspiration to deterrence. Conversely, sentence reduction may contribute to forensic goals, since only those who provide information leading to the disappeared will be rewarded with lenient punishment. The forensic principle has the potential to save lives and improve socioeconomic and psychological conditions for the family members of the missing. And to the extent that it sometimes produces incriminatory evidence, the forensic principle may even contribute to partially realizing the proportionate punishment principle.

In addition to these instrumental conditions, the priority of the forensic principle and the priority of locating the missing can be defended from the standpoint of noninstrumental arguments, which will be the focus for the rest of this section. In particular, I explore how punishment and forensic truth, respectively, honor the values of mutual respect and self-respect. As we will see, the forensic principle is of priority insofar as it consolidates relations of mutual respect as well as what John Rawls calls the social bases of self-respect (or what Martha Nussbaum calls the social bases for nonhumiliation[42]). The term "social bases of self-respect" refers to the conditions that allow citizens to regard themselves as valuable, and that give them their ability to pursue their life plans.[43]

We shall begin with the proportionate punishment principle. What is its justification from a noninstrumental perspective? Punishment has intrinsic value insofar as it is an expression of condemnation of the treatment accorded to a victim, interpreted as an affront to moral dignity. A crime, even beyond the material harm caused, relays a message of the aggressor's moral superiority; the aggressor claims the right to treat a victim unjustly and denies the victim his or her moral right to be respected. Punishment repudiates this denial of the victim's moral dignity.[44] Punishment, then, is not merely retribution; it contains moral elements that concern respect for the victim and the victim's ability to demand respect.[45]

The noninstrumental justification of the proportionate punishment principle is appealing. Nonetheless, as in the case of instrumental justification, there is an important caveat to make regarding its force under present circumstances in Mexico. Just as the dissuasive power of punishment is reduced in these circumstances, so is its expressive power. To recapitulate what was said earlier, in societies like Mexico's, punishment of the direct perpetrator (the material author) only partially counters the message of the victim's moral inferiority, since this message is expressed in a series of wrongful actions and through a chain of actors promoting victimization. In these conditions, punishment *alone*—again, unless extensive—can neither express full repudiation of wrongdoing nor fully restore victims' dignity. Selective punishment, where the criterion for selection is not properly justified, will invite the charge of moral arbitrariness. Therefore, the expressive loss arising from the failure to apply the proportionate punishment principle is greater in ordinary circumstance than in circumstances of mass violence and atrocity. Furthermore, if the value of punishment lies in its ability to convey repudiation of the wrongdoing and of the demeaning treatment of victims, then it would be acceptable to partially sacrifice it if another principle is comparatively more effective or at least as effective in conveying a similar message of expression of respect for victims. This takes us to the forensic principle.

In its own way, this principle, like the proportionate punishment principle, attributes great value to actions that express respect for the moral value of the victims. In addition to constituting material wrong—by depriving missing persons of their freedom and harming them physically—disappearances send a denigrating message to both victims and their families. The message is that their lives are superfluous, and that the ensuing consequences for the families of the missing, affecting their safety, life plans, and moral agency, are *not* of priority attention for the public authority. By contrast, the state's unobstructed search for the missing, which may entail relaxing its ordinary stance on punishment, counters these messages. Put in different terms, the harm caused to the missing and their family members can further be understood as affecting the development of social and political relations based on mutual respect, particularly respect *for* the victims, as well as the conditions that guarantee the self-respect *of* the victims. This impact can be observed at three different levels: personal, interpersonal and political. I now proceed to develop this argument in greater detail, sifting through the effects of disappearances on each one of these levels.

At the political level, disappearances trigger social and political processes that destroy any chance of building a society based on mutual respect among people. First, those who perpetrate disappearances seek more than to eliminate evidence of the crime and avoid international and state scrutiny (when the state itself is not responsible). They also seek to establish near-absolute control of the communities where events take place, paralyzing survivors and establishing dominance and order through fear. This undermines the dignity of victims in several ways. Upon silencing the families and members of the community (by terrorizing them so they will not go to the authorities or the press), disappearances deny even the most elemental possibility of demanding to be treated with dignity.

Disappearances transform people into "disposable" entities—irrelevant to the state and society, or at least less valued than others.[46] While anyone can vanish, the marginalized suffer most severely. Already invisible due to their social status, their disappearances provoke little outcry. Middle- or upper-class victims would generate far greater pressure on authorities, demonstrating how inequality shapes public outrage. Marginalization and disappearance reinforce each other: marginalized groups face financial exploitation, making them prime targets for forced labor and subsequent elimination by criminal organizations. Society compounds this violence by blaming victims—labeling them criminals or undesirables ("they must have been involved in something"). Such narratives reinforce their expendability. In Hannah Arendt's terms, these victims become "superfluous," stripped of dignity and reduced to objects.[47] Excluded from socioeconomic and political power, they endure figurative invisibility before facing literal erasure. The state and society compound this violence through indifference—even denying victims funeral rites, burying them anonymously in mass graves. This systemic dehumanization extends beyond current victims; potential future targets recognize the state's tacit approval of their fate.

Finally, and continuing at the political level, disappearances trigger a vicious cycle: bureaucratic negligence—or outright complicity—not only enables disappearances but actively perpetuates them. Claudio Lomnitz rightly claims that, although a disappearance always begins with an abduction, the phenomenon also involves the wrongful treatment by authorities of murdered bodies. By omission or commission, the police, public ministries, the prosecutors, and the Forensic Medical Services in Mexico are actively involved in disappearances in this sense.[48] Families of the disappeared often give testimony of public authorities' negligence when it comes to attending to their cases: officials who open investigations but never actually conduct them; relatives who are asked to fill forms and deliver documents to multiple government agencies, which give the appearance of being at work, unnecessarily duplicating paperwork; witnesses whose testimonies are not collected, even when it would be extremely simple to do so; failure to comply with forensic protocols as a result of which the remains of victims cannot be identified or delivered to relatives, thereby ending in mass graves; and so on.[49] All of this betrays a lack of respect for the disappeared and their families. It is unsurprising that, in its list of demands to the local authorities, the Colectivo de Familiares Unidos de Desaparecidos de Jalisco (Collective of United Relatives of the Disappeared of Jalisco) makes a significant number of requests, such as forensic classification and identification of bodies, a DNA database, proper cross-checking and verification of the data, and the enlistment of a prosecutor on duty at forensic services to monitor the arrival and departure of bodies and other remains. At the top of the list, however, sit two demands: "To treat the bodies found in graves or in different circumstances with dignity, and to hold them at SEMEFO [Forensic Services] while the families proceed to identify them, because they were once alive and had both names and identities"; and "To treat [bodies] with due diligence and respect, without forgetting to address their loved ones in a truthful manner."[50]

Now, when the state actively searches for the missing, or at the very least assists searching families in that endeavor by every means possible, including penal benefits, it repudiates the affronts to dignity that these processes inflict on victims. It expresses its commitment to ending fear and uncertainty as forms of unlawful and illegitimate dominance. Dismantling social control in this manner gives the victims their voices back, including potential victims. Searching for the missing similarly counters the message that people can be "disposed of" without encountering a strong reaction from the state. Upon embarking on a comprehensive search, the state recognizes the worth of the missing (albeit a posteriori, in response to its own negligence or inability to protect them) and acts accordingly. By extension, the search for the missing is an expression of respect for families and survivors; it sends the message that the state will mobilize support to the extent that is necessary, and that it will spare them the cruelties of forensic and legal bureaucracies.

Furthermore, given that people attach value to burying their loved ones according to prevailing cultural norms, and to themselves being buried in similar fashion when the time comes, the state shows respect for the dignity of both victims and relatives when it guarantees the conditions for the proper burial of fatal victims. From the standpoint of victims who are killed, the respect implicit in funeral honors might seem unimportant insofar as these victims are no longer able to demand respect. Nevertheless, as Jeffrey Blustein emphasizes, "survivors are thought of as legitimate surrogates or unofficial representatives of victims who did not survive, and the way the former are treated by the state and by civil society actors who collaborate with it conveys a message, belatedly, about the rightful claims of the latter, and exemplifies how the latter ought to have been treated."[51]

I now turn to discuss the harm caused by disappearances in the interpersonal sphere. Disappearances destroy the conditions of possibility for cultivating an attitude of self-respect. Simply put, having self-respect means appreciating that one has worth. Such worth can be derived from one's status as a person, as a member of a group, or as a bearer of a social role. Our sense of having worth can also come from the fact that we regard ourselves as autonomous agents. The critical point is that self-respect is fundamental for everyday life because it allows one to lead a flourishing life. Importantly, self-respect includes a desire to defend and maintain that respect.[52] Self-respect has a reflexive aspect,[53] that is, a person's self-assessment is, to a degree, contingent on the way others assess her. This idea is at the core of various philosophical arguments such as Rawls's understanding of the social bases for self-respect. His central contention is that the state must foster an environment conducive to enabling members to build a positive image of themselves and thus appropriately develop their life plans.

Stigmatization or social invisibility are classic examples of the kind of social pathologies that hinder such an environment for individual flourishment.[54] Ambiguous loss can trigger these pathologies in several ways. Ambiguous loss, a notion developed by Pauline Boss,[55] occurs when the loss of a family member or loved one is enveloped in uncertainty. The dimension of ambiguous loss that is relevant here is that of physical absence with a psychological presence. In a strictly psychological sense, ambiguous loss affects the relatives of missing persons because it freezes mourning, hinders the possibility of making decisions and coping with loss, and it affects the cognitive processes generally. Moreover, at first ambiguous loss awakens communal empathy toward the families of the missing; however, this empathy rapidly expires, and after a time people become fed up and rejection sets in.

In the long run, the relatives of the missing experience isolation, and what Theo Hollander calls *disenfranchised grief,* a "grief that is not communally acknowledged and cannot be openly mourned, publicly expressed, and socially supported."[56] In places where organized crime or even the authorities exercise social control based on fear, such isolation is immediate. People do not want to have anything to do with the missing or their relatives. A chasm opens up and deepens between families and the community—and the community embraces the absurd expectation that relatives of the missing must rapidly move past the trauma of their loss. This isolation is in itself humiliating and is further reinforced when social judgment is passed regarding the possible link between the missing and organized crime. The idea that "they were probably involved in something" stigmatizes the disappeared and their families. As an example, take the following testimony of a relative in Tijuana:

> Unfortunately society does not get involved; [I know this] because I have experienced it, I have dealt with people who know that my brother is missing and they make hurtful comments . . . they make comments like "well, something must explain why that happened to him" or "he was up to something" . . . Or . . . "Well, they didn't kill him because he was a saint." So. . . . no one knows what it feels like until they live it. Not until you go through it and feel it do you realize the suffering of the family [of the disappeared] . . . it is a very difficult and very painful suffering.[57]

Other testimonies align with the previous one:

> . . . I was ashamed to tell the people in town what was happening to me . . .

> . . . One is left without work, without friends, without family, like a pariah, [community members] think you are always going to ask them for something . . .

> . . . The blame divides the family; they all accuse each other . . .

> . . . I was overwhelmed with everything: I was forced to take my children out of school, I am both father and mother . . .

> . . . We are like stars in the sky; mine is a dull star that is burned out . . .

> . . . The archbishop told me: "it was your fault because you didn't raise him well" . . .[58]

All the testimonies above depict experiences of shame and humiliation resulting from the disappearances of loved ones.[59]

These are just some of the ways in which the stigma of disappearance upends the lives of the relatives of the disappeared, undermining the social bases of self-respect. The search for missing persons, prioritized by the forensic principle, contributes to containing or at least attenuating these outcomes. The discovery of mass graves contributes to dismantling the social narratives that connect disappearance with criminal activity by allowing forensic science to determine the method used to murder the missing persons (for example, whether such methods bespeak an extrajudicial execution, or a skirmish between two criminal groups). The mere act of finding a mass grave, more likely to be associated with mass extermination than with petty crime, helps undermine such narratives. Moreover, the testimony given by perpetrators who collaborate with authorities can also contribute to doing away with false beliefs that associate the missing with criminal activities.

Finally, let us look at how disappearances, through the effects of ambiguous loss, weaken the grounds for self-respect at the personal level. Here the relevant aspect of self-respect is not the reflexive dimension mentioned before (related to the impact of the assessments of others on the conception a person forms of herself), but the person's ability to adopt certain standards of conduct that will enable her to feel deserving of respect.[60] On this understanding, people who have self-respect can exercise morally valuable abilities that in turn make them moral agents, such as directing and assessing their own actions, reflecting on their moral values, and exercising what Robert Nozick calls a *value-seeking capacity*.[61]

Ambiguous loss freezes the mourning process, erodes the ability to confront loss, and deteriorates decision-making and other cognitive processes. In broader terms, the ensuing mental deterioration, which is far less pronounced in mourning processes that do not involve ambiguous loss, includes inter alia the following: persistent yearning or longing for the deceased; preoccupation with the deceased and the circumstances of death, and a difficulty accepting it; maladaptive appraisals about oneself in relation to the deceased; social disruption; difficulty trusting other people; feelings of being alone or detachment from other people; and confusion about one's role in life or a diminished sense of one's identity.[62] Those facing this cognitive deterioration can hardly be expected to exercise the abilities needed to have self-respect and even to demand respect.[63]

The search for the disappeared aims to counteract these effects. "Unfreezing" mourning offers family members the possibility of "recovering" their lives. This is how a mother of four disappeared people from the state of Guerrero describes it:

> After what happened to the 43 [students of Ayotzinapa], we decided to search as family members—as mothers, wives, brothers, [and] sisters of our loved ones. We launched the search on our own, risking our own lives and taking all the possible risks because we know that we are the only people who are hurting and missing our family members. . . . With all our strength we used what little we have left of our lives because right now we need help to look for our children, dead or alive. We want them alive, but we also need to identify all those loved ones who are buried in clandestine graves. We need to identify them so their families can have—I will not say happiness because we will never have that again—but at least they will [be able to change their outlook on life]. Because we have seen, [and] we have accompanied several people during the mourning process when they receive the remains [of their loved ones, and have seen] that it changes their lives; [until then] it seems that they were denied even the right to smile; they felt they did not even have the right to smile, the right to enjoy; nothing, nothing at all in life. When these people are given even a few little bones, they have a bit of peace and that is what we would all like to achieve.[64]

Those who suffer cognitive impairment because of ambiguous loss often lose the desire to live. This is accompanied by the deterioration of other important capabilities, such as autonomy:

> You cannot say that you are alive, because you are dead psychologically and emotionally; maybe physically you are moving, but emotionally you are dead. You have no idea how much we have suffered. . . . Feeling dead is not having any hope of getting up and saying, "Today I feel like eating this." No, [instead] it is: "Today you are going to eat if you're able to find something, or if you feel like eating what you can afford, or what others give you." Feeling dead is having no hope of waking up and being able to say good morning to your son. Not being able to give him a hug or a kiss; feeling dead is no longer being able to embrace the rest of your family.[65]

Retrieving the bodies, in the end, allows relatives to delineate and pursue their own life plans, recover their judgment, make decisions, integrate, and seek value.[66]

To summarize, based on this analysis it seems appropriate to conclude that the forensic principle must hold priority in contexts such as Mexico, where widespread disappearances occur; the punitive principle should be enforced only to the extent that it does not hinder the application of the forensic principle. According to the proportionate punishment principle, punishment has expressive value insofar as it publicly condemns the wrongdoing, rejects the superiority that the perpetrator claims for him- or herself, and recognizes the dignity of the victim, thus reestablishing equal footing in the relationship. This expressive power, reduced though by no means eliminated in the Mexican context, must be set against the expressive depth and width of the forensic principle in the same circumstances. Here the depth of the forensic principle lies in the fact that a relentless and unencumbered search for the disappeared affirms the worth of the victim's very existence, denied by the perpetrator, the state, and society at large. Its width is evident in its capacity to protect the bases for both mutual respect *and* self-respect. It does so by helping to remove the stigma associated with disappearance for both the missing and their relatives, and by helping the latter to heal mentally so that they can proceed to form and carry out their life plans. For these reasons, the proportionate punishment principle must be complied with only to the degree that it does not hinder compliance with the forensic principle. The latter guarantees the background conditions for a society rooted in mutual respect and safeguards for victims' self-respect.[67]

At this point we should acknowledge that the view expressed so far—extending penal rewards to reach forensic truth in Mexico is plainly justified—is not without controversy. I shall therefore address some objections that may be leveled against it. The strongest set of objections are those we may lump together under the heading of the political violence objection.[68] According to this objection, penal benefits are permissible only in situations of armed *political* conflict between the state and insurgents, which are two distinct and separate entities. In such cases, penal benefits can be justified to demobilize armed actors and negotiate an end to conflict and a political transition to democracy. Violence in Mexico, which is criminal rather than political, does not meet these criteria, or so contend those who endorse this objection. Criminal organizations are not political in the sense of waging a struggle to amend a broken social contract nor are they attempting to achieve a just objective (for example, ending oppression). Rather, they are simply seeking to make a profit. Moreover, since these organizations always control part of the state (that is, threatening or buying off public officials, usurping public roles), in such cases the state would be negotiating with actors with strong links to "captured" sectors of the state itself. This would mean that the two negotiating parties would not be clearly separated, as is usually the case in political disputes, but entwined.

Reduced sentences in contexts of criminal violence pose two further risks, following on the political violence objection. They erode the principle of equality before the law (here, penal law) because, by providing differentiated treatment to perpetrators, they distort sentencing processes. As a result, those responsible for atrocious crimes receive lenient sentences while lesser criminals receive similar or harsher sentences. Penal benefits also set a dangerous precedent, suggesting to violent criminal actors in the future that they may receive similar treatment. These risks decrease significantly in contexts of political transition, since the actors recognize that such contexts are transitory and their benefits, therefore, not transferable to ordinary circumstances.

While the political violence objection is right in suggesting that penal benefits should not be conferred lightly, I contend that its concerns can be defused or do not outweigh the dangers of *not* conferring them. Admittedly, in the Mexican case the recipients of penal benefits are criminal organizations, which pursue profit rather than legitimate political goals. However, I argue that the motivations of the perpetrators of disappearances must not determine or constrain measures or policies designed to respond to the interest of the families of the disappeared. If the benefits for victims and society more generally are significant—and I have claimed that they are because they protect and consolidate relations of mutual respect and the bases of self-respect—it is not clear why the differences in *types* of perpetrators should deny such crucial benefits to victims and their families. Or put in a slightly different form, concerns over the identity or the goals of the offenders must *not* take precedence over the needs of victims when deliberating about a trade-off that involves, on one side, something of so critical importance as the protection and consolidation of relations of mutual respect and of the bases of self-respect.

The political violence objection is also correct in noting that, by providing differentiated treatment to perpetrators, penal benefits end up meting out more lenient sentences to those responsible for atrocious crimes than to lesser or "ordinary" offenders. The comparison is misleading, however. Atrocious crimes such as mass murder and enforced disappearance are always the result of a deep transformation in social circumstances, including the breakdown of social norms, the emergence of strong criminogenic forces, and the dysfunction of state institutions, which create a strong pull toward atrocity; many perpetrators in these contexts are unable to resist this pull, which ordinary offenders do not commonly face to the same extent in normal circumstances. For this reason, putting atrocity and ordinary crimes on the same scale for the purposes of calculating the severity of the corresponding punishment is morally dubious, at least from the perspective of retributivism, according to which the severity of the punishment must match the offender's blameworthiness.[69] We cannot draw any clear moral lessons about what honors or undermines equality before penal law by comparing the severity of punishment in these markedly different contexts.

More important than the inadequacy of this ill-grounded comparison, however, is a question about the stakes of accepting or rejecting penal rewards. Why should the erosion of the consistency of sentencing practices, with the ensuing inequality before penal law, be of more consequence than the loss of the social bases for mutual respect and self-respect? We must not forget that we are before a situation in which *any* course of action will generate some unpalatable results. Penal benefits raise moral concerns but so does their absence. What is needed is an argument about the hierarchy of priorities. In this chapter, I have argued that the erosion of the bases for mutual respect and self-respect is of the highest importance.

It is true, as the political violence objection contends, that in political conflicts there are two distinct negotiating parties, while in criminal violence, where perpetrators of violence may be in collusion with the state, the line between them blurs. However, there can still be two negotiating parties amid criminal violence: parts of the state, in alliance with civil society groups, on the one hand, and the corrupt and captured parts of the state, in alliance with criminal groups, on the other. This configuration will certainly make for a more complex and encumbered "negotiation," but it still entails two negotiating parties.

Next I turn to the most powerful political violence objection—that a "negotiation with groups from organized crime is a slippery slope which other powerful criminal group might, in the future, use as a precedent to deploy more violence with the goal of obtaining a similar treatment."[70] Slippery slope arguments are plausible but always suspect because they include an empirical premise that may not be properly substantiated. In this case, the first premise of this branch of the political violence objection is that extortion of the state through violence is deeply objectionable. The second is that lenient treatment invites such extortion. The conclusion is that lenient treatment is therefore a bad and objectionable policy. The argument is unimpugnable, logically speaking, but note that the second premise is an empirical one, as such warranting empirical support. Do penal benefits always invite extortive violence? On some interpretations, they do not. Reflecting on the endemic politicization of the Mexican criminal justice system, Fernando Escalante argues that prosecutorial flexibility, including the ability to attenuate or suspend punishment, is part and parcel of the political development of postrevolutionary Mexico. Its ebullient society (socially and culturally fractured, unequal, precarious, constantly on the verge of conflict) was not pacified based on a strict application of rule of law but through a system of parasitic mediation, whereby prosecutors held significant discretion, which they in turn used to appease pressure groups (labor or peasant unions, street vendors, squatters, and so on). The pressure groups routinely *threatened* to resort to violence but refrained from doing as long as their disobedience was tolerated, thereby producing some degree of political and social stability.[71] Whether one should characterize this relationship as extortive is beside the point. The relevant matter is that, however detrimental it may have been in other regards, this arrangement often kept violence at bay rather than inviting it. There is, then, a clear precedent for arguing that some degree of flexibility within the criminal justice system reduces rather than increases violence, including crimes such as homicides and of course disappearances. It is an open question whether penal benefits could play a similar—temporary—function.

Moreover, whether negotiations with criminal groups in one domain, and in relation to one type of crime, set a precedent for future criminal activity across the board is a possibility but not a certainty. If penal benefits are circumscribed to disappearances, the worry about "other actors" threatening more violence is a moot point. Admittedly, perpetrators seeking penal benefits for disappearances *might* start kidnapping, killing, and hiding bodies to acquire some bargaining power but, given the current volume of crimes—those already committed and those in progress—reaping penal benefits might simply prompt criminals to keep track of the crimes they plan to commit anyway, rather than encouraging them to perpetrate additional ones. At any rate, this is all speculative, but we must not refrain from advancing a proposal with tangible benefits on grounds of speculation about possible detrimental effects. In fact, and more generally, penal benefits can be expected to generate a host of other perverse incentives. To give just one example: an ordinary offender guilty of femicide who happens to possess relevant information about a clandestine grave—acquired through hearsay or by witnessing another criminal burying bodies—could bury his own victim's body in the clandestine grave, allege that he belongs to a criminal organization, falsely connect his crime to those of the organization, and then reveal information about the whereabout of the grave in exchange for leniency. The proper response to this kind of perverse incentive is to gauge whether its effects are *more* concerning than the erosion of the goals and values that penal benefits help accomplish, and to devise ways of constraining the effects of these perverse incentives.

A further objection to penal benefits, somewhat related to the political violence objection, has to do with the alleged risks involved in their institutionalization. Generally, it does not follow from the moral permissibility of a sporadic practice that its institutionalization is morally permissible. This non sequitur has been pointed out regarding, for example, attempts at legalizing torture. In the long-standing debate on the subject, opponents of legalization point out that, while one might tolerate it in isolated and extraordinary situations, its legalization is out of the question because of the corrosive effect of its institutionalization, such as making it harder to subsequently abolish torture, or the creation of "torture cultures" that desensitize individuals to its harms.[72] Analogously to this argument against torture, it can be contended that, while isolated, episodic situations may render penal rewards morally acceptable, it does not follow that the practice should become part of the fabric of the criminal justice system. The institutionalization of penal benefits is harmful to the justice system, for example, in that it discourages the development of research capabilities[73] and introduces the kind of differentiation in sentencing invoked in the political violence objection. While these objections have some force, constraining penal benefits to cases of disappearances, given the gravity of the crime, tempers the potential risks of its more general institutionalization.

A final objection: Richard Lippke holds that penal benefits (or plea bargains in the US context, which is the case that he has in mind) render collaboration of perpetrators with authorities conditional on rewards, meaning that collaboration is no longer treated as their *moral obligation*.[74] From this perspective, penal benefits are the embodiment of the prevalence of self-interest and selfishness exhibited by the accused in criminal processes. In Lippke's own analogy, if a witness to a crime goes to the authorities and demands payment for informing on an event, nobody would hesitate to call this behavior immoral. For Lippke, something similar occurs with perpetrators who benefit from reduced sentences. Rewarding them for collaboration is equivalent to rewarding them for immoral conduct, which places their interests above the public interest. In the case of perpetrators, their duty to collaborate with authorities is even *greater* than that of ordinary citizens, Lippke adds, by virtue of their responsibility for the crimes committed. Hence, plea bargaining with an eye to negotiating is objectionable from a moral standpoint.

Lippke is right to claim that, through penal rewards, perpetrators cooperate with authorities out of self-interest rather than moral obligation. This is regrettable. Yet his objection can be addressed succinctly by claiming, first, that while there is indeed a moral loss here, there is also a moral loss when the bases of respect and self-respect are eroded in the absence of penal benefits. The latter is a bigger loss. Second, the benefits of perpetrator cooperation can be of such consequence with respect to disappearances that they justify the *contained* assertion of self-interest in the criminal justice system. Some offenders might be willing to share information about the disappeared in exchange for a bar of soap or chocolate or a box of cornflakes, or if they are transferred to a different penitentiary, presumably one where they perceive their life is not at risk. This kind of self-interested behavior might have to be countenanced in order to protect the interest of society in maintaining relations of mutual respect and the conditions for self-respect, as the relatives of the disappeared navigate the complex and devastating process of searching for the disappeared.

A final point. Relatives of the disappeared are already trying to elicit information from perpetrators, putting their lives at risk, regardless of whether penal benefits are implemented and promoted. Incorporating the state into the equation can allow these negotiations to unfold without imperiling their lives. In this sense, the relevant comparison is not simply between a situation where the state refuses to bargain, thus preserving, say, the integrity of the criminal justice system, and one where it does bargain, harming it. This comparison hides from view other harms that arise from the decision not to bargain. The contrast to be drawn should be between a situation where relatives engage criminal organizations without the intervention of the state, to their peril, and another where they initiate this negotiation with the support of the state, lessening the risks to themselves.

Conclusions

In this chapter, I argued that reduced sentencing poses a moral dilemma for public authorities in Mexico who seek to locate the disappeared, and that this dilemma must be resolved by prioritizing the disclosure of forensic truth over proportional punishment for crimes. Encouraging the disclosure of truth is more important, ethically speaking, than strictly protecting the integrity of the justice system and its operation in contexts of ordinary violence. In other words, the *forensic* principle (which involves making criminal law more flexible if it benefits the efforts to search for the disappeared) must take precedence over the *punitive* principle (which involves not loosening or reducing criminal sanctions to uphold the rule of law). In short, the moral cost to victims unable to find their disappeared loved ones is greater than that of a partial relaxation of punishment, a balance that principled leniency must reflect.

TWO

The Limits of Penal Benefits

On the Use and Abuse of Collaborators

Penal benefits for perpetrators are an adequate tool, morally speaking, for addressing the problem of the disappeared. They are an instance of principled leniency. This does not mean, however, that rewarding perpetrators for their collaboration is *always* the right thing to do. There are ethical limits to the use of penal benefits, which this chapter explores. Its focus is on collaborating witnesses (*testigos colaboradores*) who have bargained with Mexican authorities as well as those who have come to such an agreement with the Drug Enforcement Agency (DEA), which heavily relies on them in its operations in Mexico and elsewhere. In both cases, so the argument goes, public authorities—Mexican and American alike—acted improperly by enlisting collaborators in the service of the criminal justice system because they did so in such a way, and under such circumstances, that exposed them and others to retaliatory aggressions, thus widening rather than curbing violence.[1]

The examination of penal rewards for cooperation runs on two levels. On the most obvious level, the chapter briefly alludes to the perversions of the system of collaborators. More importantly, however, on the second level, the chapter examines the underlying philosophical problem regarding the moral permissibility of deploying collaborators in the social and political circumstances prevailing in the country. The reason to consider this deeper ethical question is that even if it turned out that the abuse of the system could be eradicated and the practice reformed, there is still room to question the morality of the practice beyond the critical case of the disappeared. Undeniably, the use of collaborating witnesses carries inherent risks. These risks are not in themselves a reason to oppose the practice. But the extent and the nature of those risks, and the willingness of the state to subject collaborators to them, ought to be regulated and constrained according to clear and defensible principles, in particular, principles of proportionality and necessity, as they are commonly understood in the literature on just intelligence. These moral principles will clarify whether the operation of counternarcotics intelligence in Mexico is morally permissible. I shall argue that intelligence involving collaborating witnesses in Mexico commonly fails to respect these principles, giving the practice a tenuous morality at best. This is partly because the country's institutional and socioeconomic conditions exacerbate the potential risk of harm to collaborators themselves and to ordinary citizens, thus raising the moral costs of obtaining intelligence through witness collaborators.

But why focus on collaborators and the perils they go through as they become state witnesses? Aren't they, after all, secondary figures in the landscape of drug violence? What does the fate of a handful of collaborators (most of them morally and legally culpable to some extent) matter compared to the plight of the hundreds of thousands of innocent victims of drug violence, some of it perpetrated by these very same collaborators?

Beyond the scholarly neglect of the subject, there are many reasons to take an interest in the state's use of collaborators in Mexico. First, it reflects some of the objectionable features of the criminal justice system, among them the inadequacy of its institutional processes and its lack of concern for the well-being of those who stand before it as the accused party and who oftentimes are believed to "deserve" whatever violence befalls them. Second, taking collaborators seriously is also critical because the refusal of potential collaborators to cooperate with law enforcement authorities or the authorities' inability to properly "administer" such cooperation can have deeply detrimental consequences for society in general.

Third, and related to this, state use of collaborators raises a moral predicament that has surfaced in related scholarly debates: whether it is acceptable to violate the rights of a (culpable) few in order to make strides in criminal investigations, thus solving specific crimes and most importantly serving collective goals such as abating crime rates and curbing violence. Political philosophers have discussed similar issues in relation to the use of torture, debating whether it is permissible to torture a terrorist to extract life-saving information from them.[2] Legal philosophers broach similar issues when they debate the proper balance between liberty and security,[3] with some arguing in defense of subjecting entire categories of individuals who are identified as "enemies" to legal standards that do not guarantee the full protections of penal law. The study of the penal benefits in the context of drug-related extraordinary violence raises some of these same concerns and should, therefore, help to illuminate them.

Finally, exploring the Mexican case can be helpful in understanding the moral implications of using collaborating witnesses elsewhere. Scholarly work on the ethics of knowledge acquisition in law enforcement contexts has advanced some ethical guidelines that ought to orient the work of intelligence-led policing[4] but paid little attention to the more specific case of rewards for cooperation in circumstances of extraordinary violence.[5] Some academic studies on plea bargains focus on their corrosive impact on the criminal justice system; others allude to the problem of "witness intimidation."[6] Yet, most fall short of theorizing more deeply the relationship between witness collaboration and social and political violence, particularly massive violence. The chapter makes a contribution in this direction.

The chapter unfolds as follows. Section one sketches the philosophical framework that sets moral parameters for subsequent sections—the just intelligence paradigm. This framework will serve to guide the inquiry in the next sections. Section two focuses on the case of *testigos colaboradores* of Mexican authorities. Section three then turns to the DEA's plea bargains.[7]

Just Collaboration

The use of witness collaborators has become standard practice in many criminal justice systems, most notably perhaps in the United States with its (in)famous plea bargains and their multiple criticisms.[8] One criticism is that plea bargains introduce distortions in the imposition of punishment, since similar crimes receive different punishments, depending on how "useful" the accused turns out to be to authorities. Penal rewards of this kind also undermine due process, so the criticism goes, since they set incentives for defendants to self-incriminate. A further criticism is that if these agreements are informal and secretive, as they usually are, they erode public transparency of the criminal justice system because they hide from the public eye the nature of agreements between law enforcement agencies and witnesses—the opposite of what occurs with trials, which involve public litigation and leave a public record. In the following lines I focus on a different problem: the potential risk of retaliation against collaborators, which state authorities promoting penal benefits, as well as the contexts in which they take place, may exacerbate or contain. Since the use of collaborators by law enforcement agencies must be understood as a form of intelligence collection, the ethical framework of just intelligence theory can be productively harnessed to address this problem.

A just intelligence framework seeks to articulate principles that "limit the harm intelligence collection causes while outlining what circumstances would be required to justify the harm caused." Ross Bellaby[9] and other scholars argue that the just war tradition in philosophy can be a useful starting point to examine the proper use of intelligence.[10] Just war theory is a normative theory that seeks to elucidate two dimensions of the ethics of war—the proper ends justifying a war (*jus ad bellum*), and the morally appropriate means to conduct it (*jus in bellum*).[11] By analogy, *jus ad intelligentiam* is concerned with the proper motives to employ intelligence services, and *jus in intelligentia* posits the morally adequate ways to do so.[12] The analogy between just war and just intelligence is not perfect,[13] and some scholars are skeptical about the fruitfulness of deploying the former theory in the context of intelligence, particularly with respect to preventive intelligence as opposed to more targeted forms of intelligence against suspects.[14] These reservations notwithstanding, the general gist of the theory can be employed to demarcate the parameters of morally permissible intelligence work.

For the purposes of this chapter, the relevant principles are *jus in intelligentia* principles.[15] They apply to agents on the field and include the principle of discrimination (liable or nonliable targets must be clearly discerned one from the other); of proportionality (the harm that is perceived to be caused by specific intelligence interventions should be outweighed by the perceived gains); and of necessity (less harmful interventions should be attempted before more harmful ones are chosen). The two *jus in intelligentia* principles of most relevance for the present discussion are necessity and proportionality.[16] Necessity may be interpreted as positing, simply, that to be permissible, a specific intelligence intervention must be the only one possible to reach a specific end. There must be no alternative means; if alternatives exist, they are worse than the proposed intervention. Put succinctly, the principle of necessity states that in choosing between two harmful means of collecting intelligence, the least harmful must always be selected—harm minimization is critical for this principle.

Proportionality is more challenging to operationalize than necessity. Proportionality tracks a relationship between intelligence action and the justifying cause. It has three components: the benefits deriving from the intelligence activity in question (for example, gathering evidence to convict a corrupt public official complicit with a criminal organization or thwarting an operation by one of these organizations), its costs (for example, the harm they cause to those who conduct it, or to civilians), and the appropriate balancing between benefits and costs.[17] While the relevant benefits must be clearly connected to the just cause, there is no parallel restriction with respect to the cost of intelligence. Every harm counts, although some harms count more than others. The "risks to agents and those to whom a duty of care is owed"; "risks of collateral damage to others"; and "risk to future operations and to institutional reputations if the operation were to go wrong" should be front and center.[18] By contrast, the harm experienced by members of criminal organizations—and this includes the witness collaborators—matters but has diminished weight since, through their actions, they made themselves liable to be affected by intelligence seeking to confront the crimes they are or were involved in. Along these lines, factors such as their complicity with, and their moral responsibility for contributing to, the crimes in question make it permissible to put them under the risks associated with intelligence; the greater their complicity and their responsibility, the more justified it becomes to impose such risks on them. In other words, the kinds of harm that count toward the proportionality assessment are "morally weighted," to use Seth Lazar's[19] term: some are more morally significant than others.

Tallying up costs and benefits in the realm of morality is, admittedly, difficult. One challenge, on the epistemic level, involves accurately identifying the significance of potential benefits of an intelligence intervention, its costs, and its unintended consequences. Embarking on an intelligence operation commonly has the goal of collecting information to determine the nature and level of a security threat or whether there is one at all. If it turns out that no threat was forthcoming, but the cost of the operation turns out to be high, the intelligence operation can be judged to be disproportionate, but this judgment can only be made retrospectively.[20] Similarly, assessing alternative intelligence operations presupposes foresight of the consequence of each alternative. Yet such foresight is frequently unreliable, as unexpected events might derail intelligence operations or even throw them in complete disarray. For all these reasons, intelligence operations involve a high degree of epistemic uncertainty. This is particularly true in nations with institutional deficits, particularly in law enforcement, since one of the essential functions of institutions is to help reduce unpredictability in social interaction, including state action. Epistemic uncertainty around intelligence activities is also heightened in nations with large socioeconomic disparities and engulfed in massive social violence. Both factors undermine the ability of law-enforcement agencies to anticipate and minimize disruptions to its operations.

Epistemic uncertainty makes balancing costs and benefits even more challenging, particularly when we are dealing with intelligence cases in the "twilight zone," by which Kevin Macnish[21] means those cases that are neither clearly disproportionate nor clearly proportionate. Most cases are of this kind. In balancing harms and benefits, according to this view, one can either take a restrictive view, which presumes disproportionality unless there are strong reasons to the contrary, and a permissive view, which presumes proportionality unless there are strong reasons to the contrary.

I will have more to say about the specifics of this paradigm further on, but for now this general framework should suffice. To anticipate the gist of the argument in the following sections, I shall contend, based on this framework, that in light of the harm inflicted on collaborators, and in some cases on the citizenry, the use of collaborators is a disproportionate and sometimes even an unnecessary intelligence measure. Although intelligence work inherently entails uncertainty, particularly of the epistemic kind, for collaborating witnesses and civilians, the degree of uncertainty varies depending on the context. In a constitutional democracy, with low levels of corruption, strong security and justice institutions, and a moderate level of socioeconomic deprivation, the uncertainty diminishes considerably. Conversely, in Mexico, where authoritarian enclaves persist within formally democratic institutions and where corrupt and unaccountable public officials, weak security and public institutions, rampant violence, and precarious socioeconomic conditions prevail in many regions of the country, the margins of uncertainty for intelligence work widen considerably, putting both collaborators and the civilian population at grave risk. In such a social setting, intelligence interventions that rely on the work of collaborating witnesses and informers will tend to be disproportionate, even if necessary, to the detriment of intelligence agents themselves as well as civilians. In situations of epistemic uncertainty arising from institutional deficits or social violence, a restrictive view of proportionality is the morally appropriate path for intelligence operations.

"Don't Bother Calling the Witness, Your Honor, He's Dead."[22]

Mexican federal authorities have increasingly used *testigos colaboradores* with the dramatic surge of drug-related violence. Their use became legally acknowledged in 1996, rising steadily but significantly during the tenure of Vicente Fox (2000–2006) and Felipe Calderón (2006–12), to decline during Enrique Peña Nieto's (2012–18) presidency, when the interest and resources allocated to them diminished considerably.[23] It is unclear whether *testigos colaboradores* gained saliency again during the administration of Andrés Manuel López Obrador (2018–24), but they are present in a high-profile case in the current criminal justice agenda—the enforced disappearance of the students from the Ayotzinapa rural teachers college. There is also some indication that informal programs of *testigos colaboradores* are in operation at the local level.[24] During the last two decades, the figure of the witness collaborator has received increasing (albeit insufficient) legal and constitutional grounding in Mexico, first in the Ley Federal de Contra la Delincuencia Organizada (Federal Law against Organized Crime)[25] of 1996[26] and then in 2012, with the Ley Federal para la Protección a Personas que Intervienen en el Procedimiento Penal (Federal Law for the Protection of Individuals Who Intervene in Criminal Proceedings), among others.

The legislation on this matter (which prevailed until 2012) did not provide sufficient parameters or regulations to guarantee a serious witness protection program. The law stipulated the protection of the integrity and identity of witnesses, but there were no clear guidelines regarding the program: its specificities were unknown—for example, the acceptance, protection, and compensation conditions on the basis of which witnesses were admitted.[27]

Worse, many of the witnesses were left to their own devices after they shared information, and some of them were even assassinated. Such treatment violates the international human rights framework,[28] which requires states to establish and enforce a legal system to oversee the use of confidential informants.[29] There are also indications that the Mexican program was misused by the federal government as a political tool to persecute political enemies. For example, former Secretary of Public Security Genaro García Luna, convicted in the United States for his assistance to "criminal enterprises" tied to drug trafficking, used statements from protected witnesses to arrest the commander of the Federal Preventive Police, Javier Herrera, who had accused Luna of precisely having those ties.[30]

Despite these regulations, then, collaborators face life-threatening conditions as a result of their cooperation with authorities. Is it morally acceptable to subject them to such risk, or is it too high a moral price to pay in the quest for useful intelligence? Following the just intelligence paradigm sketched in the previous section, necessity and proportionality are two principles to help us answer this question. The section will argue that, taking into account the institutional and socioeconomic background conditions (that is, weak political and criminal justice institutions, corruption, violence, social disparities, and so on) in which the practice is embedded, collecting intelligence through collaborating witnesses may be a necessary measure, but also a disproportionate one.

A Matter of Necessity?

Intelligence collection using witness collaborators seems to be a necessary practice in the criminal justice system. Oftentimes, law enforcement cannot fathom the details of the activities of criminal organizations without a knowledgeable "source" inside them, since these organizations operate clandestinely and commonly have enough financial or logistic resources to elude public authorities. The Mexican criminal justice system in particular might be more dependent on collaborating witnesses than other systems because of its insufficiently developed capabilities to conduct rigorous investigations. Discussing the operation of police forces in Mexico, Gustavo Fondevila rightly argues that owing to "its inadequate professionalization (the use of scientific investigation methods), the lack of a professional police infiltration system (undercover agents) and citizens' lack of trust in the police, almost all the relevant information received comes from informers." As a result, he adds, the police have been forced to "hyper-develop its informer system as its sole source of information."[31] This insight is probably true across the board in the criminal justice system, and with respect to the production and trafficking of illicit substances in particular. Thus, notwithstanding the Mexican state's responsibility to develop investigative capabilities in the long run, the dependence of the system on informers or collaborating witnesses seems to be a necessary counternarcotics strategy. Furthermore, many criminal organizations, running profitable businesses that are not limited to drug trafficking, have financial resources that match or exceed those of local and sometimes even federal authorities; the militarization of drug-trafficking combat, meant to assist and sometimes replace these authorities, does not redress this imbalance. Finally, for the purposes of crime prosecution, collaborators are the only avenue for authorities to go beyond the lower level "operators" of criminal organizations and reach their higher echelons (in administrative or authoritative positions).[32] In light of this weakness, and the muscle of criminal organizations, authorities must fall back on any legitimate means at their disposal.

A Matter of Proportion?

Are the interventions proportionate, particularly the use of collaborating witnesses? That depends, as we have seen, on the assessment of costs and benefits. Consider benefits first. *Testigos colaboradores* have a grim record in terms of the benefits they bring to the criminal justice system. Accusations based on their testimony have produced little in the way of successful prosecutions. According to a federal judge interviewed for this chapter, the use of the *testigos colaboradores* became so vitiated that oftentimes the same individual would offer testimony in several, unconnected prosecutions. The result was a contaminated prosecutorial process where convictions repeatedly rested on these dubious testimonies. Unsurprisingly, some investigations relying exclusively on the testimony of these witnesses would end up crumbling.[33] *Testigos colaboradores*, in their perverted use, dovetail with two ingrained practices in the Mexican criminal justice system—the "fabrication" of witnesses for the legal inculpation of innocent citizens and the persecution of political enemies by federal authorities.

But these results arise from a perversion of the system. There are some instances in which the use of *testigos colaboradores* does yield benefits. These are difficult to appreciate because information about the role of collaborators in criminal prosecutions is not always publicly accessible; their contributions are sometimes informal and thus fail to make it into legal records. While the federal prosecutor's office has extensively relied on witness collaborators, a former district judge interviewed for this chapter affirmed that s/he is unaware of a single sentence in which penal rewards have in effect been granted in return for cooperation.[34] Nonetheless, the case of Gildardo N., discussed in the previous chapter, furnishes an example of these potential benefits. This witness collaborator participated in the criminal investigation surrounding the enforced disappearance of Ayotzinapa students, who were abducted by a criminal organization with the complicity of local and federal security forces in the state of Guerrero. The information he shared seems to have steered the investigation away from the impasse to which it had been directed by the previous administration (deliberately some argue), and in a more promising direction.[35] Let us concede then, for the sake of the argument, that at least in some cases the use of *testigos colaboradores* can yield benefits such as locating the whereabouts of victims of enforced disappearance or, simply, abating violence. If Gildardo N. were put in jeopardy for his cooperation, but as a result Mexican society was closer to finding the location of Ayotzinapa students, wouldn't that be worth the risk?

To answer questions of this sort, we need to turn to the costs of using witness collaborators. These costs include the harm to collaborators themselves. On account of their complicity and responsibility with wrongdoing, the harm they might be subjected to as a result of their collaboration, or the risk thereof, has diminished moral weight, compared to what other actors might suffer. But just how much should the harm suffered by collaborators be discounted, morally speaking? That depends on two considerations. An institutional consideration is whether the criminal justice system possesses the tools to protect collaborators. Despite attempts at institutionalizing the practice in Mexico, for collaborators the risk involved in cooperating with authorities has always been and remains extraordinarily high. The laws that were put in place to regulate the practice were either vague or never fully enforced. Because of this lack of institutionalization, security guarantees for *testigos colaboradores*, from recruitment stage to more advanced stages in their collaboration, were poorly implemented, if implemented at all. The second consideration refers to the varying criminal and socioeconomic profiles of collaborators, from which different degrees of culpability and responsibility, as well as different bargaining advantages, ensue. I now turn to discuss both considerations in greater detail. As an illustration, I provide two contrasting examples—the case of "Venus," a low-level perpetrator, and the case of Edgar Enrique Bayardo del Villar, a.k.a. Tigre. These examples shed light on the richly textured considerations that must be made in assessing the costs of intelligence work.

Venus was a *testiga colaboradora* who began cooperating in 2010, two years prior to the enactment of the Federal Law for the Protection of Individuals who Intervene in Criminal Proceedings. She is believed to have been a collaborator for the Zetas, a criminal organization. Venus and others testified against the main leaders of the organization and 400 other individuals.[36] According to her, she was disenrolled as a *testigo colaboradora* in 2015[37] but was summoned to testify the same year, without protection. Even though a federal judge ordered the Federal Prosecutors' Office to offer protection to her, the office declined to do so, offering an obtuse legal argument to support its denial.[38] She refused to testify on that occasion, claiming she had been intimidated against doing so several times.[39] Venus reports that as a *testiga colaboradora* she was offered housing in overcrowded and unsanitary conditions, in a residence guarded by Marines and federal agents. She lived there with another thirteen *testigos colaboradores* and the families of some of them. (Incidentally, the property had belonged to drug lord Osiel Cárdenas, which the Calderón administration confiscated and repurposed.)

This case is representative of a pattern of cases where collaborators find themselves in the grips of an inefficacious criminal justice system that is unable to properly guarantee them a minimal level of protection in exchange for their cooperation but recruits them into cooperating nonetheless.[40] But the harm collaborators like Venus experience is not only the result of the institutional precarity of the witness protection figure and the institutions that sustain it. It is also the result of the socioeconomic precarity of collaborators.

Collaborators are not a uniform class of people. They differ in their socioeconomic status, their degree of involvement in crime, and the extent to which they can lever an advantage over the criminal justice system. In the case of Venus, there is every indication that she came from a disadvantaged socioeconomic background. Criminal offenders of this kind tend to be recruited into criminal organizations under conditions that cannot be described as fully voluntary, or they may have simply been born in criminogenic environments, which, as will be discussed in chapter 4 at greater length, lessens their responsibility for perpetrating *mala prohibita* crime, that is, crimes prohibited by statute but not inherently evil or wrong.[41] With some exceptions, they occupy indefinitely the lower rungs of the criminal rackets they serve and have a modest yet significant role in its decision-making processes. In a sense, they are victims of drug violence as well. Similarly, and this is also attributable to her socioeconomic condition, it is not even clear that Venus participated voluntarily as a collaborating witness, a situation that is revealed from the fact that she was enrolled into the program of witness collaborators, then disenrolled, then summoned to testify again, all the while lacking a clear sense of her legal status. Her participation seems to have been based on manipulation or even coercion, and obtained without legal assistance on her side. And because her gains are anything but secured, the bargain is unfair to her. Thus, in subjecting such collaborators to the risks entailed in serving as state witnesses, they are victimized twice over—first as reluctant, deluded, or forced participants in their criminal organization, then as potential targets for these organizations on account of their collaboration with law enforcement authorities.[42]

Contrast the criminal and socioeconomic profile of Venus to that of Bayardo—the second example I shall discuss. Before turning into a *testigo colaborador,* Bayardo held several high-ranking positions in the federal and state police forces while at the same time cultivating ties to drug-trafficking organizations such as the Sinaloa cartel and even informing for some of them for twenty years.[43] Bayardo provided a great deal of intelligence (not all of it reliable) to authorities, until he was executed in a Starbucks a year after he began his collaboration. Upon close inspection, it is clear that his execution was possible owing in part to some of the same failures of protection of collaborators described in the case of Venus. Not only was the presence of Bayardo at such a public venue a blatant security failure. An investigation of Bayardo's assassination revealed that the security agents in charge of his protection were poorly qualified as bodyguards (they were low-ranking agents), working forty-eight-hour shifts; in fact, they were subsequently imprisoned for their alleged negligence.[44] Bayardo's case is not an isolated one. Several high-ranking leaders of criminal organizations have traded penal benefits of some sort for cooperation.

Notwithstanding their similarities in relation to the deficiency of protection guarantees, which alone ought to dissuade law enforcement agencies from using collaborators, the cases of Venus and Bayardo are different. Bayardo's criminal profile warranted subjecting him to a greater level of risk than would be appropriate for collaborators like Venus and similar offenders. Contrary to low-level perpetrators, who must negotiate in lopsided and asymmetric conditions, oftentimes under coercion or manipulation, and without real power to bargain, collaborators like Bayardo have a significant bargaining advantage. Being affluent individuals, they gain access to expensive lawyers and sophisticated legal advice, which allows them to exploit the weaknesses of the criminal justice system. In short, they have the leverage to bargain with authorities on level terms. And the fact that they use this bargaining advantage to their favor is an indication that they voluntarily negotiate with public authorities. Furthermore, their stronger bargaining position should, in all fairness, come along with the acceptance of the risks that this advantage entails. Put crudely, if they are going to "game" the criminal justice system and profit from it, these collaborators must also accept the accompanying risks.

In addition, many of them, again like Bayardo, have a deep involvement with the criminal racket they worked for and subsequently informed against. They are also unambiguously morally blameworthy, as no extenuating circumstances absolve them. The state is then more justified in putting these collaborators under retaliatory risk given their responsibility in the crimes under investigation. Richard Lippke[45] is right in arguing that offenders "can reasonably be expected to make more sacrifices in helping to bring their fellow wrongdoers to justice." The kind of protection we can extend to them, he grants, is imperfect. "However, those directly involved in the wrongdoing might be thought to have a stronger duty to take the relevant risks. Hence, having to do or risk more is precisely what we should demand and expect of criminal wrongdoers."[46] Since they helped "create the mess," as Lippke puts is, they now bear the brunt of the responsibility to fix it. A corollary of this idea seems to be that the greater their involvement and the responsibility in the commission of crimes, as was Bayardo's case, the greater the risks of reprisal they should be expected to assume.

In sum, while for Mexican law enforcement authorities conducting intelligence efforts through the use of collaborating witnesses may be a necessary measure, those efforts are not always proportionate. Assuming that some significant benefit in intelligence collection arises out of the witnesses' contribution, the assessment of costs varies depending on how morally justified authorities are in exposing collaborators to harm. This is turn depends on whether witnesses collaborate voluntarily, and with some advantage in the bargain; on whether they are complicit and responsible with respect to the crimes in question; and especially on whether the state has the means to protect the collaborator against retaliation from former accomplices. When it is not clear that the costs of witness collaboration are outweighed by its benefits (the paradigmatic case of Venus being one such instance of this), the state must adopt a restrictive view of proportionality.

A "Frog Hunt" Turned Massacre: The DEA's Unethical Bargaining

Mexican law-enforcement agencies are not the only ones leading intelligence efforts that involve the use of witness collaborators. Since the 1970s, when the Ford and Carter administrations ramped up their counternarcotic efforts, the DEA has "engaged in aggressive, unregulated policing and intelligence gathering in Mexico."[47] There are many problems with the way in which the DEA routinely conducts its operations within Mexican territory, most notably, the violation of national sovereignty, as the organization has a record of carrying out its operations, some of them in an illegal manner (for example, using entrapment), without fully informing national authorities about them. I will not go over these problems in any detail here. I shall rather focus on how the DEA's use of collaborating witnesses may take a toll on ordinary citizens. While there might be gains from this intelligence, the harms to civilians resulting from them may be significant; some of these harms may have not been intended but they were certainly foreseeable, given the background conditions (political, social, institutional) that prevail in Mexico, particularly in areas under control of criminal organizations. All things considered, in this context the use of collaborating witnesses turns out to be both unnecessary and disproportionate.

Examining the use of collaborating witnesses by the DEA is warranted for several reasons. The agency is one of the most important counternarcotic actors operating in the country. In addition, the intense scrutiny of its actions on the part of the media and nongovernmental organizations offers a glimpse of its modus operandi. In the realm of intelligence services, where public information is scarce, this is a significant advantage. Finally, the DEA furnishes a useful contrast to the cases already discussed. While Mexican law enforcement agencies are, as we saw, highly unprofessional, budget-strapped, and relatively modest in the aims they pursue with the use of collaborators, the DEA is a professionalized, wealthy, and ambitious agency. For these reasons, its actions have wider social repercussions than those examined up to this point.

I shall begin by discussing in some detail one of the most egregious atrocities in Mexico's recent history in connection to drug violence—the 2011 massacre in Allende, in the northern state of Coahuila—in which the DEA played a decisive, if unintended, role.[48] The massacre was perpetrated by the Zetas, one of the most violent criminal organizations at the time, which had once been the armed branch of the Gulf Organization. Zetas have a special place in the history of drug trafficking in Mexico because they pioneered a business model that, in some respects, would later be adopted by other criminal organizations in the country. It is worth saying a few lines about the organization because some of its features serve as a background to understanding the levels of cruelty of the Allende massacre. The Zetas inaugurated a criminal business model that relied on militarized territorial control and that sought to diversify its business activities beyond drug trafficking, branching out to other extractive activities such as migrant smuggling, extortion and kidnapping, human trafficking, protection services, black markets (music and video piracy), and even theft of oil, gas, and other natural resources. The rule of Zetas over the territory they controlled was based on the recruitment of local gangs as well as on spreading fear among the population. Reliance on local gangs, as well as its strategy of terror, go some way into explaining the lengths to which Zetas went in order to punish "traitors."[49]

An intelligence operation in the pursuit of two members of the Zeta leadership—the Treviño brothers—triggered the massacre. In turn, the operation was part of the so-called kingpin strategy, which the agency enthusiastically endorses. The strategy takes the fragmentation of criminal organizations and the capture and elimination of their leaders to be the ideal mechanism to weaken these organizations.[50] A DEA agent, Robert Martínez,

had accomplished an intelligence feat that carried the promise of contributing to the decapitation of the Zetas: he had obtained the trackable cell
phone identification numbers of two of its kingpins, the Treviño brothers.
The leaker was José Vázquez, a cocaine distributor in Texas who was part of
the organization. To extract the information, the agent threatened Vázquez
with imprisoning his mother and wife (presumably with legal grounds to
do so), forcing Vázquez himself to exert pressure on other criminal confed-
erates. Charging a family member in order to pressure a defendant is commonly referred to as "wired plea"—the outcome of the family member's case
is "wired" to the defendant's cooperation.[51]

Against the explicit wishes of both the agent and the leaker, DEA su-
pervisors in Mexico City or Texas shared the intelligence with a unit of the
Mexican police. However, immediately after the unit received the information, the Zetas learned about the leak and identified the leakers, presumably
because they had infiltrated an informer in the unit. Ironically, the members
of the unit had been trained by the DEA itself and were supposed to be im-
pervious to leaks and corruption. The revelation precipitated the massacre,
and the Zetas, with the complicity of local authorities, set out to retaliate
against "frogs," as Zetas pejoratively call those who cooperate with the public
authorities. When this failed (the suspects managed to flee to the United
States), they went after their relatives, friends, and associates in Allende and
Piedras Negras. Since among them was another alleged snitch whose last
name was Garza, they targeted anyone with this last name (a common one
in northern Mexico).[52] The bodies of the victims of the massacre, in the hundreds, were burned clandestinely in a local ranch-cum-crematorium. Was
the intelligence operation in question necessary and proportionate?

A Matter of Necessity?

While surveilling the leadership of Zetas was a legitimate intervention,
it does not follow that but for the use of witness collaborators, it would have
been impossible to achieve it. Unlike Mexican law-enforcement agencies,
with chronically meager budgets and unprofessional cadres, relative to the
tasks they face, the DEA receives adequate funding (with the ensuing professionalization of its agents and cutting-edge technology) and is part of a pro-
ductive and powerful intelligence community, which includes other agencies

such as the FBI and the US Immigration and Customs Enforcement (ICE). These characteristics allow the DEA to pursue alternative, less harmful intelligence methods. As a matter of fact, the eventual capture of Miguel Ángel Treviño, carried out without a single casualty around the US-Mexico border, involved the use of commercial computer spyware, probably placed on the kingpin's computer through phishing or some other form of cyber manipulation; GPS mobile tracking devices; as well as the use of a drone facilitated by ICE.[53] The capture, then, was the result of the coordination between the DEA, with the assistance of other US intelligence agencies, and the Mexican military. Less harmful avenues of intelligence collection were available to the DEA, and therefore its actions, leading to the Allende massacre, flouted the principle of necessity.

A Matter of Proportion?

Formally speaking, the DEA abides by a stringent protocol infused with the value of proportionality.[54] According to its guidelines, for instance, the work of a "cooperating witness" must be "entirely voluntary," and the agency commits, "but cannot guarantee," that his or her identity "will not be divulged." Before engaging him or her, authorities must run a "suitability determination," which assesses "the risk of physical harm that may occur to the person or his or her immediate family or close associates as a result of providing information or assistance" to the DEA. Yet it seems clear that operations on the ground do not always abide by the protocols in the books. In the case of Allende, obtaining cell phone identification numbers (the benefit) at the expense of a massacre (the cost) was a blatantly disproportionate operation. Before settling this point, however, we must address two possible rejoinders to this view.

First, it may be argued that the massacre was of the Zeta's making, not the DEA's, and therefore one cannot hold the agency responsible and claim that its actions violated proportionality constraints. The DEA unleashed the ire of the criminal organization unintentionally when its strategy involving the collaborator was leaked. But, so the argument goes, leaks of that sort may occur in any intelligence action, and the same is true of retaliation. Both phenomena are part and parcel of intelligence work. The response to this rejoinder is that while it is true that the origin of the retaliatory violence is the criminal group (with the complicity of some state actors), and that it was certainly not the *intention* of DEA agents to wreak havoc on the local population, they should have *foreseen* the potential outcomes of their actions in view of the features of the context in which they operated. Because they turned a blind eye to them instead, DEA agents failed to properly acknowledge the epistemic uncertainty surrounding the consequences of their actions and wrongly discounted the possibility that informational leaks would have a detrimental impact on collaborating witnesses and even innocent bystanders. What were the features of the context that should have led the DEA to a more cautious approach?

One is Mexico's background institutional conditions. The Mexican state can only provide suboptimal security conditions in many regions of the country. Local security forces and law-enforcement agencies are too burdened or too corrupt to avoid informational leaks, even in the case of intelligence units trained with the assistance of the DEA. They cannot always be trusted to process sensitive information confidentially or to protect citizens adequately.

The second feature of the intelligence context under discussion relates to the kind of violence unfolding in the region. Criminal rackets such as the Zetas rely on a combination of selective and indiscriminate violence in their attempt to exercise political and social control over the territory and its population in defiance of formal authorities.[55] They recognize how destabilizing informers can be in achieving this goal, which explains why they deal with them particularly harshly. Harsh treatment of collaborators or those in their circle represents a deterrence mechanism, a way to discipline the ranks, discourage ordinary civilians from assisting formal authorities,[56] and even a strategy to emulate a state that dispenses sanctions when appropriate.[57] The Zetas "punished" collaborators for precisely these reasons.[58] In their legal testimony before US courts, several members of the Zetas acknowledge that the organization commonly killed suspected collaborators. One of them explains: "And the commander said that he was going to kill him so that people would know because he was working for the DEA so that people would become aware that nobody could betray them."[59] Such assassinations are one of the multiple sources of violence in regions like Coahuila. Where these dynamics of control are in place, failed intelligence can go awry in ways that cannot be anticipated.

The second rejoinder to the charge that in the Allende case the use of witness collaborators was a disproportionate measure is that, if one takes a broader, long-term view of the security situation in the region where events unfolded, and if one takes the massacre to be a failed step in a series of actions that eventually led to successfully ending Zeta dominance, then arguably, taken as a part of the whole, the intelligence leading to the massacre was proportionate, the long-term benefits outweighing the immediate costs. This rejoinder is unconvincing. It may very well be true that decapitating the Zetas did have, as part of a broader strategy, an overall positive impact on the abatement of social violence (although this might be disputed, as some believe that decapitation of criminal organizations leads to further violence rather than to its reduction). However, the question is whether the state may permissibly engage in any kind of action, in this case any intelligence interventions, for the sake of a greater good. It must not.

The state certainly has the duty to assist and protect citizens. Yet, as a rule, it should not provide such assistance and protection by deliberately inflicting harm on other people. This side constraint limits the range of permissible intelligence actions for law enforcement agencies. Philippa Foot articulated this view in a classical essay on political philosophy. She argued that an agent ought not to perform a positive duty (providing assistance) by breaching a negative duty (refraining from harming others). Thus, in her example, a doctor may deny a life-saving medicine at the highest dosage to one severely ill patient with grim survival prospects and instead administer it at a lesser dosage to five other patients with positive recovery prospects instead, but the doctor must not take the life of same severely ill patient to donate her organs and save five other people who need them. The latter but not the former course of action would amount to breaching a negative duty to perform a positive duty.[60] Returning to the Allende case, imperiling the lives of a few witness collaborators to achieve intelligence gains that may save lives down the line is just a case of violating a negative duty (directing harm toward innocent civilians) to perform a positive one (ridding the region of Zeta's brutal dominance), and by the same token is morally impermissible.

In sum, the DEA's use of collaborating witnesses in this case was justified neither on the basis of the principle of necessity, since less harmful alternatives were available to the agency, nor on the basis of the principle of proportionality, since it is unclear that the harm to the collaborators and civilians (through recklessness) outweighed the gains in terms of violence-reducing intelligence. For these reasons, in balancing the cost and benefits of the use of collaborating witnesses, law enforcement authorities ought to adopt a restrictive view, which presumes its disproportionality unless there are strong reasons to the contrary.

Conclusion

This chapter examined the ethical stakes of recruiting witness collaborators in Mexico in view of its institutional weakness, its significant socioeconomic disparities, and the systematic violence unfolding in its territory. The ethical assessment of witness collaboration must take into consideration the presence or absence of certain institutional and socioeconomic conditions, which may abate or increase the potential costs associated with the use of witness collaborators. Absent such conditions, the practice is bound to be disproportionate, even when necessary. In turn, this examination is crucial for understanding the limits of principled leniency: certain attempts to bargain for justice are completely inadmissible in view of their inherent risks. Incidentally, these reflections should draw our attention to some of the objectionable features of the Mexican criminal justice system—not only the inadequacy of its institutional processes but also its lack of concern for the well-being of those who stand before it as the accused party and who oftentimes are believed to "deserve" whatever violence befalls them.

THREE

Punishment without Legitimacy

Exploitation, Domination, and Communication

In this chapter, I defend the notion of principled leniency as a *via nega-tiva*: the state ought to refrain from punishing not to achieve some positive outcome, as we saw attempted in the cases discussed in the previous two chapters, but rather to avoid wrongdoing. Drawing on the consensus view that Mexican prisons are harrowing institutions, the chapter claims that it is objectionable for the state to incarcerate offenders in its own prisons when it keeps them in conditions of oppression and exploitation. Doing so robs the criminal justice system of its legitimacy to punish altogether. Such a taint to its legitimacy is wrongful in itself, but it also wrongfully undercuts punishment's goal of repudiating certain criminal offenses. All this furnishes another argument for principled leniency: rejecting punishment need not be an arbitrary demand, nor an indictment of the institution of punishment per se.[1] It is simply a reasonable response to the conditions of existing prisons and to the actual criminal justice system's legitimacy deficit.

In her chronicle/short story "Life's Not Worth a Thing," Fernanda Melchor tells the tale of two lawyers working in a corrupt legal system. They are tempted by the leader of a criminal organization who asks them to represent him, a proposal they ultimately reject, though they agree not to stand in his way. Along the way, one of them references another story, that of Andrés, an innocent man whom they recently and unsuccessfully defended against false charges. One passage of the story is worth quoting at length because it encapsulates much of what is wrong with the criminal justice system in Mexico and, more importantly, the experiences of the incarcerated:

> We couldn't do anything for the poor guy because the other judge, the one from the Sixth District Court, wiped his ass with my appeal and even after all the work we did, all the detective work to demonstrate that his so-called investigation was a load of bullshit, they still sentenced Andrés to seven years in prison, the poor fucker, and then to make matters worse it was Los Zetas running the show inside the Allende, and when they realized Andrés was inside for dealing, all hell broke loose and they went for him, beat his brains out and I think they might have even raped him, and then they started training him up, and poor Andrés—who had never been a narco or anything fucking close to one, just a regular stoner who popped his uppers just to keep up at work—ended up becoming one of them, as a matter of survival, you know, because that was the year a fuckload of inmates died in prisons across the state, supposedly hanged themselves in their cells, but those were some crazy-ass knots, real complex. So anyway, Andrés turned into a fucking hard nut, it was like a total transformation.[2]

This is the story of an innocent person, similar to that of thousands of innocent men and women who fall prey to the criminal justice system. For the purposes of the chapter, however, his innocence is beside the point. Had he been a guilty man, his experience in prison would have been equally objectionable.

Here my analysis of Mexican prisons follows the two traditionally established goals of punishment in general and imprisonment in particular—deterrence and retribution.[3] The perennial divide in penal theory is between instrumentalist or consequentialist theories—according to which punishment is valuable insofar as it contributes to a further goal, usually crime deterrence—and retributive theories, according to which punishment is intrinsically good because it imposes on offenders the treatment they deserve.[4] These questions have been profusely analyzed in the philosophical literature, and here I shall only offer a brief survey.[5]

At the same time, the discussion goes beyond the traditional philosophy of punishment, which tends to be overly individualistic, to incorporate insights from political theory. Indeed, retributive and instrumental theories focus respectively on the moral blameworthiness of an individual and on the marginal deterrence value of punishing this or that person; in so doing, they miss systemic, structural consideration, that is, "the injustice that may supervene on individual instances of punishment when they are taken as a whole, possibly even if all of the individual instances of punishment can themselves be justified."[6]

The chapter unfolds as follows. Section one argues that, in the Mexican case and many others, the preconditions for imprisonment to achieve its goals of deterrence and retribution are absent. Prisons are bound to fail at the first goal—deterring crime—because they lack the institutional and even financial means to incapacitate dangerous offenders. This is an unsurprising conclusion, as the inability of prisons to deter crime is far from an exclusively Mexican phenomenon, though Mexico is among the most egregious cases. Mexican penitentiaries have, in fact, become criminogenic institutions. This is because criminal organizations have "captured" prisons, making them cogs in the machinery of criminality. The condition of Mexican prisons renders the deterrence-based justification for prisons ludicrous, a point that has been amply recognized in the literature.

Prisons, then, fail to deter and even undermine deterrence. But the problem goes even deeper: as sections two and three argue, imprisonment is, and has long been, a tool for both criminal organizations and the state to exploit and dominate inmates, thus depriving convicts of their rights to equal citizenship (to say nothing of their human rights). Convicts anywhere in the world have their liberties curtailed simply by being deprived of some of their civil liberties (association, movement, vote, and so on), but this is not tantamount to losing their standing as equal citizens. By contractarian logic, which roots rights and obligations in a social contract between citizens and sovereign powers, they have forfeited these liberties by committing crimes. In the case of Mexico, by contrast, the loss of equal citizenship arises from the fact that prisons are spaces of exploitation and domination. This is a situation that no contractarianism can justify. For these reasons alone, even if it succeeded in deterring crime, incarceration would be objectionable, making leniency permissible if not mandatory. To aggravate matters, Mexican prisons also subject relatives and others close to inmates to relationships of exploitation and oppression, enabling criminal offenders to leverage arbitrary power beyond the walls of prisons. In this landscape, the Mexican state's legitimacy as the agent of punishment is called into question.

Section four suggests that Mexican prisons are also unlikely to advance the retributivist goals of punishment. "Classical" or, perhaps more accurately, "rudimentary" retributivism contends that offenders *deserve* to suffer as much as the victims of their crime. While this form of retributivism is fairly discredited in contemporary debates, a more convincing brand of retributivism—expressivism—posits that incarceration can be justified on the grounds that it sends a message to society as well as to the offender about the wrongness of the offense. Yet, for these messages to be effective, some preconditions must hold. Most importantly, the criminal justice process must be legitimate, from prosecution to incarceration. In Mexico, however, the criminal justice system lacks this kind of legitimacy. This deficit distorts the message of repudiation and in fact impedes the purported expressive goals of punishment: the legitimacy deficit compromises the retributive/expressivist aim of punishment. Interestingly, the negative effect runs in the opposite direction as well—(mass) incarceration compromises legitimacy because it deprives a significant share of the citizenry of the protection, stability, and opportunities to thrive in society, aspirations that, when met, confer legitimacy on the state.

Revueltas Revolted: The Wrongs of Prisons

Lecumberri palace is one of the most (in)famous prisons in Mexican history. When built at the dawn of the twentieth century, this federal prison was supposed to herald Mexico's transition to modernity: a Benthamite panopticon intended to "humanize" punishment at a moment when the alternative was an assorted menu of cruel and unusual punishments or death. Only later did Lecumberri receive the nickname "the black palace," losing its air of modernity to become a symbol of authoritarianism and the repression of political prisoners, most notably the leaders of the student revolts of the 1960s. This reputation as part of the repressive apparatus remained intact until the prison was closed and turned into the National Archive in 1982.

Among Lecumberri's celebrated political prisoners was José Revueltas, a Marxist writer and activist who reflected deeply on the carceral condition—his own and carcerality more broadly—and was imprisoned for his role in the student movement.[7] Behind bars, while staging a hunger strike protesting the incarceration of political prisoners, Revueltas penned a public letter to American playwright Arthur Miller, then president of PEN International. The point of the letter was to alert Miller of the political repression taking place inside the jail and thus build international public pressure against it.[8] In his letter, Revueltas describes the moment when he and other political prisoners were targeted by a government-instigated mob of fellow inmates:

> By then, there was no authority left in the prison; or rather, General Puentes Vargas and Major Palacios, [prison authorities] present there, represented a different kind of authority. They were there, yes, but at the head of a hundred men, standing in tight, compact ranks—prisoners convicted of "common crimes" who formed the true *élite* of power in the Preventive Prison: inmates "commissioned" to carry out the prison's most diverse administrative functions—*mayores* and *oficiales* of the cellblocks, *escribientes, galeros, recaderos, mandaderos*—each of these peculiar guilds led, of course, by the most seasoned and feared ruffian among them.[9]

Reacting to authorities who blamed political prisoners for the "riots," accusing them of demanding "privileges" that "ordinary prisoners" lacked, Revueltas wrote bitterly:

> If it were only a matter of privileges . . . the inmates would have long since rebelled against the caste of gangsters who traffic drugs; those who control the black market for all kinds of prohibited goods; those who charge for the supply of electricity to the cells; the "majors" of the prison wings who collect "rent" for the occupation of specially equipped cells where wealthy and famous criminals live; those who collect royalties that inmates with lucrative "commissions" are forced to pay weekly. In short, they would have already rebelled against that entire breed of bullies and thugs who make up the "aristocracy" of the underworld and upon whom the vile and scandalous penitentiary system in Mexico has always been sustained—despite the "advanced" theories of false criminal law experts and "social psychologists" who engage in demagogic debates at conferences, without any radical, profound, and honest reform having been implemented to change the deplorable conditions that prevail in all Mexican prisons.[10]

This chapter is not about political prisoners like Revueltas. But his testimony and indictment of the Mexican penitentiary system paint a good picture of some of the features of prisons that endure to this day, such as the complicity of authorities and their lack of accountability. Revueltas's account also foreshadows the new and more complex forms of violence that inmates ("ordinary prisoners," as Revueltas called them) now endure, rooted less in political repression than in the absence of state authority, institutional failure, and corruption. Though lacking the explicit end of silencing and intimidating dissident voices, these new forms of violence are no less political.

Conditions have only worsened since Revueltas's incarceration in a federal prison[11]—and bear in mind that *federal* prisons like Lecumberri excel in comparison to state prisons, where most suspects and offenders are incarcerated, and which are chronically understaffed, poorly resourced, and generally precarious to the extreme.[12] Mexico has the seventh largest prison population in the world, after the United States, China, Russia, Iran, Thailand, and Brazil. As of 2021, there were 222,000 inmates, 95% of them men and 5% women. Mexico has 175 individuals in prison per 100,000 inhabitants. The fact that this rate is lower than all Central American and Caribbean countries and most South American countries is no consolation. Inmates are distributed in 288 penitentiaries, 273 state and fifteen federal. 43% of these are overcrowded, some of them up to 300% over capacity. A survey of inmates shows that a third of the prison population feels insecure, more than half have been tortured or mistreated during detention, and a quarter pleaded guilty under threat. On average, one person is killed violently every day within the penitentiary system. Sporadic violent incidents with multiple victims are also the norm: forty-nine people died in Topo Chico penitentiary (in the state of Nuevo León in northern Mexico) in 2016; one year later, twenty-eight died in the Las Cruces penitentiary (in the state of Guerrero in southern Mexico), to name just two incidents. Criminal groups control 65% of the state prisons, according to reports provided by the National Human Rights Commission. Drug consumption among the penitentiary population is above 50%. Bucking international trends, the prison population increased by 10% during the COVID pandemic (at the beginning of 2019 and the end of 2021). A third of penitentiaries have inadequate premises lacking proper maintenance. This leads to overcrowding and an inability to provide basic services, such as clean water, food, and proper health care, for a population whose health is already precarious due to infectious diseases and an array of other problems. As a result, the burden of providing these services falls on the families of inmates.

With this background in mind, let us turn to consequentialist (or instrumentalist) theories of punishment. Jeremy Bentham is famous for making the claim that "all punishment in itself is evil . . . only to be admitted in as far as it promises to exclude some greater evil."[13] Consequentialist theorists like Bentham believe that punishment is justified insofar as it contributes to reaching an ulterior goal, usually that of abating crime, although reintegration (resocialization or reform of the offender) is another possible end. Crime reduction is achieved, first and most obviously, by incapacitating dangerous offenders. Those who threaten the personal integrity of others are justifiably confined. Crime reduction is also achieved through deterrence. Here the goal is not only to incapacitate offenders via involuntary confinement but to dissuade them from committing wrongful acts in the future, lest they wish to experience again the harshness of incarceration. Others who might entertain the idea of committing similar crimes in the future are also deterred. And just how much punishment is appropriate to deter crime? If the criminal offense is severe, the sanction must be harsh to be effective.

Consequentialist justifications of punishment are not without criticism. Critics may claim, for instance, that a consequentialist justification of punishment (at least a *purely* consequentialist one) would license punishing the innocent or meting out excessively harsh sentences on the guilty *if* such actions deter crime. They also argue that consequentialism does not treat offenders as autonomous agents, but merely as a means to achieving a social good. Moreover, contrary to liberal values that emphasize including all persons within the community, consequentialism is exclusionary because it treats offenders as dangerous "others" who must be isolated from the rest of the community.

Note that if one supports punishment as deterrence, there are several powerful reasons not to impose it: a goal greater than deterrence, evidence that a particular kind of punishment or punishment at a particular moment will not deter crime, or proof of alternative ways to deter crime. To give an example: in this system of justification, a perpetrator may receive a lesser punishment than deserved (or no punishment at all) if either avenue serves justice, for instance, by eliciting a confession that will help prosecute other perpetrators, perhaps guiltier ones, or deliver sensitive information to authorities.

Beyond these considerations, the critical point I wish to underscore here is that, for the instrumental justification of punishment to work, it must be shown that punishment, and specifically prisons, effectively incapacitate dangerous offenders. This is not the case in Mexico, as Revueltas warned when he referred derisively to the "advanced" theories of "false criminologists" and "social psychologists" in the passage quoted before. Admittedly, the charge that prisons do not deter is one that can be leveled against prisons in many other countries, but Mexico fails in a particularly egregious manner. Consider, for a start, a cursory comparison between prison systems in the United States and Latin America generally. The differences go beyond material conditions. In American prisons, the lives of prisoners are strictly regimented, isolated, and subject to intense surveillance. Prisons in the United States are open to external scrutiny, and their bureaucracies are formalized. Inmates have little, if any, involvement in administrating prisons. Latin American prisons in turn lack any such regimentation, isolation, surveillance, transparency, or bureaucratization. Inmates, furthermore, run or control penal institutions. As a result of these differences, the character of confinement varies significantly from one case to the other, as does incarceration's power to deter crime.[14]

One of the most alarming developments in Mexico (and other countries in Latin America), which renders deterrence arguments hollow, is what Fiona Macaulay calls *prison capture*—the informal or parallel governance exercised by those who are detained.[15] Prison capture is entwined with mass incarceration, which Macaulay traces back to two sources: primary penal expansionism (increasing the number and type of crimes on the statute books) combined with secondary penal toughening (prevalence of maximum or mandatory custodial sentencing, and application of custodial sentences to a wider number of offenses).[16] According to Macaulay, mass incarceration significantly transformed the dynamics of prison governance both among prisoners and between prisoners and staff. The influx of thousands of young inmates, unfamiliar with the complex social systems within prisons, coupled with unprecedented overcrowding, deplorable detention conditions, and systemic human rights violations, resulted in increasing violence. Furthermore, mass incarceration led to "the creation of carceral zones of legal exception and silence where prison authorities were forced either to share governance with organized prisoner groups, or to effectively relinquish control over the prison population. In response, prisoners themselves took over both the regulation of prison life, creating their own complex, pseudo-legal behavioral codes of conduct and punishments, and the exercise of coercive force over other inmates."[17] In nations like Brazil, Venezuela, or Peru, inmates take control of jails for the benefit of a particular group, using lethal force and sometimes even using prisons as operation centers to organize crime *outside* of prisons. The paradigmatic example is the São Paulo–based Primeiro Comando da Capital, a prison gang that formed to demand better treatment for inmates and then became a drug syndicate, coming to govern large swaths of the territory in Brazil from within prisons they controlled.[18] In light of these developments, Marcelo Bergman and Gustavo Fondevila are right to criticize what they call the fallacy of separation—the false claim that Latin American prisons both contain inmates, preventing them from exercising power outside of prisons, and repel outside forces seeking to influence prison life.[19]

Mexico is no exception to this pattern. The poor conditions of its prison system are by no means novel, as Revueltas's testimony shows, but most scholars agree that recent events have made things worse. Since the early 1990s, the Mexican prison population has risen dramatically, doubling and in some cases tripling over the past twenty-five years, with no sign of slowing. Between 1992 and 2017, the general population rose by 35.1%, while the prison population rose by 372%.[20] Most inmates in Mexico come from low-income populations seeking to supplement their incomes by engaging in petty theft and small-time drug dealing or transport. The main variables explaining current trends in prison population are the massive influx of inmates, mostly convicted of property and drug-related crimes,[21] and the short length of prison sentences—ranging from one to six years, shorter than averages in the United States and some European countries—which guarantee the constant circulation of inmates through prisons and a high turnover rate.[22] Primary penal expansionism and secondary penal toughening also respond to a string of reforms, as far back as a 1994 reform to the Federal Criminal Code and the 1996 Federal Law against Organized Crime. More recently, a 2019 reform, approved with multiparty support, doubled the numbers of crimes warranting automatic mandatory pretrial detention. The result has been 130,000 new detainees in just two years in the twenty-one states willing to share crime statistics.[23]

As in other Latin American countries, authorities in Mexico have ceded control of the penitentiary system to, or share it with, criminal groups, at least at the state level if not at the federal one. This modus vivendi is reflected in many ways: prisons are strikingly vulnerable to attacks from the outside; not uncommonly, inmates escape or come in and out of prison freely; and disputes among criminal groups for control of prisons, which can turn into deadly riots, are an enduring feature of the penitentiary system. To give a few, randomly chosen examples: an armed group breaks into a state penitentiary in Guerrero stripping the staff of their weapons and subduing them, and then releases a person accused of kidnapping, allowing other prisoners to escape in the confusion (2022); fifty inmates—allegedly tied to the Zetas criminal group—walk out of a prison in the state of Zacatecas (2009); as many as 151 convicts escape from a Nuevo Laredo prison (2010), in a kind of escape less spectacular than that of El Chapo, the infamous drug trafficker now serving a sentence in a US prison, but more common; a clash between rival gangs over control of a prison leaves seven dead in Puente Grande (2020);[24] finally, and most infamously, in the Apodaca prison riot, following an elaborate plan, the Zetas, with the complicity of some custodial staff, release some thirty of their members and massacre forty members of the Gulf organization (2012).[25]

Control over prisons is not just a struggle over internal resources. It is also a struggle over commerce and territory outside of prisons. The case of Piedras Negras penitentiary in Coahuila is paradigmatic in this regard. The Zetas long organized their illegal activities from within the prison: at Piedras Negras they planned drug trafficking and extortion operations, even using it as a recruitment center and a location to hide members from authorities who were not on their payroll. And since a mere sixty kilometers separates Piedras Negras from the US-Mexico border, the prison became an ideal hub for trafficking. The organization stored illicit substances within the prison, repurposing the premises for an array of trafficking-related activities, such as outfitting vehicles with secret compartments for drug smuggling.[26]

In Mexico, then, the ability of the penitentiary system to curtail or deter criminality cannot be taken for granted. To the contrary, the only certain statement about prisons is that many are schools of crime. But the failure to deter is not the only problem with prisons; it may not even be the main one, I would argue. As they currently exist in Mexico, prisons enable relationships of *exploitation* and *domination*, which in many cases extend beyond the prisons themselves. By tolerating actually existing prisons, the state relinquishes its fundamental mission of protecting citizens, not only outside of those prisons but also within them. It thus incurs a double dose of illegitimacy. I unpack this claim further in the following section.

Despotic Prisons

Thomas Hobbes features prominently in many scholarly discussions on prisons. It has been argued, for instance, that criminal governance inside prison follows a Hobbesian logic, and I have already alluded to some of these ideas in the previous section. This is right as far as *descriptive* analysis goes. But there is a further *normative* Hobbesian point that is less commonly made, one that calls into question the state's moral authority to imprison citizens. Recall that the entire point of the *covenant*—the biblical language with which Hobbes referred to the contract between individuals to form the commonwealth—is to protect each and every contracting individual from violent death, thereby allowing them to flourish. Hobbes puts it as follows in a famous passage in the *Leviathan*:

> Whatsoever therefore is consequent to a time of war, where every man is enemy to every man; the same is consequent to the time, wherein men live without other security, than what their own strength, and their own invention shall furnish them withal. In such condition, there is no place for Industry; because the fruit thereof is uncertain; and consequently no culture of the earth; no navigation, nor use of the commodities that may be imported by sea; no commodious building; no instruments of moving, and removing such things as require much force; no knowledge of the face of the earth; no account of time; no arts; no letters; no society; and which is worst of all, continual fear and danger of violent death, and the life of man, solitary, poor, nasty, brutish, and short.[27]

For Hobbes, the social covenant exists to escape such a state of affairs. Importantly, once the commonwealth is formed, protection remains the central reason for obeying the sovereign. In fact, Hobbes allows each person to object to their own punishment. No one has a duty to comply with their own punishment, for "no man is supposed bound by covenant, not to resist violence; and consequently it cannot be intended, that he gave any right to another to lay violent hands upon his person."[28] One need not endorse this last point—offenders are not bound to peacefully accept imprisonment—to agree that there must be limits to incarceration. Prisoners are still citizens—or subjects, to use Hobbes's language—who do not lose the right to be protected by the sovereign. Citizenship, as Corey Brettschneider argues from a contemporary contractarian perspective, is not a status that expires when citizens behave improperly. It is not a relationship that can be terminated once one has been convicted of a crime, but an ongoing relationship with certain entitlements. Government is born of its citizens, who cannot be cut off, even when they commit crimes.[29]

With this idea in mind, consider Mexican prisons. When offenders are thrown into these prisons, even those who are liable to be imprisoned on account of having wronged others, they are, in effect, being placed in a setting where the state can no longer guarantee protection. When the state incarcerates offenders, it thrusts them, without their consent, into a precarious criminal order. Though embedded within the larger political community and connected with it in complex ways, this order threatens at every moment to collapse into a Hobbesian state of nature. And, to repeat, all of this transpires without the offender having agreed to live under such conditions. By breaking the law, offenders forfeit their right to full-fledged freedom. They do not, however, forfeit their right to be protected by the state, which at the same time does not have the authority to place them in a criminal order against their will. When the state does so, it acts without legitimacy. This is my central claim, which I now develop at length, drawing on the testimony of incarcerated people—who, to paraphrase Hobbes, are in continual danger of violent death—and on multiple assessments of the Mexican prison system.

Distinguishing again between US and Latin American prisons, Birkbeck claims that, in the latter, prisoners are "interned" rather than imprisoned because, as in war camps, relocation centers, or concentration camps— paradigmatic cases of internment—internees are entitled to minimal, if any, political and civil rights. Birkbeck argues that the conditions of internment, as opposed to imprisonment, generate severe inequalities of various kinds. Internment reproduces—whereas well-ordered prisons block—the social inequality found in the wider society by combining the "comfortable quarters of the wealthy inmates with the squalid dormitory areas inhabited by the poor."[30] The inequalities of internment are also political. Birkbeck claims that the fact that American prisons have better supervision, where inmates do not share in custodial roles of others, results in "a greater levelling of inmates, because there are fewer positions from which to garner power or influence."[31] By contrast, when custodians give up internal control, "relations between prisoners can quickly descend into internecine warfare."[32] The point to underscore is that interned prisoners live under asymmetric power relations; this is a feature of their condition.[33]

The contrast is useful to show how Mexican penitentiaries intern, rather than imprison. In so doing, they create opportunities for *domination* and *exploitation*, which delegitimize the criminal justice system and the punishment it imposes. These two processes are intertwined, but for analytic purposes, I shall take each of these in turn. In Frank Lovett's understanding of the concept, for a relationship between persons to be one of domination, the dominated agent must be dependent on the dominator, who will also wield asymmetric and arbitrary (that is, externally unconstrained) power over them.[34] The three elements of domination according to this view—dependency, imbalance of power, and absence of external checks—are ubiquitous in Mexican prisons.

Prisoners everywhere depend on custodians in the obvious and narrow causal sense that they are a bureaucratic link in the chain of provision of the basic goods they need to survive. Similarly, it goes without saying that, by law and sheer necessity, custodians must exercise some control over inmates (to keep prisoners locked in, to preserve discipline, and so on), which means that the relationship between the two groups is imbalanced. But, in the case of Mexican prisons, an additional sense of dependency and asymmetry is at play—a political one. The *acquiescence*—not merely the labor—of custodians is required for inmates to obtain basic goods and services, even if interns are entitled to them by law. Custodians and even wealthy and powerful inmates (for example, kingpins) appropriate public goods and wrongfully place conditions on their distribution. By the same token, in Mexican prisons there is not merely an imbalance in prison regimentation; the imbalance extends to every dimension of social and political life. It is also very common for wealthy and powerful inmates to take control over prisons, particularly state penitentiaries, thereby creating and placing themselves on the better end of relationships of dependency and asymmetry. Custodians themselves are often the losers in these relationships, forced to obey the de facto criminal authorities inside the institution.

A report by the National Human Rights Commission furnishes a good illustration of the unfolding of these imbalanced relationships of dependency. The report informs that, in close to forty penitentiaries for women out of eighty-one that were inspected, inmates "exercised control over others," in many cases taking over functions that belong to custodians, such as the assignment of rooms, surveillance, the maintenance of order, the application of

disciplinary sanctions, the distribution of food, cleaning tasks, the organization of work, and educational or sports activities. In these cases, inmates also
mediated access to medical services, family and intimate visits, use of public
telephones, and so on. The report additionally noted that some inmates or
custodians charged a fee to provide security and guarantee the physical integrity of inmates, yet another service which by law must be offered for free.
There was also a fee payable for exemption from internal obligations. In some
sixty-six such penal centers, disciplinary corrective measures—the eminent
province of the state—are imposed by the custodians and even inmates
who make up the prison's internal self-government. Inmates are punished
without the right to a hearing and without being properly notified of the
sanction. Punishments, moreover, are not those defined by the state, which,
at least on paper, respect human rights. These sanctions include prolonged
isolation and restriction of family and intimate visits, telephone communications, and access to activities aimed at reintegration, such as work, education,
and sports.[35] This problem is not exclusive to women's prisons. At Reclusorio
Norte, one of the largest male prisons in the political capital of the country,
one finds the typical features of Mexican prisons such as overcrowding, precarity and insufficient security personnel (almost one hundred inmates per
custodian), and the illegal imposition of fees by both fellow inmates and
prison authorities. In all these cases, the prison administration cedes part of
its powers to some inmates in exchange for maintaining a degree of peace.[36]
As for the third aspect of domination, its arbitrary nature, the weakness of
external checks on life in prisons is a case in point. The carceral system lacks
the ability to attend to and prevent violent incidents and possesses only dysfunctional mechanisms to channel and resolve complaints regarding probable violations of human rights.[37]

Now consider exploitation, the second threat to the state's legitimacy.
Here I follow Nicholas Vrousalis's account, according to which, for a relationship between two persons to be one of exploitation, their relationship
must be systematic, and the agent who exploits must instrumentalize the
vulnerability of the agent who is exploited to extract a net benefit.[38] All three
elements of exploitation—systematicity, the instrumentalization of vulnerability, and the extraction of benefit—are present in Mexican prisons.

Few relationships are more systematic than those created in prisons,
where inmates are literally trapped, as are, figuratively, their relatives, who

must navigate a maze of norms for tasks as simple as ordinary visits. Custodians and powerful inmates in turn profit from the plight of other inmates and their families to obtain personal advantage. "Life inside the prison is too expensive."[39] This testimonial from the relative of a prison inmate conveys the fact that, inside the prison, nothing is free of charge, as it ought to be: water and food; access to showers and bathrooms, where they are available; access to health services and a decent cell; the ability to receive family visits; even the permission to bring in forbidden goods: everything has a price. Sorting out bureaucracy is another source of revenue for custodians. Strict regulations for visits, including dress codes, can be softened in exchange for a bribe.

Intimate visits (*visitas íntimas*) are perhaps the crudest opportunity for exploiting inmates. The law in Mexico City states that prisoners, "at least once a week, will have the right to a space for intimate visits" and that authorities must guarantee spaces for such visits, which "must be adequate, clean and dignified spaces" with "the conditions to respect people's privacy."[40] It is hard to overstate how precious intimate visits are for the interned. Yet such requirements are a dead letter in many cases, and the interned are made intensely vulnerable as a result. The rooms available for intimate visits at places like the Reclusorio Sur are only available for a price.[41] Moreover, in many penitentiaries in Mexico City one finds so-called cabins (*cabañas*). These are precarious tents, spread around the visitors' entrance, alongside the stalls of street vendors selling food. As an observer writes, the *cabañas* "are a popular shortcut through which inmates who do not wish to go through the long bureaucratic path to obtain an intimate visit can have sexual relations. Here, the services of a social worker to give permission are not required; the same applies to wives, lovers, girlfriends, and friends. No one will ask them for clinical tests or proof of cohabitation."[42] The only requisite is a fee: thirty, forty, fifty pesos, two hundred for an extended stay. An inmate oversees the administration of the tents, but he must of course pay a fee to the custodians.

Incidentally, the bureaucratic maze, while perhaps not *designed* to exploit the incarcerated and their families, is certainly *leveraged* to do so, through the establishment of an informal economy in the anteroom of prisons and their surroundings. *El pueblito* (the little town) in San Miguel penitentiary in the state of Puebla was a "complex" of dozens of illegally built rooms inside the penitentiary, which housed everything from a restaurant, a drug store, a convenience store, a hardware store, rooms for intimate encounters, and a hair-dressing salon. Newspaper reports estimated the weekly gains at three million pesos (roughly two hundred thousand dollars).[43] *El pueblito* has since been demolished, but its existence, as well as the existence of other informal "institutions" such as the *cabañas*, attest to the commodification of prisoners and those connected to them. Angela Davis criticized what she called the prison industrial complex, arguing that the engine for the expansion of prisons in the United States was the production of prisoners as a cheap labor force and the creation of private prisons for profit. Put differently, for Davis the point of prisons is to exploit prisoners.[44] The exploitation unfolding in Mexico is somewhat different. It is not (mainly) about creating new riches by summoning a cheap workforce, but about redistributing the wealth of the least well-off: the systematic instrumentalization of the vulnerability of prisoners and their families from which custodians, powerful inmates, and even street vendors—who sell visitors whatever item may be required of them by prison authorities—extract a benefit.

It is not just that the deprivations inside jails trigger the emergence of a black market for basic goods. There is also a black market for illicit goods or prohibited services. Sex work, for instance, epitomizes the entwinement of exploitation and domination, as well as the loss in prisons of the protections that ought to be afforded to individuals by state. According to a report of the National Commission for Human Rights (2015), inmates in at least twenty state penitentiaries reported that prostitution was common.[45] Nowhere is this better exemplified than in the infamous *túnel* (tunnel), the corridor that connects Santa Martha Acatitla, a state-level prison in Mexico City, and the courts. Within the *túnel*, prostitution (involving sex workers from outside the prison but also inmates) runs rampant and is tolerated, as authorities turn a blind eye. Prostitution, the commodification of women's bodies, can be criticized on several grounds.[46] The only plausible—but by no means unanimously accepted—defense is that it ought to be tolerated, permitted, or decriminalized when it is undertaken consensually. Many brands of feminism will rightly object that, most of the time, there is no real choice involved since women almost never freely consent to sell their bodies and instead do so out of necessity. Under different circumstances, with meaningful options, they would refuse to sell their bodies. Nowhere is this objection more powerfully instantiated than in prisons. It is hard to exaggerate the abandonment of many women while imprisoned. They oftentimes have no visitors, no safety net outside of prison, and no significant legal assistance. Sex work under these circumstances is the only avenue for generating the resources that they (and sometimes their dependents) need to survive in an environment where the most essential basics are for sale.[47] We have a case, then, in which the state puts a person in a situation of defenselessness, and where her acquiescence to being exploited and dominated is the only path to securing basic goods.

The Topo Chico and Piedras Negras prisons, in Nuevo León and Coahuila respectively, are the paradigmatic and perhaps the crudest examples of how prisons have become sites of exploitation and domination. Topo Chico prison was inaugurated in 1943 and closed in 2019 after the confrontation between Los Zetas and the Gulf organization in 2016 that left forty-nine people dead.[48] While the dispute between the groups stretched back as far as 2010, the specific causes of the 2016 riot are unclear. They may have been the result of a dispute over control of the penitentiary between two Zeta leaders, or of a rebellion of inmates. Whatever the exact reason, the events unfolded against the structural conditions I have discussed thus far. To secure some measure of governance and control, custodians (of which there was only one for every hundred inmates) had to rely on a group of internees who were willing to govern by force if necessary. Added to this was a dearth of basic necessities and a cadre of custodians who lacked qualifications and dignified working conditions. In this context, Los Zetas extorted inmates and their families, threatening and beating them if they failed to pay the fees imposed on them. The inmates were forced to work exhausting days for the benefit of the organization, which additionally monopolized scarce resources and practically left nonmembers to starve. Cells did not have locks and inmates could move freely through the patios day and night. One of the leaders had a large and luxurious room that was perfectly equipped; it included an aquarium and a bathroom with a sauna where women visited him, entering and exiting the prison at will. By contrast, other inmates lived crowded in small cells that lacked water, light, and ventilation and where they had to take turns lying down.[49] Elena Azaola reports the grueling story of an inmate on his release from Topo Chico. He had spent the last twenty-seven years in jail, until a court released him following determination that there was no proof of his participation in the homicide of which he was accused. I quote part of Azaola's interview at length:

I was there in a room with ten people, and they were killing them one by one
. . . they were killing them just like that because if you're not with them, you're
against them. They isolated me many times just for being from the neighborhood where I grew up, saying that I must belong to a certain group and had
to pay them a fee. In there, they are the ones in charge, the ones giving orders
to everyone, and a riot broke out because they wanted to set fire to those of us
in that dormitory. . . . The authorities don't want to take back control of the
penitentiary because that group collects an enormous amount of money and
gives a share to the authorities. I just wanted fair treatment—that if I did a job,
I would get paid for it—but in there, there's no authority to defend us. We were
just waiting, wondering when they would come for us to kill us. . . . [T]he very
authorities who are there don't want what's best for us; they are the first to break
the law. If someone brings in drugs that aren't theirs, they kill them. . . . I have
never seen criminals more brazen than the directors, the security chiefs. . . . Believe me, 27 years in there is a long time . . . because you see how they are killing
people, and you always think you're next, and you don't really understand what's
happening inside.[50]

A criminal investigations of prison authorities for their involvement in the
Topo Chico riot, among them the director of the penitentiary, went nowhere.
Two years after the riots, all those involved were absolved.[51]

Even more extreme was the case of the Piedras Negras prison, where the
Zetas established a brutal system of domination based on fear.[52] Here torture
was key, taking many forms: "tablazos" (beatings with a wooden board and
aluminum bats on inmates' buttocks), a custom imported from the initiation rites in military colleges attended by the former soldiers who founded
the Zetas; pouring boiling water on the backs or hands of inmates; making
them drill holes in the soccer fields and then cover them; among others.
The Zetas had a jail inside the prison, known as the "mountain," located in
the maximum-security area. It was reserved for inmates who committed an
infraction: the greater the "crime," the more severe the penalty. The "mountain" also held those kidnapped outside the prison while ransom payments
were being negotiated. Moreover, the Zetas maintained absolute control over
communications, sealing the prison to avoid leaks to the outside world about
the situation within (prisoners making phone calls were always escorted by
custodians or other inmates). Domination within prisons also allowed Zeta
leaders to hold arbitrary power over relatives of prisoners, as illustrated by
the fact that they oftentimes selected female relatives of prisoners to provide

sexual favors. The despotic rule of the Zetas, enabled by the criminal justice system, thus reached beyond the walls of Piedras Negras.

Finally, the Zetas turned the prison into a lucrative venture, exploiting every business opportunity, including prisoners themselves. Besides selling drugs to inmates on credit (severely punishing delays in payment, including by beating, hanging, or mutilation), the organization charged a weekly fee for every possible activity or service: per night spent in the marital area, for electricity and water, and for defaulting on payments. They handled the sales of telephone cards, food, and medicines and obtained income from the prison workshops and through kidnappings. Profits were high because the salaries paid to the prisoners were very low. The least well-paid person in the hierarchy was the one responsible for burning bodies, because on top of everything else, the prison was also an extermination center. As Sergio Aguayo and Jacobo Dayán put it, business was booming at the prison: the Zetas "had a captive population that they could exploit knowing that the government paid for electricity, water and the salaries of the custodians and employees who served the Zetas."[53] In other words, the state government enabled the conditions for the exploitation of inmates.

In sum, prisons ought not to be places of exception, where civic and political relations wither and die. Undeniably, the incarcerated anywhere forfeit some civil and political rights (to freedom of movement, most basically) when they offend against the law, but they ought not to relinquish all these rights. That is, however, what transpires in Mexican prisons, which rob inmates of these rights by fostering relationships of domination and exploitation. This situation calls into question their very legitimacy as well as that of the government that creates and maintains them. This furnishes us with a further reason to consider leniency, rather than rigorous punishment, as a response to drug crimes.

Self-Harm as Domination, Austerity as Exploitation

A somewhat different but equally telling example of prisons as systems of domination and exploitation is the women's penitentiary CEFERESO (Centros Federales de Readaptación Social, Federal Centers for Social Readaptation) 16, in the state of Morelos. Inaugurated in 2015, CEFERESO 16 has two peculiarities: it is the only *federal* prison for women, and it is modeled after American maximum-security prisons. In 2023, CEFERESO 16 was the location of an epidemic of suicides and other self-harming behavior among inmates. This epidemic was yet another manifestation of the relations of domination and exploitation, although under a different guise than in state-level penitentiaries.

Since its inauguration, authorities began transferring inmates from state penitentiaries across the country to the CEFERESO. Some of the women came from states along the US-Mexico border, such as Chihuahua and Co-ahuila, more than a thousand kilometers away from the inaccessible area of southern Mexico where the prison is located. Similarly, after the closure of the Topo Chico prison at the other end of the country, all prisoners were relocated to the CEFERESO. The law, however, prohibits such relocations. Inmates have a right to be imprisoned in a penitentiary near their home and may be relocated only for extraordinary reasons (for example, to preserve the security of the prison from which they are relocated or for health reasons). This was not the case for any of the relocated women. Despite having committed common offenses (*delitos del fuero común*), they were taken to a prison for offenders who had committed federal crimes (*delitos del fuero federal*), which include organized crime. Federal prisons are very different from state penitentiaries on many levels. While they are more likely to be governed by established authorities, preventing the anomalies ubiquitous in state-level penitentiaries, they are highly regimented environments: severe limitations are placed on inmates' access to phone calls and time spent outside of their cells. The prison's regulations are designed with a very specific set of offenders in mind—those who are highly dangerous or extremely rich and powerful and therefore able, if allowed, to manipulate a weak carceral system, extorting custodians or controlling the penitentiary. The women who were transferred to this prison did not fit that description.

As mentioned, a spate of self-harming behavior—thirteen women committed suicide, dozens engaged in cutting and in self-asphyxiation—alerted human rights organizations to the conditions of women in CEFERESO 16. In a report, the National Human Rights Commission concluded that most of them were in a "situation of social vulnerability":

They are mothers of young children and come from different regions of Mexico, which means they are far from their vital connections, often resulting in abandonment. Likewise, the lack of physical and mental healthcare, the absence of suicide risk intervention, prolonged confinement, obstacles to communication with the outside world, as well as the predominant approach to grief and depression treatment, among other factors, contributed to their decision to attempt to take their own lives.[54]

The commission urged the prison to improve:

> The intervention of medical, psychological, and psychiatric staff in the grieving process, along with continuous engagement in productive, recreational, and sports activities, helps prevent isolation and the fragmentation of the bonds formed among incarcerated women—bonds that become survival strategies in the face of distance from their family networks. This separation deeply fractures their identity and deteriorates their vital connections, whether familial, emotional, romantic, or even sexual. Effective management of the urgent needs of incarcerated women is essential to help them recover from the emotional climate of despair, helplessness, and perceived insignificance that has been observed. [55]

There were, of course, other causes of the epidemic of self-harm. Yet all of these experiences—deracination, alienation, depression—as well as the removal of the precarious safety nets these women might have had prior to their transfer (at such a distance, relatives could no longer visit and provide for them) all served to compound a situation ripe for mental illness, in which inmates are at their most vulnerable, and as a result more easily dominated.[56] As studies reveal, prisoners everywhere are likely more vulnerable to self-harm given their often-disadvantaged backgrounds. This vulnerability is then reinforced by custody-specific factors, such as isolation, increasing the likelihood of self-harm while in prison. Female prisoners face the added stressors of separation from family and children, higher rates of prior abuse, and bereavement.[57] Yet it seems hard to deny that, in this case, the Mexican state exacerbated the conditions that led these women to harm themselves. And public officials got away with violating the rights of inmates who lacked access to legal counsel and defense. Not only were the inmates moved without their consent; in some cases, they were moved without advance notice, under the pretense of a routine medical examination. They had no means of resistance. Thus, the self-harm in question can be viewed as an extension of the harm perpetrated by the state, the result of its exercise of domination over female prisoners.

Why were women relocated to this federal prison? The answer takes us back to exploitation within the Mexican prison system. The CEFERESO is a so-called Centro de Reinserción Privada (Private Rehabilitation Center), the term for prisons operated for profit by private agents (with the exception of surveillance and custody tasks, which continue to be the responsibility of the state and federal governments). In this case, the corporation in charge is owned by Carlos Slim, the richest man in Mexico, and his contract with the state has a profit margin of about eight million dollars monthly.[58] By 2021, CEFERESO 16 only held 806 women, about a third of its capacity. This made it a very expensive prison since, per the contract with the private corporation, the state pays a fixed amount for each bed in the center regardless of the actual number of inmates held. The Mexican government thus had a strong interest in filling the partially empty prison. Concerned with costs, in 2022 federal authorities unilaterally decided to close several nonprivatized penitentiaries and relocate inmates to the CEFERESO. When the state chooses to save money at the expense of prisoner mental health, it shows that it is willing to profit from a vulnerable population, which is rendered even more vulnerable in the process. The fact that these are public moneys does not make the act less exploitative. If this were not enough, women in this prison also face exploitation in the prison "workplace." The only job option women can aspire to at the CEFERESO is at the textile workshop, though the availability of positions is limited. There, they can work from eight in the morning to six in the afternoon for the minimum wage. Importantly, they cannot collect the money they make. Instead, they receive a "credit" to be redeemed at the prison "store," which, according to testimonies, inflates prices. In effect, this means that they are grossly underpaid.[59]

To recapitulate, like inmates in state-level prisons, inmates in the CEFERESO 16 are thrust into a situation of defenselessness and likely domination. This is not, or not to the same extent, because the state has ceded its authority to powerful groups.[60] It is because the penitentiary is structured and governed in such a way that inmates adopt self-destructive behaviors. Rather than tolerating powerful criminal groups or corrupt custodians who harm inmates, the state creates the conditions for despondent inmates to harm themselves. We must include suicide among the violent deaths from which the Leviathan ought to protect subjects when it is a response to the environment they have been forced into. The sources of exploitation are also not the same as those found in state-level prisons, whose masters extract every cent possible from the meager earnings of inmates and their relatives. Instead, by relocating prisoners to save state funds, an objectionably austere state cuts expenses to the detriment of the mental health of prisoners, against the backdrop of an unjust contract between the state and a private actor. In state-level prisons, low levels of statehood result in the institutionalization of a criminal social order that entrenches relations of domination and exploitation. In this federal prison, a higher level of statehood prevents such an institutionalization, but exploitation and domination enter through another door.

Two objections may be raised against the arguments presented so far. First, one might agree that offenders never lose their standing as moral agents and that, therefore, punishment must not degrade them to such an extent as to impair their dignity.[61] And one might further agree that offenders never lose their standing as political agents who must not be denied equal citizenship and, therefore, must not be thrust into a situation where they are dominated and exploited. Yet, so the first objection would run, retaining prisons and incarcerating offenders is required because this is the best mechanism we have to protect the citizenry, however imperfectly, and we must prioritize the interest of victims, actual and potential. The most obvious rejoinder to these claims is that prisons do not genuinely deter crime and might even exacerbate it. The idea that prisons protect citizens is dubious at best. The argument from protection justifies imprisoning only a fraction of perpetrators, perhaps leaders of criminal organizations whom police intelligence, if available, has identified as extremely dangerous and unlikely to be deterred otherwise.

A more challenging objection goes as follows: both sides, victims and offenders, stand to lose from prisons, assuming conditions in them will not change. But offenders must bear the brunt of the harm if no other solution is possible, because they are implicated in the wrongdoing in question. Punishing offenders (and in effect wronging them) may be the lesser evil because offenders committed the crimes that landed them in prison, even if attenuating circumstances might diminish their responsibility. Victims, on the other hand, are innocent, at least in most cases. Those advancing this objection view the agential differences between victims and perpetrators as the only possible criterion for allocating consequences. This objection fails to reckon with the fact that, when the state imprisons a wrongdoer under the degrading and oppressive conditions already discussed, it itself commits wrongdoing. Admittedly, it is also objectionable for the state to refrain from punishing dangerous offenders who may end up victimizing others. But note that while in this case the state is implicated in an injustice, its implication is of a different kind than when it forces offenders into the internment camps that prisons are. In the first case, the state is merely an intervening agent, in the sense that its actions are necessary for wrongdoing to occur, but its intention need not be for the wrongdoing to happen. In the second case, the state is both the causal agent and intends the action that results in wrongdoing. It seems, then, that the state must choose between impermissibly *wronging* offenders and impermissibly *allowing offenders to wrong* their victims. Neither scenario is palatable. At any rate, in the current conditions, the state cannot prevent wrongdoing without committing wrongdoing. However it acts, it will dirty its hands. And there is no way around this stain on its legitimacy without profoundly overhauling the criminal justice system.

No Uptake without Legitimacy

Let me now turn more briefly to the alternative theory of punishment, retributivism. "Giving offenders their just deserts": this phrase sums up the retributive justification for punishment. As I will explain here, however, retributivism can be interpreted in various ways, the most promising of which are communicative or expressivist theories.[62] For these theories, criminal offenses warrant a message of repudiation from the state. Importantly, expressivist theories presuppose that, for such a message to be effectively communicated, the state must be legitimate. The problem in the case of the Mexican state is that its claim to legitimacy is, and has always been, strained. My claim, then, is that in Mexico the state, and particularly the criminal justice system, lacks the legitimacy that would render repudiation credible to its intended audience.

For retributivists, the effects of punishment, such as its ability to deter crime, are not relevant. Punishment is justified insofar as it imposes on the perpetrators the harsh treatment they deserve. Deserved punishment is an intrinsic good. In short, retributivism upholds what Thomas Scanlon calls "the Desert thesis": "the idea that when a person has done something morally wrong it is morally better that he or she should suffer some loss in consequence."[63] There is a further claim that such suffering compensates victims. As then President Felipe Calderón (2006–12) pointed out in a typically (and rudimentarily) retributivist speech defending his overly punitive strategy against drug-trafficking organizations, punishment is a way "to compensate, even in part, those who have suffered mistreatment through crime."[64]

This is a classic characterization of retributivism. Decades of discussion have produced different versions of retributivism. To mention just a few: retributivists differ on whether they believe that desert is not only a necessary but also a sufficient condition for punishment. They also debate whether the notion of desert makes punishment simply permissible or, more demandingly, obligatory. Some retributivists might also be forfeiture theorists, asserting that, for punishment to be permissible, it must be shown that offenders have forfeited their right not to be punished. Then there are the hybrid theories of punishment, which include retributivist and consequentialist elements. One can be a consequentialist about the *aims* of punishment but a retributivist about the *constraints* that such aims should respect. I leave aside all these considerations to settle on a broad view of retributivism.

The core idea of classic retributivism—that wrongdoers deserve to suffer in proportion to the suffering they have caused—has fallen into disrepute, with Scanlon, for example, calling it "morally indefensible" and equating it with vengeance. Furthermore, this kind of retributivism runs into several theoretical problems. For example, retributivism is firmly committed to proportionality in punishment, but in mass atrocity, which involves egregious crimes, proportionate punishment defies calculation: what kind of prison sentence is proportional for members of an organization that routinely commits homicide, dismembers and disappears bodies?

There is, however, a more palatable understanding of retributivism according to which punishment is worthwhile because it has expressive value.[65] It conveys a message of repudiation of the wrongdoing. This is, incidentally, an insight that instrumentalists and retributivists can agree on, albeit for different reasons. Instrumentalists will endorse the expressivist argument if it can be shown that such repudiation has some effect in discouraging crime. But for retributivists, this is not the point. Repudiating wrongdoing is just what the state ought to do, regardless of any possible benefits of doing so.

Let me elaborate on the retributivist account in its expressivist or communicative version. Punishment, in this view, is the *deserved* response to a crime because it is the main way for a society to censure criminal activity. The state is the representative of society and even its moral exemplar. Failure to express repudiation would indicate that the state does not take seriously the law, which condenses the values of the community. Anthony Duff, an influential advocate of the communicative theory of punishment,[66] claims that repudiation of wrongdoing is owed to the victims of crime as a recognition that they have been wronged. Censure also publicly expresses what the community at large considers to be wrong. Along these lines, Duff states: "To remain silent in the face of their crimes would be to undermine—by implication go back on—its declaration that such conduct is wrong."[67] Furthermore, condemnation reasserts the legal and social equality that ought to prevail in society, which perpetrators repudiate through their actions.[68] Disregarding the demands of victims amounts to telling them that their expectations of equal treatment before the law are in vain. Doing so would be a violation of the principle of "mutual recognition" among citizens.[69] Crucially, proponents of this view argue that it holds even when we acknowledge that the justification for punishment in modern societies does not exclusively or even mainly depend on the retributive desire of victims and their relatives.

One final aspect of the communicative approach is worth mentioning. Duff contends that we should not only focus on the message that punishment sends to society but also on the message that it sends to the perpetrator. Accordingly, punishment communicates the gravity of the harm to offenders, allowing them to repent. This secular penance, Duff and others argue, provides a chance for perpetrators to be reintegrated into the political community.[70] Punishment must be meted out in such a way that it encourages the offender to be an active participant in the penal process, answering for crimes in a public forum (the trial). Punishment must be undertaken, not undergone. Moreover, on this view, criminal law is a distinctive practice whose aim is to respond adequately to public wrongs in conjunction with the idea that citizenship entails rights and responsibilities.[71] Even "offenders" have civic roles to fulfill.

For expressivist justifications to work, however, a critical condition must hold. Condemnation is only credible if the agent who condemns has credibility. Admittedly, receipt of a message is never fully in the control of the communicator, but the space for ambiguity widens when the communicator lacks credibility. In the case of punishment, for the message of repudiation to be effectively communicated, the speaker—in most cases the state—must have legitimacy. Otherwise, repudiation may not be received as intended. There are, of course, many ways to understand and acquire legitimacy. In a Hegelian vein, scholars like Jean Hampton claim that legitimacy derives from the state's status as representative of the community's shared moral values.[72] This is a very high bar for legitimacy, or at least one that is very difficult to operationalize. An alternative notion of legitimacy is democratic legitimacy. A democratically legitimate state justifies its actions to those affected by them and displays equal basic regard for all members of a society.[73]

Let us adopt this understanding of legitimacy, with which we may turn to the case of Mexico. For punishment to carry its message of repudiation, the Mexican state, and particularly its criminal justice system, would need to possess some substantial degree of democratic legitimacy. This is not the case. Every stage of the criminal justice system is punctuated by a set of ingrained practices that work against such democratic legitimacy.

Consider the investigative and prosecutorial processes. A survey of suspected offenders reports abuse at every stage of these processes. Nationally, an average of close to 44% claimed they had been falsely accused. When apprehended, they reported being disrespected, abused, humiliated, and, in the worst cases, tortured. After detention and before being presented to the public prosecutor's office (*ministerio público*), around two-thirds of those who were apprehended claimed to have experienced some kind of violent act perpetrated or tolerated by authorities (being held incommunicado, experiencing death threats or threats to family members, and so on), and a third were threatened with being falsely charged (this is a national average; in many states the average is much higher). Around a third were kicked or punched, and over 20% were asphyxiated. Close to half were robbed by the authorities that detained them. Once before the public prosecutor's office, around 20% pleaded guilty under threat and, again, a substantive number of respondents claimed they had been assaulted, some of them sexually. On a national level, almost half of the accused (closer to 70% in some states) took more than a year to be sentenced.[74] Academic research confirms that coercing some citizens into confessing, imposing disproportionate sentences, and denying defendants adequate legal representation are all part and parcel of the Mexican criminal justice process, particularly since the start of the War on Drugs (and particularly with the increasing involvement of the military in security functions, bringing with it the systematic use of torture as an interrogation method).[75]

A recent survey's finding that a significant part of the population distrusts judges and courts should come as no surprise. Only 57.7% of respondents trusted prosecutors and 60% judges. Conversely, 62.4% and 65.4% respectively thought prosecutors and judges were corrupt.[76] Roughly 78% of Mexicans have a high degree or some degree of trust in public universities and public elementary schools; close to 70% in public hospitals; and 60% in NGOs and religious institutions, to name just a few public or semipublic institutions. Meanwhile, only around 40% trust judges, magistrates, and prosecutors, and policemen struggle to reach 40%.[77] All these figures speak to an illegitimate criminal justice system. Neoliberal economic reforms, as well as those tied to the transition to democracy in the late 1990s and early aughts, attempted to transform this landscape. However, despite twenty years of much-vaunted state and federal democratization, authoritarian enclaves remain within the criminal justice system, including the prosecutor's office at the federal and state levels. Hoping for a powerful message of repudiation under these circumstances is disingenuous at best.

But it is not only the practices that prevail in the investigative and prosecutorial process that taint the criminal justice system. As was discussed extensively in the previous section, the conditions of prisons are harrowing. I already made the case that tolerating or encouraging such conditions calls into question the legitimacy of the state, which forces citizens to live under conditions of domination and exploitation. This situation raises other problems for the expressivist theory of punishment. If, as expressivists believe, punishment is an invitation to perpetrators to initiate a secular penance, life in prison must allow for that experience. However, it is hard to find a prison environment that facilitates such a process, not just in Mexico but in the world at large. Advocates of punishment who rest their case on the supposed expressivist virtues of incarceration tend to downplay, as a former inmate in a US prison puts it, the "psychic and physical toll that accrues from decades of social exile, the affronts to dignity that 'corrections' regularly imposes, and the injuries to one's sense of themselves and their relationships."[78] In Mexico, with its high turnover of inmates, not all prison sentences are long enough to produce social exile, although some are, but life in prison is most certainly dominated by affronts to dignity. Under such conditions, there cannot be the kind of civic uptake that Duff envisions as the ultimate justification of punishment. The message that prisons send is one of degradation.

Further eroding the legitimacy of the criminal justice system is Mexico's slide toward *mass* incarceration. By mass imprisonment, what is meant here is "a rate of imprisonment that is markedly above the historical and comparative norm," and where the trend "ceases to be the incarceration of individual offenders and becomes the systematic imprisonment of whole groups of the population."[79] In absolute terms, Mexico has one of the largest prison populations in the world, behind only the United States, the world's top incarcerator, several fiercely authoritarian nations, and a few others. As noted, Mexico incarcerates 175 individuals per 100,000 inhabitants. These are not the figures of El Salvador, which boasts a ghastly incarceration rate of 1,000 people per 100,000, or Cuba, with 700 people per 100,000. Yet, when one looks at state-level data, imprisonment rates begin to approach mass incarceration rates. The states of Baja California and Sonora have incarceration rates of 351 and 336 per 100,000, respectively, and Mexico City of 284 per 100,000. Several other states are at or around 200 per 100,000. Furthermore, disaggregated by sex, many states have a rate of roughly 600 men per 100,000.[80] Unsurprisingly, most incarcerated persons are men, and more than 70% do not have a high school (*preparatoria*) degree.[81]

Mass incarceration erodes state legitimacy in many ways. It imposes all the costs of incarceration, but on a much more severe scale and, in the case of Mexico, without even of a hint of benefit in terms of crime prevention. These costs are the opportunity costs of allocating resources to the carceral system rather than, say, the educational or health systems; the costs of errors within the criminal justice system, when it convicts the innocent, imposes harsh penalties on the guilty, or punishes the undeserving under laws that overcriminalize; the potential for abuses of power when the system is used for political purposes, such as the persecution of political opponents by those who wield control; and the collateral harm of punishment, most notably to the dependents of convicts, who are deprived of the support of those who are punished.[82]

These problems are severe enough on their own, but mass incarceration undermines state legitimacy from another, contractarian, perspective. A state that uses incarceration widely imperils its legitimacy because it creates conditions antithetical to a flourishing life, most notably an environment of diminishing liberty, which undercuts the goal of the contract. As Raff Donelson puts it, in Hobbesian terms, "each of us has a valid objection to the level of incarceration when that level is such that each of us no longer receives something they have contracted for, namely a free society."[83] Moreover, mass incarceration is a strong indication that a chasm has opened between the rules of society and the ability of citizens to abide by them. This is also a problem from a contractarian perspective: "A society which puts penal sanctions to heavy use may lose its claim to allegiance from those people who suffer from those sanctions, and perhaps it should."[84] This is because "if a society has not made it possible for someone to flourish or be happy outside of committing a crime, then that society may lose its normative ability to punish that crime." Even if rules are just, "a society's expectations for compliance with rules [might be] too high: accordingly, society might have to tolerate some crimes that ideally it would not."[85] Excessive punishment is a threat to the ongoing legitimacy of the state, and this in turn distorts the expressivist goals of punishment.

Conclusion

In the early days of the War on Drugs, then-president Felipe Calderón professed his faith in the value of prisons as a tool to combat organized crime. He declared that, "what needs to be done is to increase penitentiaries. [If] the law determines that there is one, a thousand, ten thousand or one hundred thousand inmates, the state must have spaces so that the law can be complied with: spaces must be adapted to the rule of law rather than reducing the rule of law to the availability of spaces."[86] Such trust in and reliance on punitivism is deeply objectionable without what Revueltas demanded more than fifty years ago: "a radical, deep, honest reform to transform the deplorable conditions that reign in all of Mexico's prisons." Absent this fundamental reform, opting for leniency is ethically justifiable, and indeed preferable, in the vast majority of cases.

FOUR

Punishing "Crimes of Infirmity"

After defending principled leniency based on its promise to deliver what must be deemed a greater good than punishment and on a consideration of the objectionable conditions surrounding prisons, we turn in the next two chapters to an altogether different basis for justifying it. This chapter explores the idea that many perpetrators in the criminal turmoil of the "war on drugs" have diminished moral responsibility, which ought to be reflected in the severity of the punishment imposed on them. To begin the exploration, I shall invoke again the ideas of Thomas Hobbes. His reputation as the philosopher of unrestrained executive power tends to obscure his views on punishment, which, contrary to what those unfamiliar with Hobbes's ideas may believe, show great restraint when it comes to identifying the permissible aims and recipients of punishment. Let me begin by quoting a passage of the *Leviathan* at length:

> The severest punishments are to be inflicted for those crimes, that are of most danger to the public; such as are those which proceed from malice to the government established; those that spring from contempt of justice; those that provoke indignation in the multitude; and those, which unpunished, seem authorized, as when they are committed by sons, servants, or favorites of men in authority. . . . But crimes of infirmity; such as are those which proceed from great provocation, from great fear, great need, or from ignorance whether the fact be a great crime, or not, there is place many times for lenity, without prejudice to the common-wealth; and lenity when there is such place for it, is required by the law of nature. . . . To be severe to the people, is to punish that ignorance, which may in great part be imputed to the sovereign, whose fault it was, they were no better instructed.[1]

I quote this passage because many of the crimes related to drug trafficking are "crimes of infirmity," as Hobbes calls them, arising from sources such as provocation, ignorance, fear, or need and as such warranting "lenity." The view that many of the perpetrators of drug violence in Mexico, particularly those at the lowest rung of the criminal hierarchy, grew up in criminogenic environments and that this fact should bear on our assessment of their guilt is by no means novel. It is reflected, to go no further, in the equally popular policy prescription that the problem of drug violence should be confronted not with further violence but by addressing its root sources, vaguely understood to be background conditions of socioeconomic inequality. But arguments along these lines are usually presented in too coarse a fashion to offer any moral guidance regarding the question of principled leniency. This chapter seeks to unpack this conventional view to gauge its precise implications and its limits.

The chapter examines some of the most frequent pathways that have led thousands of individuals to join and participate in activities linked to drug trafficking violence. Competition among drug-trafficking organizations, the violent disputes to which such competition leads, and the response of authorities to imprison or kill members of such organizations have produced a perpetual and insatiable demand for new recruits. The chapter examines pathways for recruitment to identify the forces that, to put it in a Hobbesian manner, "weaken" the ability of recruits to resist the pull toward crime, putting them in great moral hazard.

The existence of these enormous pressures to commit wrongdoing makes harsh punishment objectionable in three ways.[2] First, these pressures generate excuses and justifications that diminish the legal and moral responsibility of perpetrators. Second, these pressures undermine the value of fairness. A fair society is one in which the burdens of cooperation, both benefits and costs, are distributed justly. If a group of citizens systematically encounters more pressure to commit crimes than others, for no other reasons than social disadvantage, a claim of unfairness arises. The overwhelming pressure to commit a crime, in other words, creates unfairness in the opportunity to avoid punishment. Last, if these pressures go uncurbed, it is to a large extent because the Mexican state has "infirmities" or weaknesses of its own, and we must therefore attribute some of the responsibility for the crime to it. If so, it is an open question whether an agent that does little or nothing to alleviate the infirmities of its citizens has the moral authority to punish them severely for the outcome of these infirmities. The first of the three aspects is familiar to moral and legal theory, which is, for the most part, concerned with examining individual action. The second and third aspects, the province of political theory, take a less individualistic perspective insofar as they incorporate concerns about fairness and state responsibility, where social and political relationships are the critical subject matter.

It is worth noting before proceeding that what I offer here is a general framework to assess criminal and moral responsibility, the prescriptions of which may apply with greater or lesser force or not at all, depending on the circumstances. Consider the following caveats. One is that the logic and dynamics of criminal violence are exceedingly hard to fathom, varying from year to year, criminal market to criminal market, region to region, and even neighborhood to neighborhood. When it erupted at the beginning of the century, drug violence attracted public attention as open clashes between criminal groups, or between the military and criminal groups, spread throughout the nation. While this kind of confrontation is still a source of violence, other forms have emerged. Jalisco, a current epicenter of criminal violence, is a case in point. From 2018 to date, only one in forty fatal victims of organized crime there has died in such confrontations. Many criminal organizations, such as Jalisco Nueva Generación, have opted for a strategy of massive but silent extermination of alleged rivals. Raids (in which an armed commando blocks access to a town and enters to take away anyone it considers a possible enemy) have become the predominant methods of this extermination.[3] The moral relevance of distinguishing between confrontations and carefully meditated extermination lies in the fact that confrontations *may involve an element of provocation*, which is *typically absent* or *lessened* in cases of premeditated extermination. In the face of this complexity, and others similar to it, it is impossible to draw conclusions about reduced blameworthiness that apply to all wrongdoers in the present circumstances of violence engulfing the country.

Relatedly, the arguments of the chapter apply more decisively to acts of criminal violence that result from disputes between criminal groups locked in disputes for territory, markets, or influence.[4] Put differently, its focus is not on state crimes, but on crimes that occur when the state is not involved. Admittedly, it is difficult to draw a clear line between the two, as oftentimes state authorities at the local or even national level are complicit in crime that on its face might seem attributable to nonstate actors only. One might go as far as to say that the state is always implicated in criminal violence insofar as it neglects its duty of protection.[5] Notwithstanding this reservation, excluding state crimes for the purposes of analysis reflects the concern that crimes committed by state actors, for instance, extrajudicial killings by the army, which are not rare events,[6] warrant a separate moral examination.[7] Such an examination must reflect the fact that members of the army or other state actors took the responsibility to protect citizens. The moral standard for qualifying their blameworthiness for crimes must be higher to reflect the fact that they have violated the responsibilities attached to their roles.[8] Similarly, many of the motivations or pressures we will explore in the chapter do not apply to them or do so with lesser force.

Finally, while I shall lay out the conditions for moderating the responsibility of perpetrators for *criminal violence* in general, such mitigation needs to be qualified by a consideration of the specific kinds of acts under discussion. Whether or not a wrongdoer receives a lenient sentence should reflect not only their diminished moral responsibility but also the moral quality of the crimes they committed. The killing of innocent and unarmed civilians or political candidates has a radically different moral quality than the killing of an adversary in a crossfire between criminal organizations. The leniency resulting from reduced blameworthiness must itself be tempered by due consideration of the kind of wrongdoing in question.

The chapter unfolds as follows. The first section lays out the notions of excuse and justification, which are the two most common appeals for justifying or eliminating the moral and legal responsibility of perpetrators, relieving them from the full brunt of punishment; the section also discusses the relationship between fairness and punishment. Once this conceptual framework is in place, each of the following sections examines the excusatory or justificatory potential of the pressures or conditions that put hundreds of thousands of Mexican civilians in a state of infirmity, to use again Hobbes's terms, and as a result, trap them in trafficking organizations and networks. We begin with pressures that have partly excusatory potential (although in many circumstances, there may be grounds to appeal to both justifications and excuses). Section two discusses coercive and quasi-coercive recruitment. Forced recruitment is the most predictable pressure and the one that has been most discussed in academic and journalistic literature. More diffuse pressures arising from circumstances that closely resemble what classical sociology calls anomie (crudely, the breakdown of collective values that leads to social instability) have also been recognized, although to a lesser extent, by specialized literature on the subject. Section three discusses mental illness/addiction: offenders frequently perpetrate crime under the influence of drugs or after addiction has wrecked their ability for adequate decision-making and self-containment. Section four discusses circumstances with justificatory potential. In particular, I examine what I shall call all *impure* justifications: wrongful action that is interpreted by those who undertake it as a form of imperfect self-defense. Section five then turns to the case of women and children who engage in criminal behavior because they have been brought up in and inhabit a rotten social background, a context of deprivation and insecurity that scars individuals cognitively and emotionally, impairing their moral development. Section six briefly makes the case that once offenders are integrated into criminal organizations, their ability to steer clear from atrocity is severely impaired, which constitutes a further consideration in reckoning moral and criminal responsibility. Finally, having discussed various states of infirmity, section seven discusses the infirmities of the state in Mexico, which can be said to bear some of the responsibility for the crimes of offenders by failing to provide them with tools to resist criminal organizations and by failing to develop the tools to assess the responsibility of offenders properly, all of which calls into question the state's standing to punish them.

States of Infirmity: Responsibility and Fairness in Punishment

Discussions about the social and political circumstances that mitigate responsibility have a long lineage. I shall offer an extremely brief sketch of such discussions here. The goal is to set up a minimal conceptual framework of the different sources of mitigation, which will then help us determine whether they apply to criminal offenders in Mexico's drug violence.

Criminal responsibility presupposes moral responsibility. Attributing criminal responsibility independently of moral responsibility is the basis of the doctrine of *strict liability*, which is too rigorous a principle because it does not take into account the mental state of the perpetrator of the crime. In contrast, the opposite principle, epitomized by the Latin maxim *actus non facit reum nisi mens sit rea* (the act will not render the person guilty unless the mind is also guilty), considers the mental state of the perpetrator to be a fundamental factor for determining criminal punishment.[9] From the perspective of this doctrine, criminal responsibility must be a reflection of moral responsibility. This is why any legal and moral theory worthy of its name recognizes that certain features of the individual or her circumstances may assuage or qualify her responsibility for wrongdoing, with an impact on how the criminal justice system ought to address her wrongful actions. Diminished moral blame implies diminished legal guilt and, therefore, lenient punishment. More specifically, there might be grounds for *exculpating* or *justifying* those actions, which in turn are decisive in determining the proper state response.

Exculpation and justification are different concepts with different implications, legally and morally. As philosopher J. L. Austin puts it in his classic examination on the subject, someone who *justifies* her acts accepts responsibility but denies that they were bad, while someone who *excuses* her acts admits that they were bad but does not accept full or even any responsibility.[10] Exculpation denies blameworthiness but acknowledges wrongdoing; justification denies wrongdoing but acknowledges responsibility. Insanity is the clearest example of an exculpating condition. The insane person lacks the kind of autonomous decision-making that is necessary for the attribution of blame; she lacks, in short, reflective self-control. Other examples of excuses include involuntary intoxication. Self-defense, in turn, is an example of a justified action. The person who engages in it acts autonomously and, therefore, takes full responsibility for, say, murdering her aggressor. Yet no legal system or moral theory would regard such an action as wrongful as long as it considered to be proportionate and necessary to save her life.

While insanity and self-defense are clear excuses and justifications, respectively, the excusatory and justificatory qualities of other conditions, such as duress and the so-called rotten social background, are more controversial; other conditions, such as provocation, may share both qualities in part. It is worth examining some of these conditions in some detail because they are relevant to the cases I shall discuss.

Most scholars regard duress as a paradigmatic excuse.[11] For them, duress works as an excuse because people acting under it lack the cognitive or volitional capacity, or the fair opportunity, to avoid acting wrongly or unlawfully, and by extension they also lack the attendant moral agency. This is why duress removes blameworthiness and delivers a complete defense in prosecution for any crime. By contrast, some authors regard duress as a justification rather than an excuse because, they claim, duress does not impair in the way that conditions like insanity do and hence does not remove autonomous agency. People acting under duress, in fact, choose between two evils, which opens up space for the exercise of choice. Finally, some authors reach the compromising conclusion that duress has partly exculpatory and partly justificatory components.[12] For the purposes of this discussion, we do not need to settle this matter.

Another controversial form of excuse that seems relevant to many of the cases under discussion is the rotten social background consideration.[13] According to this defense, conditions of social destitution and deprivation, such as those prevailing in the environment of a favela, a slum, or a ghetto, create the lack of individual self-control that is behind the excuse defense. In a ghetto, for instance, daily existence "creates a reservoir of rage, which, if tapped, can take control of the individual's actions. . . . The actor's conduct is not voluntarily determined, but rather directed by the dominating emotional force of rage."[14] In the ghetto, other conditions debilitate self-control: "mental or emotional trauma"; "physical and physiological changes associated with early poverty and deprivation," which can "alter perception and interpretation, causing the person to perceive incorrectly the nature or consequences of his or her actions"; and socialization "to behave in a manner necessary for survival in the ghetto [whereby] he or she does not see the wrongfulness of his or her conduct."[15]

Aside from *complete* excuses and justifications, there are *partially* excusatory and *partially* justificatory conditions. While entirely exculpatory or justificatory defenses are mutually exclusive, partial ones are not. Provocation is a clear example of the latter. Imagine A kills B because B murdered A's son. This makes A's response less wrongful than A killing B over a financial disagreement. B's prior killing partially justifies A's retaliation; while wrongful, it is, to repeat, less wrongful. Add to this that A acted immediately on learning B was the murderer; B sadistically informs A himself. A was understandably enraged. The fit of rage, insofar as it made A lose control, making her less blameworthy than if she had carefully plotted her retaliation, partially excuses him.[16] Interestingly, it might be argued that these components do not provide sufficient grounds for mitigation unless they are jointly present.

Together, they are necessary and sufficient conditions for mitigation. The mitigation that flows from partial excuse and partial justification is cumulative; when both are present, the perpetrator is less deserving of punishment.[17]

The critical point that I wish to underscore here is that excuses and justifications must attenuate punishment. Erin Kelly put the point thus with respect to excuses:

> People who think carefully about criminal justice must address the problem that the *legal* criteria of guilt do not match familiar *moral* criteria for blame. Conditions that excuse moral failings—such as ignorance, provocation, and mental illness—have limited application in law. This demonstrates a lack of alignment between law and morality. . . . Some criminal defendants have diminished moral culpability and others should not be seen as morally blameworthy at all, yet such factors have no bearing on determinations of legal guilt.[18]

Beyond the diminishment of responsibility, the conditions just sketched also create a situation of unfairness. The value of fairness is usually associated with punishment in the sense the punishment contributes to achieving fairness. If we regard society as a system of cooperation, those who reap its benefits without making their appropriate contribution—without accepting their burden—take advantage of those who do contribute. Punishment discourages such abuses; it "restores the equilibrium of benefits and burdens by taking from the individual what he owes, that is, exacting the debt."[19] This relationship between punishment and fairness seems less relevant in our case. More important is the idea that, if we understand the exercise of restraint from engaging in criminal behavior as a burden of cooperation, then in a fair society it must not be the case that exercising such restraint turns out to be more taxing on some citizens than on others.

Admittedly, all individuals must resist "strong temptations" to act illegally. Yet there is a problem when this temptation falls disproportionately on a group of individuals, such as the socially deprived, who constantly encounter some of the pressures discussed before, compared to others, such as the well-off, who do not do so: "the socially deprived much more often find themselves facing hard choices about whether to engage in some form of illegal conduct or to remain law-abiding."[20] These trying circumstances generate for them a set of hard choices that others do not encounter or not as persistently, and, "It is precisely the difficulty of the choices they face combined with the ubiquity of such choices that presents a challenge to our thinking about the extent to which the socially deprived should be held criminally responsible for their actions."[21] Put shortly, all individuals must have the same opportunity not to commit crime. This is the idea of fair opportunity to avoid crime.

This sketch on criminal and moral responsibility and some of the most common extenuating circumstances should suffice for the task ahead. In what follows, I explore the grounds for excusing or justifying (or both) the actions of some offenders involved in (or, in many cases, engulfed by) drug trafficking, including some who have committed very serious offenses.

Forced and "Soft" Recruitment

The most obvious case of an exculpating condition—an instance of duress—is forced recruitment. Data on forced recruitment in Mexico are highly speculative, but journalistic investigations attest to the fact that criminal organizations employ deceptive recruitment methods such as false advertisements to force individuals into joining and serving them without the freedom to leave (frequently under threat of harming family or friends). Forcible recruitment into (and retainment in) these organizations, always in the lower ranks of drug-trafficking organizations, is grounds for full exculpation.

But not all individuals are driven into the drug-trafficking business by coercion. There are other less obvious but weighty forms of pressure. These "soft" pressures—compared to coercive recruitment—include the deterioration of local institutions, the consequent loss of traditional socialization spaces that once discouraged violent behavior, and the emergence of new spaces of negative (re)socialization that promote such behavior. These pressures attenuate moral and criminal responsibility because they undermine individuals' ability to resist the allure of criminal groups that promote violent or antisocial behavior, inhibit the development of skills that are fundamental for the exercise of moral reasoning (for example, self-control or empathy), and deprive them of healthy and ethical sources of guidance. The pressures provide, therefore, a partial exculpation for some of the actions that result from them. These pressures also rob those who face them of a fair opportunity to avoid the kinds of behavior for which criminal punishment is the ordinary response, raising a problem of fairness. Let us analyze some of these pressures in more detail.

Social norms structure individual behavior. Individuals base their behavior on community codes established long ago, such as those articulated by the local priest, parents, single mothers, neighbors, and teachers. What is considered ethical conduct is usually a part of the local normative fabric. When reflecting on right and wrong, few men and women do so in a vacuum; their conclusions are usually strongly influenced by dominant opinions and views that surround them. Such community codes are often a safeguard against basic crimes, such as murder or theft. Their erosion bodes ill for peaceful coexistence.[22]

Ethnographic evidence shows that such codes have collapsed in many parts of the country where crimes associated with drug trafficking are rampant. The border municipalities of Sonora, one of many regions where social relations have become increasingly violent in recent years, have experienced a dramatic increase in homicide rates. Drug trafficking routes across the border, once communal roads, are now owned and managed for private profit by a variety of regional criminal organizations. On the other hand, illegal migration, once organized locally, is now controlled by these same criminal organizations. One of the consequences of this "regionalization" phenomenon is the emergence of a criminal bureaucracy that manages both the use of roads and the smuggling of undocumented migrants. It is made up of very young men, and their meager salaries are paid by external organizations. Some of these young men charge fees to migrants and *polleros* (people smugglers); others guard roads; others are hired assassins. The moral consequences of this new work model are profound: by carrying out orders for a regional organization in the municipality, the youths break their family and community ties. They no longer respond to local social controls against violence; instead, they are effectively outside the local ethical order. The sources of local authority (family, church, school) no longer exercise power over them.[23]

We find a similar pattern of erosion of local authorities and their ability to regulate social behavior in other states of the country. Guanajuato, once a peaceful state in the center of the country and a source of immigration to the United States, is in the grips of massive violence. A study of a transnational community in southern Guanajuato, connected to southeastern Pennsylvania and forming a migratory circuit where people, money, culture, and, more recently, drugs and arms flow between locations, shows how in these communities immigrants visiting their homeland, voluntarily or after forced deportation, began to introduce drugs and drug use behaviors to their home communities, thereby contributing to the emergence of a drug use culture.[24] To cater to it, a major drug cartel made marijuana, cocaine, crack, and crystal methamphetamine readily available in *tienditas*, or "little shops."[25] With this background in mind, the study contends that "transnational migration has weakened the traditional family and kinship bases in transnational communities that once served as important deterrents to improper behaviors, including substance abuse." These communities, the authors of the study claim, "find themselves ill-prepared to deal with unruly adolescents and their drug use" because "traditional forms of social control, such as the traditional family which in the past served this purpose, are no longer effective." As the authors claim, tri-generational family groups were prevalent in the past, but "transnational migration and emigration have reconfigured either temporarily or permanently these traditional tri-generational living arrangements." As a result, "males—husbands/fathers, older sons, and older brothers—are often missing for years." Moreover,

> the permanent loss of kin . . . has truncated kinship ties in the community and the kinship bases of many families. . . . Relatives have always looked after each other, especially the children in the extended family, and have made sure that proper behavior, customs, and traditions are learned, practiced, and passed on to the next generation. The absence of kin, especially close kin, has eroded this important social safety net in the communities.[26]

Not only are fathers and other male kin (uncles, godfathers, and older brothers) absent or present in insufficient numbers when it is time to intervene to prevent the violations of community norms. Local authorities, including municipal police forces, lack the ability or the will to cope with problems once resolved by families. Members of these communities are well aware of what is happening and fear for their young, but they are afraid to go to the authorities, concerned about whether the authorities are complicit with criminal organizations and are fearful of reprisals, giving these organizations free rein.[27]

In these same communities, drug-trafficking organizations are also targeting at-risk youth, turning them into drug consumers and recruiting them to sell drugs. This takes us to another dimension of the problem. While many local and more traditional institutions are showing signs of deterioration, others are (re)emerging to capture the loyalty of people, particularly the youth. Scholarship and journalistic reports have shown to the point of exhaustion that acquiring money and status is a powerful motivation for joining criminal organizations. This kind of motivation (which should not be exaggerated, since the remuneration of some of these low-ranking perpetrators can be relatively low[28]) provides only frail bases for exculpation. However, wealth and fame cannot on their own explain the resolve to join criminal organizations. For further explanation, an ethnographic investigation directs us to the importance of what it calls the *collective trajectory*. This term captures the idea that, in contexts where a community has crossed a certain threshold of criminality, novices perceive their future/destiny as being inexorably tied to the group in which they are already embedded. This research shows that "intimate, personal, and face-to-face social relations characteristic of kin and friends were antecedents to participating" in criminal organizations, as was "group connectedness," understood as "the collective experience of being attached to intimate groups." When potential recruits decide on their future, the "desire to remain attached to their immediate group narrowed their options."[29]

The yearning for group connectedness is fertile ground for manipulation. Recruiters, who share biographical similarities with those whom they recruit, are ready to exploit this yearning and the shared background "by portraying the transition to a criminal organization as a logical step in the trajectory of those around them with whom they share a common past." Recruiters seeking to win the trust of potential recruits use "intersubjective and instrumental empathy," the study claims, "in selecting messages that reinforce the appeal for group belonging."[30]

> This makes it easy for recruiters to traffic in, and relate to, the aspirations of a novice perpetrator. . . . In doing so, they appeal to a particular segment of a well-known population from the same neighborhoods who are inclined to accept cartel work because of a *mental preparation* from those around them. Recruiters draw upon personal experiences to employ a shared perspective regarding the desire for exiting poverty, fulfilling expectations of manhood, and more importantly linking DTO [drug trafficking organization] membership to group affiliation.[31]

The importance of group connectedness also explains why abandoning criminal organizations is so onerous. "The same factors that facilitate recruitment act as an inhibiting mechanism for exiting criminal organizations. The risk of retribution from the cartel makes desistance possible only if a member is willing to undertake complete self-ostracism from intimate groups."[32]

In sum, processes such as the collapse of local norms and the weakening of traditional forms of control, which in turn are owed to multiple social processes, including the transformation of the intensity and the quality of (return) immigration as well as the emergence of regional actors and novel drug cultures, put individuals in great moral hazard. They render them more vulnerable to accepting and undertaking behaviors they would have rejected in the past and to manipulation by recruiters from criminal organizations. Judgments of blameworthiness must be sensitive to all these facts.

"War," Mental Illness, Addiction

The use of the label "War on Drugs" is deeply objectionable because it frames drug trafficking, as well as the social and political processes it triggers, as a major threat that legitimizes extraordinary—and oftentimes violent—counternarcotic measures. But the ample availability of drugs and the unavailing attempts at curbing their circulation does resemble a war in one respect—the psychological toll they inflict on users. In the previous section, I alluded to a budding drug-use culture in communities in Guanajuato in the 1990s. Today, this culture is in full fruition across the country, with fentanyl use as the latest iteration of this phenomenon. A problem in and of itself, drug abuse, along with the inability of the state to counter it and the shortcomings of nonstate institutions when standing in for the state to pursue this goal, are important engines of violence and a critical consideration for attenuating the moral blameworthiness of perpetrators. Being an addict in Mexico furnishes perhaps the clearest partially excusatory defense: offenders in the grips of addiction fall into a condition close to that of mental insanity, and their actions may be involuntary in an important sense of the word. If they are fortunate enough to emerge alive from a life driven by addiction and its consequences (for example, committing wrongdoing while under the influence of narcotics), they are left in such a state of material and psychic deprivation that they become easy prey for recruiters. Addiction is "debilitating" several times over.

Usually hidden by authorities, addiction and mental illness have seen a sharp increase in Mexico in the last two decades, particularly among adolescent males.[33] Even drug-consumption-related mortality rates have increased in Mexico since 2015, particularly in the northern states of Baja California, Chihuahua, Sonora, and Sinaloa, rising annually by 10.49% at the national level. Opioid-related mortality was the chief driver of this increment.[34] Many reasons account for the rise in drug consumption. It is likely a spillover effect of increased drug trafficking. Criminal organizations have promoted consumption because, to accommodate excess production, they constantly seek to expand markets. As important, criminal organizations dedicated to drug trafficking have a broader "business portfolio," as it were, which includes the sale of protection. Indeed, criminals sell protection, and they create "disorganized" petty crime from which they protect the citizenry. Drug addicts (*drogadictos*) are the main perpetrators of this kind of crime.[35]

It is hardly novel or controversial to claim that offenders who commit crimes under the influence of drugs are not fully responsible. After all, addiction produces cognitive and affective changes that impair rationality. This warrants mitigation, morally and criminally.[36] The deeper question is about the extent of such mitigation. Admittedly, addiction does not furnish a full excuse neither for the decision to consume drugs nor for subsequent criminal activity, especially serious wrongdoing. "Social causal variables, or any other kind of causal variables, cannot excuse addicts who are individually responsible without threatening all individual responsibility."[37] Even poverty or subcultures that celebrates the use of drugs "do not excuse unless they produce sufficient irrationality or a sufficiently hard choice."[38] Offenders under the grip of addiction may be said to be responsible, notwithstanding its devastating effect on decision-making and self-control, for two reasons: because the addict knowingly "took the risk that he or she would become irrational" and is almost always aware of "alternative possibilities"; and second, because "almost all addicts have lucid, rational intervals between episodes of use during which they could act on the good reasons to seek help quitting."[39]

While it is true, then, that addiction provides a partial excuse only, a thorough consideration of the prevailing socioeconomic background of addicts in Mexico makes it plain that the force of the excuse, however partial, is significantly strong there. Consider one of the reasons just discussed for why addiction is ruled out as a full excuse: addicts can always seek help quitting in their moments of lucidity. This assertion presupposes that addicts receive some assistance (ideally from the government) to quit. But in Mexico such help might not be forthcoming, it might be available only haphazardly and in insufficient quantity, or even worse, it might be provided by criminal groups, although not without the expectation of receiving something in return, as will be seen shortly.

Indeed, despite the severity of the problem of addiction, resources allocated by the state to address addiction and mental health are notoriously scarce, particularly when it comes to assisting individuals from low-income strata. The sole institutions that have emerged to provide psychological or psychiatric assistance for the poor are so-called *anexos*, private centers for residential treatment of addiction, of which there were between 1,000 and 4,000 in 2016.[40] Angela García's ethnography shows that *anexos* in Mexico City are harrowing places. *Anexados* are self-described alcoholics, drug addicts, schizophrenics, and neurotics who are forcibly taken to *anexos* by their relatives, although some enter voluntarily. They can be interned for months, and they are confined in the *anexo* until claimed by a relative or are deemed successfully rehabilitated. Sometimes consisting of a single room, the facilities of *anexos* tend to be precarious, obsolete, unhygienic, and overcrowded. They are seldom inspected (let alone certified, funded, or supported) by public health officials, and their operators are untrained.

Anexos are morally ambiguous institutions. In the best-case scenarios, they help some men to overcome or control addiction.[41] But in many other cases, they are spaces that reproduce violence. Beyond forcible internment, many inmates experience violence within them. Violence is, in fact, part of the treatment in some of these institutions. There is abundant testimony of relatively minor maltreatment, like giving interns cold showers, to more serious episodes of sexual harassment and even rape. Whatever physical, sexual, and verbal abuse *anexados* experience, it is meant to humiliate and "humble" them, with "the intention of making the men controllable and labile as a mechanism of treatment."[42] Some men are indeed "tamed," but others are left to repress their rage. An *anexado* explains: "every time I went in I was more resentful, right? Angrier, every time I wanted to recover less and less, right? I was there because I was forced to be there, not because I wanted to."[43] *Anexados* become inured to violence if they were not already inured to it.

Sometimes the only assistance for addicts comes from criminal organizations themselves. The most emblematic case is that of La Familia Michoacana and the Knights Templar, which consistently recruited from the *anexos* and eventually created their own rehabilitation centers.[44] The leader of both organizations, Nazario Moreno El Chayo, called on young Michoacanos and especially drug addicts to join the organization "with a message of salvation and self-improvement, [and] to free them from the slavery of drugs." Membership in the Knights Templar, as Claudio Lomnitz shows, was touted as a path out of addiction. An evangelical pastor, no less, guided some of these processes of transformation, claiming to have brought nine thousand individuals out of their addiction. The process of personal transformation, with its adherence to the Templar code of ethics, "would move recruits from the abject dispossession that is addiction to serving in the 'Order of the Temple.'" These recruits transitioned from "servitude to positions of manly power;" and "from being a slave of addiction to being a drug lord." A critical phase of this transition away from addiction and into membership, however, required proof that one was capable of killing, then butchering, even "cooking" and handling butchered bodies. As Lomnitz argues, rehabilitation came at a price:

> To rehabilitate an addict and give him a spot in the organization is to rob Death of someone who had already given himself up to her. This substitution is carried out in exchange for other lives . . . the life regained by the newly recruited Templario, stolen away from Death, shall be paid back to Death with that knight's first victim. This exchange is also at times figured as an act of divine justice, wherein the man who was humiliated and slighted, and is now resurrected as a knight, takes his vengeance on those who had humiliated him.[45]

According to authorities, *anexos* are hiding places or operation centers for criminals with arrest warrants; safe houses to inflict torture on debtors or adversaries or to extort financially well-off relatives of addicts; or drug points of sale. This might be an exaggeration on the part of authorities, eager to criminalize as much as possible any sphere of social life touched by drug trafficking. What is certain, however, is that the effect of *anexos* on those that populate them is deeply consequential. Interns are taken there while in the grips of addiction; they are subjected to degrading and traumatizing treatment and even afforded narratives that justify the wronging of others. Their condition is the paradigm of infirmity: their will is weakened to the point of undermining their ability to exercise self-restraint. *Anexos* are a rotten background within the rotten background found in many contexts in Mexican society.

"Just Wars"

In previous sections I sketched a number of full or partial excuses for crimes related to drug trafficking. Membership in criminal groups may also furnish a full or partial *justification*, or what I shall call an impure justification. We first need to understand that joining such groups may be an imperfect act of self-defense. Some individuals may choose to become members of criminal organizations believing that, despite their questionable or objectionable nature, these groups offer the best chance for protection. In turn, there are two ways of approaching imperfect self-defense. Individuals may join criminal organizations because they are immersed in territories where the threat of violence is very tangible and immediate, with public authorities often being complicit in it, or at least reluctant or unable to intervene to stop it. These very immediate threats make membership in such groups a matter of life and death. Not all those who join criminal groups face imminent threats, however. Even then, some of them may act on a set of beliefs shared by some strata of local societies and by specific groups that give a positive meaning to violence and hermeneutical tools to members for interpreting their violence as self-defensive. These beliefs, from which it is not at all easy to detach oneself, form a cultural backdrop that affects their capacity to see and label their actions as morally reprehensible and are a consideration that must be factored into judging their blameworthiness as well as their opportunity to eschew crime.

Gangs and self-defense (*vigilante*) groups are two instances of social groups that emerge and persist in reaction to imminent threats to life and limb to those who form them. Their increase in the country has been a well-documented issue for well over a decade, and it is tied to the rise in drug trafficking.[46] Organizations dedicated to the drug-trafficking business often opt to subcontract local gangs to act as hitmen or to support their own hired assassins. The gangs in question go by names such as Los Artistas Asesinos or Los Mexicles. In Ciudad Juárez, for instance, three gangs became involved in disputes between drug-trafficking organizations, and in some cases brutally attacked each other.[47] One of the gangs is Barrio Azteca, which has links to the organization once led by El Chapo Guzmán.

There are, of course, different types of gangs, some more violent than others. Importantly, though, to a certain extent individuals do not "choose" the type of gang they join. Their local neighborhood context is a determining factor. The formation of criminal gangs occurs in violent neighborhoods where there are already integrated criminal networks, where generational overlaps among gang members allow adults to "teach" the gang business to young people, and where some community leaders are also involved in the violence. What is most important for the purposes of this chapter is to point out that membership and participation in some gangs entail what members consider to be obligations, which take precedence over other moral responsibilities and commitments.[48] To the extent that the gang is an adopted family and an organization that allows members to survive in a society that, to some extent, excludes them, gang members develop a very peculiar sense of their ethical duties. They believe, not always unreasonably, that their fates are tied to that of the gang.

Something similar can be said about self-defense (*vigilante*) groups that emerged in states such as Michoacán and Guerrero in 2013. Ioan Grillo interviewed a man who joined the vigilante fight in the town of Parácuaro in Michoacán.[49] The man's name was Manuel and, surprisingly, he hardly spoke Spanish. His first language was English because he grew up in Oregon in the United States before being deported to Mexico. In his neighborhood in the United States he joined the Barrio 18 gang, which fought with other gangs and even clashed with them at gunpoint. After his deportation, Manuel arrived in Parácuaro, where his family had roots. He found the town under the control of the Knights Templar, which was extorting from the local population. Manuel stated: "Almost everyone here worked for the Templars. Either you were with them or they could kill you. . . . The head boss was a guy named Sierra. He found out I knew how to use guns, so he recruited me." Manuel divided his time between cooking crystal meth in the nearby laboratories and accompanying hired killers to collect debts, and he admitted that collection events usually turned violent. When the vigilante groups arrived in Parácuaro, Manuel, like most of the other community members, "flipped" and joined a vigilante group.

The threat need not be imminent for the argument of imperfect self-defense to apply. There may be circumstances where individuals believe themselves to be under a threat that is latent and diffuse, but no less existential in their eyes. They may be immersed in environments that cultivate this sense of threat and that encourage—or at least do not discourage—

violent attitudes and behaviors as a response to such threats and that provide resources to conceptualize their actions as morally permissible. Here, too, there is an argument about imperfect self-defense to be made. I now turn to explain in general terms how the argument would unfold.

Individuals are epistemically dependent beings, which means that they need certain beliefs to orient their relationship with the world and, above all, to guide their social relations. Their moral judgments, particularly, are based on their beliefs, as social moral epistemology contends.[50] Take an extreme case: the commandment "thou shalt not kill thy neighbor" is only intelligible based on beliefs about who counts as a neighbor and who does not. For example, although far removed from the case at hand, the Nazi regime did its best to disseminate the belief of Jewish racial inferiority and its harmful effect on German society. If Jews were almost subhuman and, moreover, dangerous, then in dealing with them, the ordinary German citizen was no longer bound by the moral guidelines that governed his conduct with respect to his fellow human beings. Some authors have characterized this process as a "distortion of normativity": certain abstract moral principles remain intact but are impaired and damaged in their social manifestation.[51]

Such distortions can be particularly harmful when they interact with what Yang Su calls, in his work on collective killings in Mao's China, "wartime frames."[52] These frames are a set of beliefs articulated and delivered by the state to citizens to understand social and political problems. In the case of China, for example, these frames unsurprisingly cataloged social and political problems in class-struggle terms, identified class enemies as responsible for them, and advocated collective action against these enemies.[53] Su claims that a crucial point about this wartime frame was its lack of specificity in a very crucial respect—it provided a problem frame and a diagnosis frame (class enemies are on the loose, and they are a threat), but, significantly, no action frame (what citizens should do about that is X or Y). In other words, the state clearly identified a national "menace" and then left citizens to their own devices to "fight" against it. Ambiguities about what to do in the face of threats, particularly lethal ones, compounded with the distortion of normativity, put individuals at great moral risk.

Many of the elements just sketched form the cultural backdrop of the violent environments associated with drug trafficking in Mexico. Many perpetrators are born into and spend their entire childhood and adolescence in toxic epistemic environments that distort their moral judgment. The pervasiveness and force of such beliefs allow them to characterize their actions as self-defensive. Examples are Sinaloa, the birthplace of narcoculture,[54] or the "regional ranchera culture" of Michoacán.[55] These are not marginal subcultures. In the case of Sinaloa, narcoculture is the result of a decades-long development and institutionalization process. Narcoculture began as a subculture to resist the negative stigmatization of the drug-trafficking trade and quickly became a widespread and robust belief system that legitimized the drug trade.[56] Such a belief system establishes symbolic incentives for participation and creates ways to justify activities linked to drug trafficking.

Consider narcoculture in Sinaloa in more detail. *Narcocorridos*, or ballads about drug trafficking, which since the 1970s have contributed to the spread of narcoculture in the north of the country, offer some insights into narcoculture. *Narcocorridos* mythologize drug traffickers, transforming them into role models. Luis Astorga points out that a corrido is a "musicalized socio-odyssey of a social category that went from being marginalized to being omnipresent, and which [is] in the process of building a new identity for itself, trying to get rid of the stigma that had been attached to it since its inception."[57] *Narcocorridos* recount tales of traffickers, businessmen, and convicts who are portrayed as powerful individuals; they are loved, respected, and feared in their homelands. The canonization of local traffickers in some regions of the country, such as Jesús Valverde in Sinaloa, is a case in point. *Narcocorridos* also depict lavish lifestyles and glorifying acts of violence. Thus, thousands of Mexicans live immersed in a symbolic order that through music and other artistic expressions "exalt the adventures of the leaders and traffickers of the drug industry."[58]

But there is obviously much more to narcoculture than *narcocorridos*, with their glorification of drug trafficking. Another set of beliefs relates directly to the day-to-day operations of criminal groups and is the basis for the indoctrination processes of their members. According to these beliefs, traffickers are soldiers in a "just war" combating their nefarious enemies (rival traffickers and gangs, especially). The term "war" fuels strong-arm rhetoric and justifies violent measures that often fail to respect human rights. To paraphrase the unfortunate words of an adviser to Felipe Calderón's regime, the fight against drug trafficking "is a war, and in war, there are always 'casualties.'" But a warlike discourse has also been established in the confrontations between criminal organizations. There is not only a "war" between the state and "drug traffickers" but also a war between traffickers.

It is worth zeroing in on the Familia Michoacana and its splinter group, Caballeros Templarios, to illustrate and elaborate on the points just made. The Familia Michoacana, whose name, not fortuitously, emphasizes familial and communitarian bonds, emerged as a response to the brutal and violent dominance that the Zetas were beginning to exert in Michoacán. Shortly after its gruesome public debut (they left five human heads in a disco bar in Uruapan as a "message"), the organization published a leaflet in local newspapers asking for social support and clarifying that the Family was made up of "workers from the Tierra Caliente region motivated by the need to end the oppression [and] humiliation to which they were subjected by the people who had always held power." They also indoctrinated young men with ideas Moreno published in a book called *Reflections of the Familia*.[59] Along similar lines, it is noteworthy that the leadership (or so we assume) of the Knights Templar took the time to draft and distribute among its members the "Code of the Knights Templar of Michoacán" ("Código de los Caballeros Templarios de Michoacán"), a brief pamphlet that not only establishes strict rules of behavior for members of the organization but also states that the organization's purpose is nothing more and nothing less than "to protect the inhabitants of the free, sovereign and secular state of Michoacán" from the corruption of local authorities and, particularly, criminal groups. All of this is the groundwork for indoctrinating their lower rank-and-file members.

Claudio Lomnitz has conducted a careful examination of the ethos of the Knights Templar, its implications, and the reasons why it resonated with so many young Michoacanos. Familia Michoacana and Caballeros Templarios developed an identitarian strategy for seeking local support against the Zetas. This entailed making a pledge to protect the interest of locals and, in the case of the Caballeros, into forming a quasi-religious order, a regimented organization structured around the Code of the Knights Templar of Michoacán. La Familia and the Caballeros adopted a familistic and communitarian face in a deliberate strategy of differentiation in a competitive environment. The Knights Templar in particular developed an ethical code assembled by Nazario under the influence of *Wild at Heart* by American evangelist John Eldredge (the Spanish translation of the book became compulsory reading for recruits), which touted masculinity as a virtue in need of recovery. Many Michoacanos were bound to be receptive to these ideas since Michoacán had undergone deep demographic and social transformations associated with migration and return migration, which resulted in phenomena such as the enshrinement of a culture of ostentation; the reconfiguration of family morality, with absent father figures; and the lingering unease at having performed demeaning ("feminized") jobs in the United States.

Admittedly, the moral code of the Knights Templar was implemented for a brief period of time and without much system. This means that the degree of its institutional consolidation is very much in question. It is, therefore, unclear whether the Code became a regulative force for members of the organization or whether it was a document merely for public consumption and for building a public reputation.[60] Be that as it may, and summing up, the preceding discussion raises the question whether the perpetrators have the ability to break free from the criminal environment in which they are immersed. Seeking a way out would require a moral reckoning about the acceptability of their actions, but this ability—moral competence, so to speak—is precisely what the cultural context has distorted and made difficult. In such conditions, the effort to disengage and leave a criminal context would be the equivalent of pulling oneself out of a swamp by one's bootstraps. In short, certain actors face extraordinary obstacles to freeing themselves from violent contexts. This serves as justification to lessen their moral and criminal responsibility, as well as eroding the ideal of fair opportunity to avoid wrongdoing.

Before concluding this section, let me address a potential objection to the claim that the existence of a cultural framework such as the one described ought to attenuate moral blameworthiness. There are many people exposed to narcoculture, and yet not all of them end up joining the ranks of a drug-trafficking organization. Why reduce the responsibility of some people if others in the same circumstances steered clear from drug violence? The answer to this question is that exercising what one might call epistemic caution (being cautious about what one believes) may be more demanding for some individuals than for others. Many individuals who live and act under contexts of mass atrocity make decisions in trying and uncertain circumstances, undergoing extraordinary amounts of stress. Some are even complex victims,[61] at once perpetrators and victims, and inhabiting what Claudia

Card, following Primo Levi, calls "gray zones"—they are the victims of some evil, are implicated through their choices in perpetrating the same or similar evils on others who are victims like themselves, and act under extreme pressure. All these elements make it unclear which actions are avoidable and at what cost. As Card writes, "We may not know how to assess the power of the threats facing the agent or the agent's powers of endurance. The agent may have to make difficult, irreversible decisions quickly and in the absence of relevant information."[62] So being cautious about what one believes is an ability that not all can exercise with the same ease. Thus, we are back at the original point: many of the contexts where narcoculture dominates offer the possibility of distancing and disengaging oneself from toxic beliefs, but only at a very high cost; some may be able to pay it, but not all.

The Digital Allure of Narcos

As in all other contemporary social interactions, those between youth and criminal organizations in Mexico increasingly take place on digital platforms. Criminal organizations use platforms to recruit youth in two ways—by deception or persuasion. Deceptive digital recruitment is grounds for full exculpation insofar as it lures the youth into drug trafficking against their will. The Jalisco Nueva Generación organization, for example, used Facebook to make spurious job offers as interviewers, bodyguards, security guards, or local police officers. Once recruited under false pretenses, individuals were taken to a municipality in the outskirts of Jalisco's capital, Guadalajara, where they "trained" them to be *sicarios*.[63] There are also a handful of documented cases of recruitment via video games like *Grand Theft Auto* or *Call of Duty*.[64] By contrast, persuasive digital recruitment is harder to grapple with, morally, because while it need not involve sheer coercion, it does rely on a method of persuasion that is harder to resist than traditional persuasive methods. There is a case to be made, then, for reduced blameworthiness when some forms of digital persuasion are at work.

Increased use of social media by criminal organizations is owed to its growing popularity and penetration and to the limited access these organizations now have to traditional communication outlets. Prior to 2011, they could rely on traditional media to disseminate the content of *narcomantas* (blankets with messages for rival groups or the government) or publicize their atrocious acts. After 2011, however, the government and broadcasting companies reached an agreement to restrict the flow of such information to the public. Criminal organizations had to find alternative ways to reach an audience, and thus, *narcomantas* and staged atrocities receded in favor of videos on YouTube with scenes of brutal killings, torture, and beheadings of members of rival cartels.

Criminal groups do not only use platforms to sow terror among civilians or weaponize them against rival groups. They also try, depending on the circumstances, to garner social support and, relatedly, to attract recruits. They may do so by relying on some of the strategies discussed in the previous section, for instance, by making the world of drug trafficking seem appealing, exulting the lifestyle of narcos or whitewashing criminal organizations, which in turn is accomplished by portraying them as altruistic social institutions or by normalizing their violence. Already in their early stages, it was common to find some platforms where Jesús Malverde was depicted as a patron saint with a halo-like light over his head.[65] *Corridos tumbados* and other inheritors of *narcocorridos* (*trap*, *reguetón bélico*, and so on) are novel musical genres that have flooded digital platforms such as YouTube.[66]

The main difference between traditional styles of persuasion and those prevalent in digital platforms is that the latter are more difficult to resist. Algorithmic influence in platforms can boost persuasive strategies. Platforms, as is well known, run on personalized recommendation algorithms that promote certain content while at the same time removing or discrediting content that might rival or contradict it. They can create "criminogenic positive feedback loops of information consumption,"[67] whereby a user who has interacted with content that validates or promotes "antisocial" behavior or who has joined online groups that do so will subsequently continue to be exposed to such content.[68]

Speculatively, since sustained empirical investigation on the subject is scarce, it is plausible to argue that algorithmic influence renders the allure of drug trafficking more powerful than in the past. The persuasion of traffickers becomes more effective because their message can reach a broader audience and allows for more convincing publicity stunts, as when, during the COVID-19 pandemic, the organization Jalisco Nueva Generación recorded and uploaded its carefully staged deliveries of food and other basic goods to poor individuals. Instagram, Facebook, and TikTok have been teeming for years now with "hedonistic publicity,"[69] that is, content promoting and ideal-izing the life of traffickers, showing expensive clothes, cars, pets, houses, and so on. The content is engaging and goes viral.[70] Finally, in creating content, rather than unilaterally producing a message and circulating it through the platforms, some organizations have used the platforms to establish a space to interact with the public in those regions where they vie for dominance; thus, as early as the aughts, criminal organizations (Sinaloa and Juárez) interacted with civilians of Ciudad Juárez on YouTube through the comments section, initiating a dialogue in which they appeased them (we do not want to target the innocent), blamed rivals ("pigs") for violence, accused authorities of cor-ruption, and of course attempted to recruit the youth. In this way, they cast themselves as organizations in the service of people.[71]

Digital persuasion constitutes a uniquely potent form of manipulation—more resistant to detection and harder to counter than traditional methods. This enhanced efficacy creates compelling grounds for alleviating responsi-bility when such techniques enable wrongdoing.

Engendering *Mulas* and *Sicarias*

Men are responsible for generating most of the violence in Mexico, but women are also perpetrators of crimes. While men dominate drug-trafficking circles, like most other criminal circles, consistently occupying positions of leadership, women remain in the lower rungs of the social and political hi-erarchy in a subordinated role, with poor and Indigenous women, who sit at the intersection of multiple inequalities, situated at the lowest level. Women are increasingly involved in criminal groups, making up from 5% to 8% of a criminal group's composition.[72] Ethnographic work has identified the following among the recruitment pathways for women who participate in drug-trafficking circles as *mulas* (as female smugglers are usually called), cell organizers, saleswomen, collectors of money, or even *sicarias*: a romantic rela-tionship with a partner; drug addiction; or the assessment that participating in drug trafficking is the sole and most effective means for self-preservation.[73] Each of these pathways provides a different kind of reason for mitigating the culpability of women who participate in criminal wrongdoing.

The participation of women in criminal offenses tied to drug trafficking (including the most serious ones, such as homicide and kidnapping) may emerge out of an emotional relationship with a male partner structured around unjust gender norms. In a common scenario for mules, a dire economic situation will lead a man to smuggle drugs. He will then ask his female partner to join him, an offer she will reluctantly accept out of a (gendered) sense of having the duty to obey her husband and the duty to provide for her child at any cost. When caught, she will acquiesce to becoming a *pagadora* (payer), taking the legal blame for the offense and covering up for the partner, on the understanding that while she is imprisoned in lieu of him, he will provide for the common child. Importantly, women face greater obstacles exiting criminal milieus because they carry the burden of child rearing, while men are less reluctant to leave their children behind. Dynamics like this reveal how a background of expectations about their obligations as wives and mothers constrain their decisions on whether to participate in drug trafficking.[74] As Corina Giacomello argues, the role of women "in a context of victimisation makes the difference between consent and coercion to commit a crime more complex. [T]he context of their involvement conveys a 'forced choice' rather than free, willing and full consent."[75]

The claim that women lack the ability to act autonomously due to patriarchal constraints can be disputed by claiming that, save for exceptional cases, women are responsible for choosing to remain with their abusive partners. Feminist philosophers have carefully explored the problem of women's autonomous agency in settings of oppression. In the stylized example of the deferential wife, the question is to what extent a woman who apparently "chooses" to be self-effacing, sacrifices her desires, and assumes a submissive role is genuinely an autonomous agent. On a superficial level, since she "decides" to subordinate herself to her husband and make his decisions her own, her behavior is autonomous. But in a more demanding, more robust understanding of her autonomy, her behavior is not autonomous, because a servile character cannot produce autonomous decision-making. And a common feminist contention is that in the case of women, this kind of servility arises out of a set of gender norms women internalized as girls. It is as a result of gender oppression that women assume servile roles and refrain from even forming their own desires, blindly embracing those of their partners.

In the most extreme cases, however, questions about servility and its relationship with autonomy are beside the point. Even if it turned out that women offenders were able to overcome the oppressive gender norms that tied them to criminal networks, other circumstances partly excuse their actions. The point of departure for most women who participate in drug trafficking is a rotten social background. Giacomello summarizes their life trajectories punctuated by violence and abuse as follows:

> First, as children, violence is perpetrated against them within their family, mainly in the form of sexual and physical violence, neglect, and verbal violence. When they attempt to share details of these episodes of sexual violence they are not believed; on the contrary, they are accused of being liars or blamed for provoking their stepfathers or other male perpetrators. Other reactions—usually from their mothers—include battery. Two main scenarios develop before them: becoming involved in a cycle of gender-based violence in the context of relationships with older men, drug-use settings, and institutional settings (police stations, prisons and drug treatment centers); this usually leads to multiple pregnancies—as teenagers first and adult women later—and, sometimes, sex work, partner-induced sex exploitation and crime. They might also end up living on the street. In either case, fleeing from violence opens up new means of abuse.[76]

Furthermore, many mules and *sicarias* become drug users. For them, as Giacomello explains, "drugs are clearly a coping mechanism against the pain caused by neglect and abuse in the household and in intimate partner relationships. When dependence develops and life starts revolving around drugs, their reference points—mainly family—fall apart and riskier situations occur, such as living on the street, sex work and exposure to criminalisation and incarceration."[77]

In addition to these partial excuses, women who are implicated in the actions of criminal organizations may also have an impure justification for their actions. In many cases, these organizations provide protection for women that they desperately need. This protection becomes necessary because the state is absent and unwilling or unable to provide it. Joining criminal organizations is, in some cases, an act of self-defense. It is, admittedly, a very imperfect and flawed form of self-defense, but one such act, nonetheless. One former member of a criminal organization put it this way:

> From a very young age, I understood that you have two options: either you become a *cabrona* or you get fucked up. . . . It's not like you say, "Oh, I'm going to be a thug," but you realise that you can't go around naively, that if you want to live you have to know how to defend yourself and know who you are with. One thing leads to another, and you end up like this.[78]

This is not to say that *all* women who participate in drug trafficking become helpless victims. This view would deny women agency, making it dubious, and would be factually wrong as well, because, as a study in the US-Mexico border region shows, for some women, activities such as drug smuggling can become "a vehicle for female empowerment."[79]

In sum, as women steadily increase their participation in criminal organizations, we need to realize that their actions are partly excused and justified. They are excused insofar as their offenses may be the result of a life of social deprivation or of acting while in the grips of drug addiction—the epitome of nonautonomous decision-making—which impairs judgment and more generally debilitates character, especially since drug use may be a habit acquired to cope with the devastating effects of a rotten background. Women in criminal organizations are justified in participating in criminal groups as an "imperfect" self-defense against the wrongs of an unjust society.

Incidentally, the involvement of women in organized crime has led to an increased recruitment of their children. Children and youth have played a role in criminal organizations for a long time now. Among the first cases that gained public visibility in the early aughts were those of Rosalío Reta Jr. and Edgar Jimenez Lugo, alias El Ponchis, both of whom worked with criminal organizations and were eventually imprisoned in the United States and Mexico, respectively, for their complicity in atrocious crimes. Already in the administration of Felipe Calderón, crime statistics revealed an intense participation of minors and youth in surveillance, monitoring, and assassinations for criminal organizations. However, the presence of children and youth in criminal organizations has soared ever since.[80] Every indicator regarding arrests, pretrial detentions, and convictions of youth in the Enrique Peña Nieto (2012–18) and Andrés Manuel López Obrador (2018–24) administrations reveals an increment of significant magnitude,[81] and estimations about the future are grim.[82]

Like many women, children may be justified in joining criminal organizations. Many of them are left unprotected after their mothers are incarcerated and, without other means of support, they gravitate toward these groups as, yet again, a strategy of self-preservation.[83] Children may also have what comes closest to a complete excuse for their actions. Sometimes criminal organizations forcibly recruit the children of mothers who attempt to leave the organization, as a form of punishment. Beyond this, as is well known, children lack cognitive and noncognitive skills (emotional and impulse control) that are considered prerequisites to being full moral and legal subjects. In fact, abundant evidence from the neurosciences shows that during adolescence, the brain is still unstable in terms of its structure and functioning. Adolescents, for example, are more prone to adopt riskier attitudes than adults.[84] Because of their immaturity, children and adolescents must be judged less severely, both on moral and criminal grounds, than adults.[85] For this reason, an extremely important consideration in moral and criminal discussions of the culpability of low-ranking perpetrators is whether their initiation and first exposure to violence took place during their childhood or adolescence.

Training for Atrocity

Up to this point, I have mainly discussed the motivations behind offenders joining criminal organizations. Were they forcibly recruited? Were they in the grips of addiction? Did they have an alternative, or was their participation a matter of self-preservation? And so on. But it might be argued that for the purposes of attributing blame for atrocious crimes, we should examine first and foremost the acts they perpetrated, not the conditions under which they were recruited. After all, notwithstanding the reasons they have for joining criminal organizations, they retain the freedom to refrain from participating in heinous acts.

My concern about focusing solely or mainly on the acts that perpetrators commit is that time and again, journalistic reports and academic investigations show that perpetrators of mass atrocity tend to act as members of an organization, and one could argue that organizations involved in atrocity forcibly turn their members into perpetrators of atrocity. As soon as recruits become part of these organizations—be they armies, militias, paramilitary groups, or criminal syndicates—the freedom of members to decide whether and when they may refrain from committing wrongdoing, let alone the freedom to leave, begins to slip away from them even if they never lose it completely. These despotic and hierarchical organizations subject their rank and file to a simultaneous process of deindividuation and intra-individuation that extinguishes their ability to act freely. Deindividuation removes from them their sense of themselves as separate individuals: personal identity is superseded by a collectivized identity. Atrocity-producing organizations erase the identity of members by humiliating them, forcing them to shave their heads, making them wear uniforms or tattoos, mandating in-group slang, and so on. They also exploit their ordinary human impulses to obedience and conformity. In intra-individuation, the self is compartmentalized into noncommunicating "functions," as a result of which one's relationship to other persons is mediated by a specialized professional role. Executioners see themselves as professionals, no different from lawyers or doctors, and in that way, they are able to acquiesce to the requirements—the "morality"—of the job. Finally, these organizations make available to members narratives for the dehumanization of others and for self-absolution.[86]

Criminal organizations in Mexico are no exception when it comes to training their members for atrocity in these ways. In videos confiscated from La Familia Michoacana by public authorities, one of its leaders is shown slitting the throat of a corpse in front of a group of young men who were beginning their "training." The same leader also narrates how, to train members, he forced them to kill and dismember "captured enemies." Overcoming their initial reluctance, the new recruits obeyed.[87] In this manner, La Familia dehumanized the recruits. We have also seen how many recruits of La Familia, in a despondent condition owed to addiction, credited their recovery to their incorporation into the organization and were encouraged to believe that they exchange their newly "recovered" life for the lives they took in a kind of metaphysical trade-off. Similarly, Mexican low-level traffickers articulate narratives that normalize torture or the disposal of bodies in an economic logic, where such atrocities are viewed as an inherent and inevitable part of the drug-trafficking business and as the proper way of conducting it.[88] Organizations also use digital resources "to establish military and moral superiority" and to produce "*moral disengagement* through the 'displacement of responsibility,' the 'dehumanization of rivals' (in the case of Mexican cartels, this involves calling members of rival cartels 'pigs,' 'dogs,' and so on), the use of 'euphemistic language,' the 'attribution of blame,' and other discursive devices."[89]

Cannibalism is a paradigmatic (and morbid) example of atrocity training. Instances of cannibalism have been documented since 2014, arising from the initiation rituals of the Familia Michoacana and the Caballeros Templarios, which sought to recruit reliable (and dependent) novices from the most diverse extractions in a context of rapid organizational growth, but cannibalism seems to have spread to other organizations, such as Sinaloa and Jalisco Nueva Generación.[90] The practice occurs in a context where competition between rival organizations is extremely violent as they vie for dominance. With cannibalism, novices must demonstrate that they are willing to violate well-entrenched moral codes. As Claudio Lomnitz puts it, cannibalism "implies a radical—and brutal—moral transgression that could serve to consolidate an internal order and lift an insurmountable wall between inside and outside members."[91] Cannibalism seeks to produce loyalty, the pursuit of which prompts leaders "to develop rigorous recruitment methods that make it difficult or impossible that new recruits return to 'normal' society."[92]

In other words, atrocity training is training to weaken, if not annihilate, the moral agency of individuals. And when moral agency is so diminished, a plausible argument for reduced responsibility can be articulated.

The Infirmities of the State: "Imputing the Sovereign"

As can be gleaned from the foregoing discussion, which outlined the many "infirmities" of offenders and how they may ground a claim of diminished culpability and unfairness, the Mexican state has infirmities of its own. Every time, the state is in the background as the agent enabling offenders by shirking its duties toward them and other citizens. When not flouting its duties, the state appears to be ill-prepared or reluctant to properly assess the behavior of offenders: their motivations, their worldview, their constraints, their deprivations, and so on. In all, four infirmities stand out, and they bear on the question of the moral and criminal blameworthiness of offenders as well as raising difficult moral predicaments. The first set of infirmities call into question the standing of the state to punish at all. The last infirmity undermines its ability to judge blameworthiness properly.

The first is a *welfarist* infirmity. The state provides little to no assistance to socially vulnerable individuals who lack a safety net, which in turn puts them at severe risk of gravitating toward criminal groups. We see this happen in the case of individuals in the grips of addiction or of women whose socioeconomic plight prevents them from providing for their dependents. There is little controversy about the existence of this infirmity. More controversial is what follows from it. Does a state that neglects its citizens in this way have the moral standing to appear later as a prosecutor and judge to punish offenses?

It appears at first sight that the state's standing to blame and punish is compromised due to its complicity in the wrongdoings in question. Federal, state, and local governments have done their part, by inaction or direct involvement, to cultivate criminal environments and are, therefore, materially and morally co-responsible for the crimes that take place. And because the state is a co-conspirator, it should not be authorized to determine criminal responsibility. The state should not act as a judge because it should instead be a co-defendant.[93]

At the same time, if the state refrains from prosecuting and punishing perpetrators of egregious offenses, it commits an injustice against victims. Blame and punishment are a means of publicly condemning crime, which in turn reaffirms legal equality by vindicating the victim's rights to proper treatment. From this point of view, disregarding victims' demands for retribution amounts to rejecting citizen equality and telling them that their expectations of fairness before the law are in vain. This is true even if the justification for punishment in modern societies does not exclusively depend on the retributive desire of victims and their relatives.

Thus, the Mexican state faces a double moral dilemma, one that is irresolvable. First, it must punish offenders to publicly condemn their transgressions, but it must also *not* punish them because it lacks the moral authority to do so. Second, the state must punish (that is, incapacitate) dangerous offenders to protect actual and potential victims' basic rights but must simultaneously refrain from doing so because in the past it denied these offenders a fair opportunity to avoid punishment and, more generally, because it contributed to the serious injustice many of them suffered.[94] Even if we argue that, from a retributive perspective, the injustice to victims far outweighs the injustice to perpetrators, we are left with a "taint of injustice."[95] Whether or not it assigns criminal responsibility to low-ranking perpetrators, the state acts in a morally reprehensible manner.

There is a related *political* infirmity of the Mexican state: its sheer inability to provide protection to citizens in many regions of the country. Many criminal organizations now control local authorities to such an extent that they can be said to be de facto authorities. Excluding these cases and considering the perhaps more extended cases where formal authorities retain some degree of independence, it is still the case that the state lacks the ability to enforce the law because the police, the military, and prosecutor's offices, to name just a few institutions, have been overpowered or "captured" by criminal organizations. The question then arises whether the state retains the standing to punish offenders under these circumstances. Arguably, it does not because its justification to punish rests on its ability to protect citizens. In a contractarian view of the justification of punishment, Hobbes asks, "By what door did the right or authority of punishing in any case come in?" He responds that "the foundation of that right of punishing which is exercised in every commonwealth" is that the sovereign uses it "as he should think fit, for the preservation of them all."[96] Add to this Hobbes's view on political obligation, according to which, "The obligation of subjects to the sovereign, is understood to last as long, and no longer, than the power lasteth, by which he is able to protect them."[97] The implication of these views is that since the state does not command efficient law-enforcement and security institutions, it lacks the moral authority to punish.

The third infirmity is an *epistemic* one. This infirmity is less evident than the previous two but no less critical. To unpack it, let me return to the lengthy passage quoted at the beginning of the chapter, where Hobbes "imputes the sovereign" for failing to "instruct" its subjects, who may have committed crimes out of ignorance of the law. By this Hobbes intimates that the state has a duty to promote critical thinking among the citizenry. In turn, promoting critical thinking entails fostering epistemic virtues that allow citizens to properly weigh the evidence against false social and political beliefs so that they can better resist their pull. Or, to put it less strongly, critical thinking must at least try to eradicate epistemic vices that predispose people to accept harmful beliefs. The duty to promote critical thinking can be conceptualized as part of the broader duty to protect citizens since critical thinking can guard them against moral risks.

In the case of Mexico, the readiness with which youth accepts narcoculture is the result of several epistemic vices, which are within the realm of the state to combat, analogous to how the proliferation of fake news on social media renders state intervention—the contours of which might be debated—permissible and even obligatory. Consider the three facets of *narcocorridos*: those that exalt opulent lifestyles, those that glorify the deeds of traffickers, and those that normalize and glorify violence. A positive attitude toward these messages is the result of various epistemic vices such as *closed-mindedness, carelessness, or obstinacy*, which imply a disposition to consider certain standpoints, sources of information, or evidence haphazardly, superficially, or partially, and the reluctance to revise beliefs.[98] In turn, this can lead to self-deception. It is tempting to see these dispositions as *personal* vices or flaws of character, and they are that to some extent, but they are also an indication of a level of epistemic degradation that transpires on the state's watch. The point to underscore is that because the state tolerates such degradation, the state's standing to blame and punish is weakened.

There is one final state of infirmity. While this infirmity is also epistemic, it is not an infirmity pertaining to the state's inability to provide citizens with tools to think critically. Rather, it is a deficiency with respect to its capacity for assessing the legal culpability of suspected offenders. All states face the challenge of adequately gauging an offender's criminal blameworthiness. Some authors go as far as to say that it is unlikely that "the state *can* properly assess what wrongdoers justly deserve in all, or almost all, relevant cases." This is because "the state is epistemically and practically compromised in a number of important ways," which include the inability "to dedicate the time, resources, and effort needed to accurately assess desert and blameworthiness in most cases, cognitive biases that cloud our judgments, and the general difficulty of knowing how addiction, diminished capacities, social injustice, and other relevant factors should affect judgments of desert."[99] Put succinctly, the state—*any* state—is hardly ever in the proper epistemic position to know what an agent deserves and is, therefore, unable to justly distribute legal punishment in accordance with desert.

For the Mexican state, these challenges are herculean and ultimately insurmountable as it lacks even the most basic tools to make fine-grained assessments of culpability. It has been amply documented that the criminal justice system, when not captured by criminal organizations, lacks the human and infrastructural expertise, budget, and willingness to investigate crime. This has been its condition for decades if not centuries. The (sometimes deliberate) lack of professionalization and resources was less of a problem when criminal violence was moderate to low. But as violence erupted at the beginning of the century, the shortcomings had devastating consequences. For a system that struggled with ordinary crime, grappling with systematic and widespread criminality soon became overwhelming. To mention an example, "macrocriminality" of the kind that has emerged and consolidated in Mexico (involving complex networks of complicity between private and state actors, widespread and extraordinary crime, and high financial stakes) requires judges with knowledge of human rights law and even physicians with forensic and therapeutic training.[100] All these features are a sine qua non in the pursuit of truth in contexts of extraordinary crime, which includes revealing perpetrator guilt. This infrastructure is glaringly absent in Mexico, leaving the motivations, and, consequently, the blameworthiness, of perpetrators of massive crime unveiled.

In sum, for different reasons, all these infirmities diminish the state's standing to attribute responsibility or undermine its ability to produce adequate judgments of criminal and moral culpability.

Conclusion

This chapter set out to consider the long-standing argument that some offenders are the product of socially and economically precarious backgrounds and cultural environments conducive to violence. Various social processes come together to promote the recruitment and participation of adults, youth, and even children in the drug-trafficking world. These include a disconnect from the local social system, participation in gangs that are linked to trafficking organizations, and the abandonment of drug addicts who are willing to join trafficking groups to escape the vulnerability imposed on them by society (due to the absence of support networks, for example). All these means of joining and recruiting into the "reserve armies" of trafficking organizations require us to question the idea that all "narcos" are fully responsible for their actions. The drug-trafficking army is not an army of volunteers or enlisted men but of foot soldiers who joined for reasons that lie somewhere between free will and coercion. No one chooses to be born in a town or city where local authority structures have been replaced by violent ones. No one chooses to be born in a neighborhood where a criminal structure operates and will eventually co-opt the local gang. Not all individuals in precarious situations or those who fall prey to addiction have the resilience to resist the promise of a less destitute life. The preceding argument does not imply that individuals in extraordinarily violent settings lack "agency."

Proper reflection on the problem requires that distinctions be made between different types of perpetrators, even if it is extremely difficult to put these distinctions into practice. The point is not to exonerate individuals because of the precarity of their past or present life conditions but to assess the nature of the factors that influenced their decision to become involved in drug trafficking, as well as to determine what real options they had to resist and behave differently. In these instances, a case-by-case assessment will always be used. And above all, the point is to underscore that the complexity of determining the degree of blame and responsibility should not be underestimated.

FIVE

Forgetting the Forgotten?

When the State Shows (or Feigns) Compassion

Previous chapters made the case for principled leniency based on consider-ations such as the importance of recollecting information about the disap-peared, the existence of circumstances that mitigate personal responsibility, and the conditions of imprisonment. This final chapter adopts a slightly dif-ferent approach. It assesses the plausibility of an additional argument for leniency—compassion—while simultaneously examining how, in practice, it can serve as a disguise for perpetuating punishment-as-usual. The justifi-cation for leniency based on compassion differs from the legal defenses ex-plored in the previous chapter. Compassion refers to the idea that something about the background or the life of the accused should elicit an empathetic response from authorities and would make it excessive or unjust to impose punishment of a severity that we would otherwise accept.

The focus is on the 2020 amnesty promulgated during the presidency of Andrés Manuel López Obrador. I take this amnesty to be, in the letter, an embodiment of the value of compassion.[1] While the 2020 amnesty delib-erately excluded offenders who committed serious crimes such as murder, kidnapping, or enforced disappearance, it sought to extend a compassionate or "humanitarian" treatment for low-level perpetrators who have been drawn into drug trafficking out of desperation, particularly in the case of members from two paradigmatic groups that have endured background injustice since time immemorial: Indigenous peoples and women. The amnesty, as it was enacted, was very capacious and benefited not only drug offenders but also, in its compassionate zeal, women who had an abortion and had been imprisoned as a result, and even those who committed theft. Women ought to be granted amnesty, accordingly, on account of the existence of gender-based domination, including the absence of a safety net for single mothers, victims of domestic violence, and so on. In turn, Indigenous groups, the main focus of the chapter, were granted amnesty on account of the history of discrimination they have been subjected to, including socioeconomic discrimination that may have cornered them into committing drug-related offenses such as the transportation of drugs.

On its face, then, the amnesty seems like a tenable justification for principled leniency insofar as it commits the state to refraining from punishing some offenders in the name of compassion.[2] However, when taking into consideration the wider context of state policies enforced concomitantly as well as the virtual inaction with respect to the operation of the Mexican criminal justice system, the amnesty reveals itself as an ill-disguised form of *un*principled leniency. The amnesty is not unprincipled in the sense of arbitrarily selecting individuals for its benefits without justification or failing to apply its standards impartially. Rather, it is unprincipled in the sense that it functions as a smoke screen, obscuring the inherently punitive nature of the criminal justice system. Put succinctly, it is a demagogic amnesty of feigned compassion.

The chapter also makes a historical digression about amnesties in Mexico to develop two further claims, which reinforce the argument about the unprincipled character of the amnesty. The first is that the choice of the particular legal instrument, amnesty, to instantiate compassion is rather striking because, historically, amnesties in Mexico had been used as bargaining chips to stave off or quell social or political conflict; they were extended to members of belligerent groups, most notably discontented factions of armies that challenged the state, and they targeted political crimes (sedition, insurrection, and the like) in return for disarmament and demobilization. While there are some remnants of this rationale in the 2020 amnesty, which seems to analogize political armed conflicts of the past to current criminal violence, this time the beneficiaries are notably disarmed and relatively harmless individuals. There is, however, one precedent of an amnesty that introduces the same language, associated with compassion and cognate terms such as mercy, clemency, equity: the amnesty of the so-called Dirty War. This amnesty was extended in 1978 to members of the left-wing guerrilla groups that challenged the state in the 1970s and were fiercely repressed by it. While couched in a pragmatic language of appeasement, this too was an amnesty of compassion, with interesting parallels to the amnesty of the Drug War.

The second claim points toward another resemblance between these two amnesties. In the case of the amnesty of the Dirty War, the aim of the regime was to retain power and shore up its legitimacy by modestly increasing the participation of left-wing voices in political institutions. Many of those who were granted amnesties went on to become public officials at the local or national level. At the state level, however, some governors used the amnesty to lure in guerrilla members and assassinate them. Likewise, in the case of the amnesty of the War on Drugs, what little the government has offered with its left, progressive hand, it has withdrawn with its right, punitive one, as it entrenches dubious and cruel practices in the criminal justice system like pretrial detention, which affects some of the same groups that are shown compassion with the amnesty law. Pretense, in other words, plays a major role in the enactment of the two amnesties.

The chapter is structured as follows. Section one develops a brief philo-sophical discussion about compassion: what makes it valuable, what makes its relationship to criminal justice so tense, and how its invocation can be used ideologically, in the Marxist sense of the term. This is done to make the case, in section two, that the amnesty of the War on Drugs extends a com-passionate treatment of women and members of Indigenous communities who committed drug offenses while coexisting with policies that contradict the amnesty's compassionate spirit. Section three examines the justifications for and the uses of traditional amnesties (promulgated in the late nineteenth and twentieth centuries), showing how authorities conceived of them in strictly pragmatic ways to deactivate conflict. By contrast, section four shows that this legacy was interrupted by the amnesties of the Dirty War, which, much like the present amnesty, professed to be compassionate law but was also, in some instances, a subterfuge.

Compassion and Criminal Justice

Political philosophers have long discussed the importance of mercy (clemency, compassion, or equity, as it is also commonly called[3]) and its relationship with justice, from Aristotelian *epieikeia*[4] and Senequian *clementia* to the discussions of Aquinas, Anselm, and a handful of contemporary authors.[5] Seneca thinks clemency should incline the observer (or judge) toward comprehension and leniency during the imposition of sanctions. He does not deny the importance of moral and penal responsibility but asks that we look at the perpetrator's circumstances. For Seneca, the antithesis of mercy is cruelty and the legal rigorism that grows out of retributive anger. For him, imposing a strict punishment is a vice rather than a virtue. Thus, Seneca defines *clementia* as a "tendency of the mind to leniency in exacting punishment" or as "moderation that remits something of a deserved and due punishment."[6]

Building on this tradition, John Tasioulas describes mercy as "the putative ethical value that justifies leniency in the infliction of punishment that is due in accordance with justice." But, Tasioulas adds, "not every suspension or relaxation of a just punishment is an instance of mercy; instead, leniency must be shown for the right reasons[:] these are [in the mercy tradition] typically glossed as reasons of charity (or, equivalently for our purposes, compassion or humanity) that have their source in the value of relieving a wrongdoer's plight."[7] From a merciful perspective, in some cases, the imposition of the sentence warranted by retributive justice would constitute an excessive hardship. What underlies compassion is a concern for the impact that a proposed punishment will have on the offender's well-being "in light of a searching and empathetic scrutiny of their character, life history and the broader context of their wrongdoing."[8]

To illustrate this view of compassion, consider a battered woman who kills her tormentor. In taking her tormentor's life, she wished to bring her intolerable situation to an end. Yet the wrong of murder remains. But rather than focus on the gravity of the offense, we focus on the character and the circumstances of the offender: a morally decent person subject to systematic abuse. This rightly leads to compassion. Her suffering created a powerful incentive for her to escape her situation by killing her abuser, the sort of incentive most law-abiding citizens are fortunate not to experience.[9] To offer a recent example, the criminal justice system should respond empathically to, and therefore impose lenient punishment on, the nurse who consumed the fentanyl-based painkiller she was supposed to administer to her patients, leaving them in excruciating pain. After all, she was a victim of the highly addictive and massively marketed substance, which she began taking to cope with extreme hardship in her personal life: she was going through a crippling divorce, the legal bills were mounting, her partner was unwilling to pay child support, and all of that in a society that structurally disadvantages women. Put briefly, then, mercy reduces punishment to less than what is deserved and, importantly, it does so on the grounds of caring for the plight of the offender, particularly if they repent for their actions, for repentance entails a repudiation of one's acts and an admission that a different course of action may have been more appropriate.

As can be gleaned from this extremely brief philosophical account, mercy and justice are often characterized as standing in tension. Some authors resolve this tension in favor of mercy, positing it as a supra-ethical value beyond (or above) justice. As Aquinas puts it, a merciful God is not under an obligation to punish sinners because the sins he dismisses, if he chooses to do so, are against himself, the supreme common good of the whole universe.[10]

However one resolves the tension, the key point to underscore is that amnesties can serve as the legal instrument to materialize compassion. This was the case in Mexico with the 2020 amnesty, as I now turn to explain.

An Amnesty of Compassion (and Deceit)

The amnesty was promulgated two years after Andrés Manuel López Obrador's landslide electoral victory in the presidential election. It had been one of his campaign promises, along with a change of course in the state's strategy to combat drug-trafficking organizations. Candidate López Obrador rightly claimed that part of the reason why previous administrations failed to curb violence should be attributed to the punitive character of their strategy. More specifically, the strategy consisted, among other things, of increasing sanctions, eroding the rights of the accused, creating new penal categorizations (for example, the crime of *halconeo*), and so on. Unsurprisingly, punitive measures of this kind disproportionately targeted marginalized populations, and the penitentiary system was soon filled with poor, Indigenous, and even men and women with disabilities. This trend was by no means novel; the least advantaged members of society have always been easy prey for the criminal justice system, but the trend was exacerbated in the last decade. An amnesty, López Obrador concluded, represented the first step away from the punitive path.

No one put it more clearly than López Obrador's then-surrogate, Olga Sánchez Cordero, who later became secretary of the Interior and senator. In 2018, during the presidential campaign, López Obrador's mention of a possible amnesty for perpetrators generated public outcry. To contain it, Sánchez Cordero wrote in a national op-ed that Morena, the president's party, "does not seek a pact with the *capos*, it does not seek their pardon; Morena seeks alternatives to the failed models, it seeks an amnesty for the millions who have been recruited and co-opted by organized crime for not having the opportunities that every Mexican should have."[11] Sánchez Cordero explicitly mentions transitional justice as a model of conflict resolution that inspires the proposal. Transitional justice, a term of art that refers to a set of proposed principles, policies, and institutions, is a popular program of reforms for societies emerging or aspiring to emerge from social conflict. The transitional justice "tool kit" considers some forms of amnesty as a possible tool to build peace, and the candidate and its campaign seized the language of this program to appease the human rights community.[12]

To illustrate the point, Sánchez Cordero used the example of Sebastiana, a Tzotzil Indigenous woman from Chiapas, who was imprisoned while smuggling cocaine as a "mule" (that is, a drug smuggler). Men and, more often women like her, Sánchez Cordero argued, were the intended beneficiaries of the amnesty:

> Sebastiana might not have been sentenced to 14 years in prison, and thousands of Mexicans would not have lost their lives or their freedom if we had sought to provide them with education, health and work. Violence is not fought with violence. The best policy is to address and resolve the social causes that have led us to this violence by seeking prevention and social improvement.[13]

The choice of Sebastiana was an implicit recognition that the kind of discrimination suffered by members of vulnerable groups is intersectional, by which I mean that it is a kind of discrimination that does not occur only along one axis of identity. In the presence of overlapping membership to different groups, disadvantages from discrimination on account of belonging to one group might be aggravated by disadvantages flowing from belonging to another group.[14] Thus, the likes of Sebastiana are the subject of an intersectional compassion: a kind of empathy arising from being a woman, Indigenous and poor at once.

Along these lines, once elected, López Obrador and his administration issued the National Development Plan of 2019–24, which asserted that "the files of accused and sentenced individuals will be reviewed in light of the peace-making approach in order to determine whether their cases may be subject to amnesty or pardon, conditioned in all cases on compliance with the four pillars of transitional justice: truth, justice, reparations and guarantees of non-repetition."[15]

Roughly, the spirit of the amnesty that the López Obrador administration eventually passed was faithful to the original proposal.[16] As we shall see, considering its target population and the offenses it covers, compassion must be viewed as its driving force, particularly with respect to the plight of poor women and ethnic minorities. In keeping with its predecessors in nineteenth- and twentieth-century Mexico, the amnesty benefited those who committed politically motivated crimes (sedition), excluding terrorist acts, as well as crimes perpetrated with firearms and that harmed the integrity of another person. But politically motivated crimes, listed as the last in the law, do not seem to be the priority of the amnesty. Contrary to what was the case with the previous amnesty, the main beneficiaries of this one are not members of belligerent organizations to which the state attributes political standing. No such organizations exist in the current political horizon. While not in the original proposal, the amnesty was extended to include women who had had abortions, an act considered a crime in most Mexican states when the amnesty was passed, as well as to the physicians and relatives who assisted them in the process. More importantly for the purposes of the chapter, the amnesty contemplated offenses against public health (*delitos contra la salud*), granting amnesty to offenders who committed them while "in poverty or extreme vulnerability due to exclusion and discrimination [from society], or because they have a permanent disability, or when the crime has been committed at the suggestion of a spouse, common-law husband or wife, sentimental partner, blood relative or relative without any separation limitation, or out of well-founded fear, as well as those who were forced by organized crime groups to commit the crime." Notably, members of Indigenous or Afro-Mexican communities who committed drug offenses are also eligible for the amnesty, presumably under the premise that historically these communities have faced and continue to face socioeconomic, cultural, and political discrimination. Individuals from these groups may benefit from the amnesty if they were denied interpreters or defenders/lawyers familiar with their language and culture, which would be considered a violation of their due process. In short, the motivations at the heart of the amnesty allude to correcting prior procedural injustices (for example, violations of due process) but also showing compassion for the plight of those who historically have been the subject of structural injustice, especially women and Indigenous groups. The law initiative by a Morena legislator calls it an amnesty "for humanitarian reasons against the victimization of poverty."[17] This, then, is an amnesty whose beneficiaries were selected on humanitarian grounds, not qua members of a political organization.

The process of granting amnesties had a lethargic start and raised initial signs of concern, some of which were addressed much later.[18] One concern is that to be far-reaching, the *federal* amnesty would need to be replicated at the local level, since many of the crimes committed by the groups in question fall within the remit of local jurisdictions. Another concern, right from its inception, was the process to grant the amnesty to its beneficiaries. Rather than creating an autonomous body, as has been the case of paradigmatic amnesty commissions (for example, South Africa), the amnesty commission was integrated by members of the government—the heads of three ministries (Interior, Security and Citizen Protection, Welfare) and of two national agencies or institutes (on women and Indigenous peoples). Sessions were held at the discretion of the presiding member (Interior). Human rights activists complained that the commission was working arbitrarily and opaquely—for a long time there were no transcriptions of the sessions and no criteria for determining which or how many applications would be considered in each session.[19]

The results of the amnesty at the time of writing were underwhelming, to say the least. By June 2024, the commission had met some fourteen times and granted amnesty to 424 people, of which the judges finally accepted 374.[20] In line with the original spirit of the proposal, the vast majority (98%) of those released had been accused of *crimes against health*, as the legal technical terms describes an assortment of offenses related to drug trafficking, and most of these were related to transportation of drugs. Of those amnestied,

126 were women. A score of them committed drug offenses because they had received pressure from their partners or organized crime. There was, for instance, Domitila, a Mazahua Indigenous woman who was sentenced for drug transportation and had been detained since October 2019. She claimed that she was coerced by a man who threatened to kill her son unless she agreed to transport a suitcase containing marijuana. She was discovered and detained in Huitzo, Oaxaca, during a routine federal police inspection, while traveling on a bus bound for Mexico City. The public prosecutor, the judge, and even her defense ignored the fact that she had been forced by a third party who threatened her. She was sentenced to six years and eight months in prison but was released after serving two years in a women's prison in Oaxaca.[21]

Domitila's is a paradigmatic case of duress, more in line with what was discussed in the previous chapter, but in most cases those who benefited from the amnesty, according to official documents, did so on account of committing drug offenses while "in a situation of poverty" or "extreme vulnerability by exclusion and discrimination," a justification more in keeping with compassion. Among the beneficiaries were members of Indigenous communities (Mixteco Nahuatl, Cora, Chol, Tzotzil, Amuzgo, Zapoteco, and Tzeltal ethnicities, to name a few) who transported marijuana, cocaine, methamphetamines, and other drugs. Consistent with the idea of intersectional compassion, the recipients of the amnesty are characterized as disadvantaged from the ethnic (they are Indigenous) as well as the socioeconomic (they are poor) perspective. However, only a fraction (thirty-five) of those released fit the profile of Sebastiana, the victims of intersectional discrimination on account of their identity as poor, Indigenous, *and* women. Such was the case, for example, of three Tzeltal women who were amnestied and released from a penitentiary in Guerrero.[22]

All these shortfalls are minor compared to the larger problem that, as it were, stained the amnesty—its incongruency with other policies of the current administration. Despite implementing the amnesty and advocating for related measures,[23] the López Obrador administration also passed a set of policies that openly contradicted the amnesty's compassionate spirit. The most obvious example is a reform in 2019 that strengthened *prisión preventiva oficiosa* (mandatory pretrial detention) and broadened the kinds of offenses that fall under this category (automatic "preventive" imprisonment for twenty crimes, more than double those allowed before, including imprisonment with only a complaint for theft).[24] Far from cultivating a compassionate approach, mandatory pretrial detention is a part of a regime that openly espouses the harsh treatment of those suspected of criminal behavior. It is therefore unsurprising that the current administration oversaw the fastest growth in prison population in fifteen years, with 300 persons imprisoned every day. The detainees belong to the most disadvantaged segment of society: people who have a high school education or less, who work in informal commerce (for example, taxi drivers), and who have a public defender who handles up to 300 cases[25] at the same time.[26]

Even more strikingly, there has been a notable increase in the detention of individuals from the group intended as the primary beneficiary of the amnesty. By the end of 2023, 8,175 individuals deprived of liberty—representing 3.5% of the total incarcerated population—identified as belonging to Indigenous communities. The majority were held in state prisons, with only a small fraction in federal penitentiaries. Compared to 2022, the number of incarcerated Indigenous individuals rose by 8.9% in 2023.[27] While these figures are presented in absolute terms, the trend is concerning: rather than witnessing a decline or even stabilization, the data reveal a troubling upward trajectory. This raises critical questions about the aspiration to address the vulnerability of Indigenous communities within the criminal justice system.

The deepening of the militarized strategy to combat drug trafficking further contradicts the compassionate thrust of the amnesty by exacerbating the problems that the amnesty purports to address. Despite vowing to the contrary, the López Obrador administration accelerated the involvement of the military at every stage of crime prevention. This involvement is controversial for reasons that have been amply documented. Empirical analysis has shown that rather than abating violence in every instance, military intervention may sometimes exacerbate it.[28] Even granting for the sake of the argument that military intervention may contain violence in the short run, it will do the opposite in the long run by instituting what may be described with little exaggeration as regimes of military occupation across the country. At any rate, a military approach to combating drug trafficking is not bound to cultivate a compassionate treatment of participants in most of the links in the drug-trafficking chain. Enemies of the state, which is how members of the army are encouraged to view citizens in most of this chain, are seldom viewed as deserving of compassion.

In conclusion, beyond the fact that its implementation was marred at the outset by bureaucratic inefficiencies, the amnesty's impact was undermined by contradictory policies, such as the expansion of mandatory pretrial detention and the deepening militarization of public security, which disproportionately target the very populations the amnesty seeks to protect. The rising incarceration rates among Indigenous communities and other vulnerable groups highlight the dissonance between the administration's rhetoric of compassion and its punitive practices. The amnesty was a symbolic gesture rather than a meaningful expression of compassion.

Prudential Amnesties

With the 2020 amnesty, the state acknowledged the plight of disadvantaged members of society and, in a supposed exercise of compassion, vowed to "forget" their offenses. By contrast, compassion had not been the motivation of amnesties in the past. They had usually been crafted during a stalemate or in the aftermath of victory to appease or reintegrate the insurrectionists, members of militia groups, and the like. This makes the choice of amnesty somewhat perplexing. The next two sections make a brief historical digression to elaborate this point.

Amnesties are commonly proposed and conceded in times of conflict. Public authorities have traditionally used amnesties as strategic assets to appease social, political, and military conflict. During or in the aftermath of existential threats, states extended amnesties as if to wave a white flag. Often, they did so aware that combating an armed group would drag violence on endlessly, even if the belligerent group had no clear chance of succeeding. Or, in more symmetrical combat, both parties acknowledged that there would be no clear winner. In yet another scenario, the winning side used amnesties to gain the allegiance of the rank and file of belligerent groups, for without them governance or stability might not be possible.[29] This is true for some of the earliest amnesties recorded.[30] Carl Schmitt articulates these ideas very clearly in an extremely short albeit provocative piece, "Amnesty or the Power of Forgetting,"[31] which he wrote in the aftermath of World War II, advocating for the use of amnesties in Germany's postwar criminal prosecutions. While Schmitt's advocacy in this specific instance is objectionable,[32] and while he has in mind amnesties in interstate war, not intrastate conflict, he aptly captures the traditional underlying rationale for amnesties when he writes: "The word amnesty means forgetting. And not only forgetting, but also the strict prohibition to rummage in the past, and finding occasion there to further acts of revenge and further compensation."[33] Put briefly, for Schmitt, amnesties are the only mechanism available to societies to stop potentially endless cycles of violence resulting from postwar revenge. Note that when an amnesty is understood in this way, it is in direct contradiction with basic ideals of criminal justice. Prudentially offering an amnesty for the reasons described requires that justice be put aside. It might be tempting to think that when the motivations of the belligerent groups are just, such as when such groups are fighting an oppressive government, amnesties are not unjust. Yet it should be acknowledged that something is amiss when an injustice is corrected with tools that imply, at least conceptually, another injustice.

Amnesties, then, have been understood as a means to bring the political and social unrest that results from a challenge to state authority to an end. To work, they require a minimal degree of trust among the relevant stakeholders. And, again, they imply a repudiation of criminal justice, since a beneficiary of an amnesty is a perpetrator who ought to have been punished but gets off scot-free. Importantly, in this view amnesties need not make emotional appeals to compassion or reconciliation. They can be framed as strictly prudential, transactional measures that bring peace and stability.

Most amnesties in nineteenth- and twentieth-century Mexico fit the model of prudential amnesties just described and were extended in the face of significant challenges to state authority. In the nineteenth century, they made their appearance in the aftermath of the war that defeated the second Mexican "Empire." Benito Juárez and Sebastián Lerdo de Tejeda decreed two amnesties in 1870 and 1872, respectively, extinguishing criminal liability for crimes such as "*infidencia a la patria*," sedition, conspiracy to overthrow the government, and other "political crimes" (*delitos del orden político*); desertion was also covered in the case of members of the military. Juárez, however, denied it to "the regents and lieutenants of the so-called empire" and "the generals who, while commanding divisions or army corps, switched to the [side of the] invader." These were typical amnesties via which the vanquishing party turned a blind eye toward the crimes of the small fish but was rigorous toward those of the big fish; recall that Emperor Maximiliano of

Habsburg and his inner circle were the first against the wall in 1869 when the empire was defeated.

Some decades later, amnesties reappeared in the legal and political landscape in the wake of the violence of the Mexican Revolution. Perhaps the most momentous one was extended to the Cristero movement, a massive grassroots movement that challenged a set of state policies it considered to be anticlerical and antireligious. The Cristero amnesty is exemplary of a kind of prudential amnesty that would prevail in much of the twentieth century. With it, public authorities sought to deactivate a social and political conflict that was very much alive, regardless of the causes of the insurgents or of whether authorities believed they deserved punishment. This was reflected in the fact that the amnesty involved a negotiation during every step of the way—from the initial approach between the warring parties to the outside agents allowed in the negotiation to the terms of the amnesty. In addition, the Mexican state's betrayal of the amnesty crudely inaugurated a course of action that would persist in time. I unpack these claims in the remainder of this section.

The regime emerging from the revolution unleashed Catholic resentment with a set of anticlerical laws, which restricted the role of the Church in both schooling and politics, and even regulated religious services. Shortly after, the unrest turned into armed insurrection against the state. The ruling cadre wanted to bring the Cristero military threat to a halt and began negotiations with the Catholic Church. *Los arreglos* (the arrangements or the deals), as the negotiations that ended in 1929 came to be known, involved secret and open agreements between the highest echelons of the government (including President Emilio Portes Gil, as well as generals Álvaro Obregón—until his assassination—and Plutarco Elías Calles, the power behind the throne), the Catholic Church (in Mexico and the United States), and even envoys from the Vatican and the US ambassador to Mexico. In the end, the president and a representative of the Catholic Church struck a deal whereby the latter would resume services and the government declared its intention not to "destroy the Church." The government would tone down, without abrogating, some of its anticlerical laws. Before the Church could accept the terms of the agreement, however, it sought approval from the Vatican, which accepted it on the condition, among others, that an amnesty be extended to Cristeros.

Indeed, the amnesty came as an explicit request from Rome, and Portes Gil conceded. The Liga even secretly discussed the terms of the disarmament (*licenciamiento*) of the Cristero army (the "Guardia Nacional," as it came to be known).[34]

The Cristeros accepted the amnesty provisions, although many of them grudgingly, as they were skeptical, and rightly so, of a legal measure they had little participation in crafting, and of the sincerity of the government's intentions. Ultimately, the government went against its word and continued to execute the Cristeros in their strongholds. With the amnesty, religious conflict subsided but remained an issue.

After the presidency of Pascual Ortiz Rubio (1930–32), and until 1937, the government continued its religious persecution. In that year, Cárdenas passed yet another general amnesty, with the main beneficiaries being members of the Second Cristiada.[35] Even though the approval of the amnesty was a prerogative of Congress, this time it was passed in a special session using the exercise of emergency powers. It did not merit parliamentary discussion because it was considered of "urgent and necessary resolution."[36] The amnesty targeted the crimes of rebellion, sedition, and riots or mutiny.

Dirty Wars, Dirty Amnesties

As can be gleaned from this history, the choice of an amnesty as the instrument to remove the brunt of punishment from low-level drug traffickers of the War on Drugs is rather odd. Perhaps choosing amnesties for this purpose can be traced to the popularity among human rights circles of transitional justice programs, which may include narrowly targeted amnesties as tools to reckon with civil conflict. However, there is one precedent in Mexican history for the kind of compassionate amnesty we are discussing—the amnesty extended to the members of guerrilla groups that challenged the Mexican state in the 1960s and 1970s. Perhaps on close inspection the parallel between the Dirty War and the War on Drugs should not be striking. After all, there was a direct line of continuity between the two "wars," or put more specifically, between counterinsurgent strategies and the emergence of drug trafficking. As Alexander Aviña puts it, several military officers engaged in counterinsurgency efforts in Guerrero "seamlessly coupled the brutal repression of peasant guerrillas and social activists with direct participation in the growing and trafficking of narcotics during the 1970s." Aviña underscores "the blending together of practices and epistemologies of counterinsurgency, on the one hand, and counternarcotics, on the other, into a broader praxis of militarized rural governance."[37] Like the amnesty of the War on Drugs, the amnesty of the Dirty War tried to build a foundation on the basis of an appeal to compassion. And like the amnesty of forty years later, its underlying motivation was deeply political.

In 1978, the José López Portillo administration promulgated an amnesty whose justification deviated from the traditional transactional rationale. Authorities portrayed it as an exercise of mercy, and as an opportunity to repair social and political relationships in the aftermath of Mexico's internecine conflict. In turn, many segments of society and even armed groups (or what remained of them after they had been savagely repressed by the state) rejected the sincerity of the state in pursuing these goals. Beyond the authorities' rhetoric, the reality is that the state faced a momentous legitimacy crisis. The amnesty was a strategy to improve a sullied reputation.

In the 1960s—if not earlier—social unrest began to brew in Mexico, including student demonstrations, workers' strikes, and rural demonstrations. By the end of the 1960s, significant portions of the country were already engulfed in violence. Guerrilla groups quickly spread throughout the country and gained strongholds in several regions, most notably in Guerrero, Jalisco, and others. Among the insurgent organizations were Asociación Cívica Nacional Revolucionaria, Partido de los Pobres, and the Liga Comunista 23 de Septiembre (LC23S). Authorities dealt with most forms of dissent by students, workers, and peasants through repression. The style of the military and paramilitary response to protest was exemplified during the Tlatelolco massacre of 1968 and the Halconazo of 1971, which violently quashed peaceful student demonstrations. The state's militarized campaign against rural and urban insurgents—the state-sponsored terrorist repression that acquired the controversial designation as the Dirty War—was even more brutal, particularly throughout the 1970s, as the military and paramilitary groups increased pressure to annihilate insurgent groups, which had themselves stepped up their campaigns against authorities, conducting ambushes against the military, and targeting high-level public figures such as Rubén Figueroa, a cacique from Guerrero, and Eugenio Garza Sada, a businessman in Nuevo León, who was assassinated by the LC23S in a failed kidnapping attempt. Counterinsurgent strategies included conducting house searches without a warrant, arbitrary detentions, extrajudicial killings, and torture.[38]

This is the historical background for the federal amnesty of 1978 and the state-level amnesties that followed it. The hope behind these amnesties was to usher in a new political era free from the social conflict and armed violence that had spread throughout the country in previous years. They were part of a broader set of policies that sought to attenuate dissatisfaction with the authoritarian, militarized grip of the PRI on some sectors of society, and its economic model of development.[39]

The crimes included in the 1978 law were sedition, rebellion, conspiracy, and other crimes committed as part of groups with political motives. Likewise, the amnesty took into account crimes against life, bodily integrity, and kidnapping, as long as the perpetrators did not represent "high levels of danger" (*alta peligrosidad*), based on the judgment of federal prosecutors. Those who surrendered their weapons within a period of ninety days from the law's implementation were considered. Since many of the crimes insurgents were charged with fell within the local jurisdiction, states had to enact their own amnesties to effectively extinguish criminal responsibility of insurgents. The terms and the beneficiaries of the amnesties were set by public prosecutors, but in a small concession to human rights activists and relatives of insurgents, some amended their amnesty proposals to include insurgents who had committed homicide, whom the original version explicitly excluded.[40] It is unclear how many dissidents received an amnesty. On February 5, 1979, an official source counted 559 individuals. Of those, 252 were included in the federal amnesty, and 317 in those promulgated in fourteen states.[41] On September 2, 1982, forty individuals were offered amnesties.[42] Most guerrilleros who benefited from the amnesty were men.[43]

So, how was the amnesty justified? One of the main architects of the amnesty was Jesús Reyes Heroles, secretary of the Interior and the man behind the broader political reform in which the amnesty was embedded. He touted it as a token of reconciliation and an exercise of compassion. Amnesties in Mexico, he affirmed, are a "traditional method of reconciliation and harmony applied in our country to overcome political and ideological difficulties of the past."[44] He also wrote: "If amnesty means forgetting, hopefully it will bring about reconciliation, without partisanship of any kind. It is intended to heal wounds. Let us not get bogged down in yesterday. Let us think and build today for tomorrow. Shackled to yesterday, we lose power to build the future."⁴⁵ For Reyes Heroles, an amnesty is a healer of wounds; it allows citizens to look and move forward.

President José López Portillo tells a similar story. While Emilio Portes Gil and Lázaro Cárdenas found no need to provide a reason to justify their amnesty proposal, let alone to make an emotional appeal, by contrast López Portillo had much to say in his annual address to Congress. There, he claimed that the amnesty

> [should] benefit those who, thinking of the solution to their own problems and those of others, overcame social and economic marginalization, which unfortunately still exists, [and] expressed their dissatisfaction via the misguided road of crime. With [the amnesty] I seek for these Mexicans to return to their homes, to reintegrate themselves into the civic activities that the country demands and to participate in the responsibilities of the national agenda. . . . We have carefully and responsibly considered this serious matter, in which the great national harmony may be at stake; and upon seeing the mothers who go on hunger strike in search of their children, and others in mourning—all the Mexican children, all the young people, just like our own children, our own children!—I have reaffirmed my decision: the minuscule groups or interests that we have not yet identified and pulled apart cannot thwart the possibility that the country, forgetting [and moving forward] in all areas, has the right to begin new virgin times. I am certain that today, just as yesterday, with Juárez, Lerdo de Tejada and Cárdenas, an Amnesty Law will make our social and political peace more solid and productive.⁴⁶

In his speech, López Portillo acknowledged the legitimate cause of guerrilleros while at the same time repudiating their methods and emphasizing the need to forget their "ill-advised" deeds in order to reintegrate them, thus opening up the possibility of a new beginning with peace. And to achieve this, the president offered compassionate treatment. Nowhere is this more clear than when López Portillo finds words of compassion for the searching mothers of the time, like Rosario Ibarra de Piedra, who led a decades-long effort in an unsuccessful quest to find her disappeared son.

The congressional debates that followed López Portillo's intervention leaned unanimously in favor of the amnesty. In unison, representatives of the entire political spectrum in Congress endorsed the "courageous" initiative of the president—from the right-wing and Catholic Partido Acción Nacional (PAN) to the left-wing "satellite" parties such as the Partido Auténtico de la

Revolución Mexicana and Partido Popular Socialista (PPS), and including, needless to say, the PRI. (While endorsing the amnesty, the PPS also claimed that the amnesty was part of a CIA conspiracy; this is the context of the Cold War, after all.) All agreed that the amnesty was a sine qua non for social peace; that it was a critical piece of the Political Reform; that in most cases the ends sought by insurgents were noble, but the means inappropriate. And all found reasoning and justification for the amnesty in calls for unity, peace, reintegration, and more clearly in some cases than others, for compassion.

A PAN representative, Francisco J. Peniche Bolio, expressed reservations about some of the procedural aspects of the amnesty. For example, he takes issue with the fact that the amnesty considers crimes that go beyond the political crimes that amnesties tend to include, such as sedition, insurrection, and conspiracy to overthrow the government. Furthermore, he worries that the amnesty vests the authority to grant it on prosecutors within the executive branch and not on judges. These observations notwithstanding, the congressman notes that his personal conscience forces him to turn a blind eye on these objections. The amnesty, he says following closely in the footsteps of Thomas Aquinas (he is, after all, the member of a Catholic party), "has a teleology that far exceeds the limited field of law and jurisprudence. It encompasses the unlimited realm of mercy, it encompasses the unlimited realm of benevolence—and between these two values, each as great as the other, it is undeniable that the hierarchy of the ethical value of mercy must prevail over the also ethical value of law or that of justice."[47]

The language of compassion was not confined to Congress. It resonated in the public opinion. One example of its indirect invocation is that of *guerrilleros arrepentidos* (repentant guerrilla members), as insurgents who abandoned the armed struggle came to be known, usually in a pejorative sense. By the time the amnesty was enacted, most insurgents had been annihilated. The rural guerrillas had been decimated through military and paramilitary repression. And urban guerrillas, including the LC23S, had been severely fractured during the years prior to the amnesty, in part through state repression but also due to internal disputes. Some of these disputes related to the question whether the guerrillas should continue to pursue armed struggle. Since the death of Ignacio Salas Obregón, leader of LC23S, a group of guerrilleros initiated a "process of rectification"; they objected to the militaristic attitude of the guerrilla, its rejection of unions, its reluctance to consider institutional avenues for political participation, and so on.[48] These dissidents embraced the amnesty and participated in the institutionalized political process with the Partido Socialista Unificado de México (PSUM) to win a handful of seats in Congress over the years to come. In addition, some of these former members joined forces with a faction of the Asociación Cívica Nacional Revoluciona-ria (the guerrilla group commanded by Genaro Vázquez Rojas) to form the Partido de la Revolución Democrática (PRD), the left-wing party that had a deep influence on Mexico's transition to democracy. Other former members of guerrilla groups joined political parties and held public office at the local level. Yet other guerrilleros simply defected to the side of the repressing regime.[49] At any rate, an extended opinion was that because these insurgents "repented," they had benefited from the compassionate amnesty.

But like the amnesty of the Drug War, this amnesty left intact the root of the problem. While many *exguerrilleros* supported it,[50] they also rightly criticized it for its narrowness and its arbitrary character. Commenting on the content of the amnesty proposal, which, with few amendments later became the law, Rosario Ibarra de la Piedra argued that it was "unfinished justice" because it was very restrictive (it had very few beneficiaries) and because "the intellectual authors of the repression" (prosecutors) could determine the high or low risk (*peligrosidad*) of potential beneficiaries.[51] She added: "Why is there no punishment for the police officers who made attempts on the lives and bodily integrity of hundreds of people? Why is there no mention . . . of the disappearance of the bodies by parapolicemen? Why is there no mention of those detained without judicial process by police and military forces?"[52] Along similar lines, a former member of the LC23S put his dissatisfaction with the amnesty law as follows: "The heads and agents of the security forces, as well as their superiors, were not subject to amnesty, probably because there was no reason to include them, since the government did not admit that they committed crimes or were committing crimes in the fight against the guerrillas. . . . Including members of the security apparatus and the leaders themselves in the amnesty would have implied recognizing what the government vehemently denied: the excesses of the 'dirty war.' "[53]

In sum, while the rhetoric of compassion was central to justifying the Dirty War amnesty, and was used by public authorities and critics alike, its underlying motivation was to clear the political regime's reputation, tarnished by human rights abuses. The source of those abuses, however, was left unrecognized. Thus, while couched in compassionate rhetoric, the 1978 amnesty—much like the 2020 amnesty—was merely a superficial performance of compassion.

Conclusion

The chapter argued that despite the Mexican state's declarative rationale for the 2020 amnesty—to benefit disadvantaged communities, particularly Indigenous groups, in line with principled leniency—this display of compassion was swiftly contradicted by incongruous policies. This incoherence suggests that the amnesty served as a smoke screen to deflect attention from the state's inaction to dismantle enduring punitive structures that harm the least well-off, including Indigenous peoples. The chapter also traced how political discourse in Mexico refashioned amnesties from strictly strategic legal tools into allegedly compassionate ones.

CONCLUSION

Morality and Leniency in Times of Atrocity

A Fool's Errand?

The toll of violence in Mexico is staggering, its spectacle horrific. The atrocities speak for themselves. In the Sierra Tarahumara, members of a criminal group ambush a military convoy with a drone, their leaked audio capturing triumphant cheers as the soldier's bodies are dragged from wrecked vehicles. Elsewhere, military troops spray machine-gun fire at unarmed civilians, on mere suspicion—executing survivors point-blank before staging a cover-up. Hitmen leave dismembered bodies in an abandoned car along a major avenue, a gruesome public display meant to intimidate the citizenry. Recruitment camps operate hidden in plain view, and their administrators execute or torture those forcibly recruited men and women who refuse to be "trained." Faced with such brutality, leniency toward perpetrators, principled or not, might seem an objectionable response.

I agree that some cases should not even begin with a conversation about leniency. However, it is crucial to recognize that not all cases are as unambiguous as these—except, perhaps, in the editorial lines of some traditional media outlets or in the news feeds of social media. The difficulty of distinguishing between cases that warrant leniency and those that do not makes it tempting to ignore the difference and assume that all offenses—and offenders—merit the same treatment. This would be as misguided as thinking that *all* perpetrators deserve leniency.

As this book has outlined, the argument for principled leniency rests on at least three foundations. It serves a higher goal: contributing to efforts to address the humanitarian crisis of the disappeared. It extricates the state from addressing wrongdoing through further wrongdoing, given the dire conditions of Mexican prisons and more generally the corruption of the criminal justice system. It evaluates the mitigating circumstances that stand in the background of perpetrators' actions. At the same time, the book identifies the limits of principled leniency as well as cases that may appear to qualify as such but do not.

By way of conclusion, I offer a few final reflections. The first is that prospects for improvement in many of the phenomena discussed in this book— the crisis of the disappeared, the squalor and oppression within prisons, and the underlying socioeconomic background conditions of many men and women—remain bleak. The persistence of these phenomena underscores the importance of seriously considering the merits and limits of principled leniency. Take, for instance, the crisis of the disappeared. There is no end in sight to this tragedy. Violence persists, the backlog of cases continues to mount, and the response from authorities remains inadequate. Efforts to locate the missing grow increasingly desperate, and the aspiration of bringing peace to grieving families seems achievable not because of the Mexican state, but despite it. Given this horizon of hope, the tool kit for locating the disappeared should not exclude penal benefits of the kind that principled leniency prescribes.

Something similar can be said about the state of Mexico's prisons. As discussed earlier, the penitentiary system is a disgrace. Governments of all political stripes have held power at both the federal and state levels, yet improvements have been modest at best. Reforming this entrenched system is undoubtedly difficult, not only due to financial and administrative hurdles but also because its current condition appears to be a structural feature of the political and criminal justice systems themselves. A recent judicial reform to democratically elect judges and magistrates only exacerbates the situation, ushering in a period of uncertainty that will likely further weaken already fragile judicial institutions—perhaps even making them more susceptible to influence from organized crime. This reality renders a discussion of principled leniency even more urgent.

The broader background conditions that shape criminal behavior are also unlikely to undergo the radical transformation needed to counter centuries of deprivation. The state is unlikely to transform criminogenic environments in the short term and, in fact, the state itself plays a contradictory role—co-creating criminogenic conditions and then appearing as the coercive apparatus tasked with punishing those who emerge from such conditions. To avoid hypocrisy, the state must take responsibility for its complicity in creating the conditions for crime. In some situations, this entails extending lenient treatment to offenders without thereby disrespecting victims or failing in its duties toward them, which requires an extremely complex and delicate balance.

My second point is that even where strides can be made to reduce violence and promote accountability, a discussion about principled leniency remains relevant. Any plausible attempt to curb the criminal behemoths operating in large swaths of the country will require coordinated intervention from both Mexico and the United States. These organizations draw their power from their ability to muster resources—money, weapons, and personnel—from both sides of the border, necessitating bilateral action. Moreover, criminal organizations in many regions often outpower the Mexican state, meaning it needs all the assistance it can get, particularly from a nation with the world's most sophisticated intelligence apparatus. This only underscores how intelligence, already critical, can only grow in importance, and rightly so. But its acquisition needs to be conducted ethically, which takes us back to the limits of leniency.

To illustrate this, consider the case of Ismael "El Mayo" Zambada, a notorious kingpin who evaded both Mexican and American authorities for decades. For reasons that remain unclear, he boarded a plane alongside the son of another infamous cartel leader, El Chapo Guzmán. Guzmán's son may have been used as bait in a US operation—allegedly orchestrated by the DEA—to lure El Mayo onto the aircraft. Regardless of whether this constituted an abduction, the episode is significant for another reason: it ignited a wave of violence in Sinaloa, as members of the cartel waged a brutal war of retribution. As discussed in chapter 2, which focused on the ethical use of collaborators, state intervention to confront outsized criminality needs to respect certain constraints. As Mexico and the United States deepen their collaboration in law enforcement, criminal investigation, and intelligence capabilities, it becomes increasingly pressing to determine which methods of intelligence gathering principled leniency permits—and which ones it rules out.

My third reflection is that the themes of this book—focused as they may seem on narrow and isolated issues such as penal rewards, the moral blame-worthiness of perpetrators, and prison conditions—raise broader questions about the state's pursuit of justice in contexts of mass atrocity and of weak and captured law-enforcement institutions. Take, for example, the issue of penal rewards. This theme is an instance of a more general topic—to what extent can the state "negotiate" stability and public order with criminal groups? What if the state, instead of attempting to eradicate these organizations entirely, were to negotiate with them—allowing them to operate as long as they reduce violence? The knee-jerk reaction is that these groups must not be treated as legitimate negotiating parties. The state, it is argued, must subjugate them, using force and intelligence to dismantle their operations. Along these lines, President Andrés Manuel López Obrador, reflecting on the willingness of searching mothers to negotiate with criminals for truces, declared: "I'm glad that the mothers of the disappeared maintain this attitude and that criminals are willing to listen, although we cannot guarantee that action will not be taken against those who violate the law."[1] The president's (rhetorical) reluctance to guarantee immunity from prosecution reflects a common objection to any form of negotiation with criminals: such actions risk exacerbating impunity. While this may be the right approach in a world where the state can keep criminality at bay, it might not be appropriate where it is beleaguered by it. In nonideal conditions, where state institutions are weak or compromised, negotiated solutions may emerge as the lesser evil. The cynical rebuttal—that this observation is true but hardly novel, since politicians have always bargained for peace—misses the point entirely. Such a modus vivendi must not be understood as a deviation of morality but as what morality dictates under the circumstances. Nor is the arrangement to be conducted in the shadows but as part of a public discussion. These are precisely the presuppositions behind principled leniency.

A final point. Leniency must be a sustained and careful subject of inquiry for political morality in academic and public debates, particularly in times of atrocity. Some might dismiss this as a fool's errand. What can societies struggling to contain criminality gain from a fine-grained moral discussion of atrocity, apart from a byzantine scholarly reflection? When faced with

massacres, extermination camps, disappearances, and given that such societies appear to be operating in survival mode, do ethical subtleties not seem
frivolous. Shouldn't effort instead focus on research on the root causes of
crime or policies to disincentivize it? All one can respond to such concerns is
that moral and empirical inquiries are not mutually exclusive, and that not
enough energy is ever spent in pursuing both, especially when done together.
Furthermore, to deem normative inquiry as irrelevant is to surrender political
morality as another casualty of mass atrocity. There is nothing foolish about
an errand that tries to resist this outcome.

Acknowledgments

This book has benefited greatly from the feedback and support of numerous individuals and institutions. I presented individual chapters at several seminars and conferences, including the Latin American Political Philosophy Seminar at the National Autonomous University of Mexico, the American Philosophical Association, the American Political Science Association, the Midwestern Political Science Association, and the Pennsylvania Council for International Education. I am deeply grateful to the audiences at these venues for their thoughtful questions and constructive critiques.

I would like to extend my heartfelt thanks to Claudio Lomnitz, Fernando Escalante, Ernesto Azuela, Cristian Pérez, Blanca Heredia, and Tom Donahue-Ochoa, for their invaluable feedback on various parts of this project. I am especially indebted to Claudio Lomnitz for his intellectual generosity. Mauricio Tenorio also provided much-needed encouragement at the early stages of this book's development. I am grateful to Gustavo Fondevila, Moisés Vaca, and Mónica Serrano for their insightful comments. I am deeply appreciative of the editorial assistance provided by Miguel Bautista and Víctor Manuel Morales, whose keen eyes and attention to detail strengthened the manuscript. Teresa Davis and Kiran Stallone also deserve my thanks for proofreading and translating some of my words.

At Stanford University Press, I owe a special debt of gratitude to Marcela Maxfield for her editorial guidance and commitment to this project. The anonymous reviewers offered incisive and constructive criticism that significantly improved the manuscript. I would also like to thank Justine Sargent for her assistance during the production process.

This book would not have been possible without the financial support provided by the research grant PAPIIT IA400523 and the APSA Centennial Center Research Grant. I am also grateful to the Institute for Philosophical Research at the National Autonomous University of Mexico for providing the intellectual environment and resources necessary to complete this work.

Above all, I would like to thank my family for their unwavering support. As always, to my parents, Rachel and Juan Manuel, thank you. To Ezra, Vera, and Miwa, I dedicate this book.

Some sections of chapter 1 originally appeared in "Bargaining for the Disappeared? Rewarding Perpetrators in Transitional Justice Contexts," *Journal of Social Philosophy* 53 (2): 143–289 and in "Entre la inmunidad y la verdad: Beneficios penales y desapariciones en México," from Juan Espíndola y Mónica Serrano, *Verdad, justicia y memoria: Derechos humanos y justicia transicional en México*, El Colegio de México, 2023. Both pieces are published by permission of the publishers, Wiley and El Colegio de México, respectively. Sections of chapter 2 appeared in "Bargaining with Criminals: The Morality of Witness Collaboration in Mexico's 'War on Drugs,'" *Theoretical Criminology* 27 (1): 5–22 and is published by permission—and an exorbitant fee—of Sage Publishers.

Notes

Introduction

1. *Halcones* bear colorful or derogatory terms in different regions of the country: in Tamaulipas *marucheros*, if they are men, *sirenitas* or *campanillas* if they are women; *punteros* in Michoacán and Sinaloa (Caballero 2021).

2. Mendoza Rockwell 2012.

3. Article 188 bis of the Penal Code (Gobierno de Tamaulipas 2016).

4. For an account of how an unjust social context can be grounds for mitigating culpability, Stuart Green 2011.

5. Aguayo et al. (2016) provides evidence of this kind of forcible recruitment.

6. Degree of contribution and endorsement of the plans of the "principal" agent are two important conditions for attributing moral responsibility to accomplices (Lepora et al 2013).

7. Herzog and Zacka 2017. On the development of empirically oriented political theory, see Ackerly et al. 2024.

8. On the perils of the use of the label of "narcotraficantes," see Astorga 2005, 90; Astorga 2007, 283; Escalante 2012, 39–68.

9. Lomnitz 2019, 97.

10. In what follows I draw on Zepeda Gil 2018, who offers a good summary of these approaches.

Chapter 1

1. The law in Mexico distinguishes between enforced disappearances and disappearances perpetrated by nonstate actors. Throughout the text, I will refer to disappearances to encapsulate both, unless I indicate the contrary.

2. Tzuc 2023.

3. Guillén et al. 2018.

4. OSJI 2016, 37.

5. The closest and yet very distant precedent in terms of the magnitude of the problem are the cases of enforced disappearance during the 1960s and 1970s. De Vecchi Gerli 2023.

6. See Elster 2004b.

7. This dilemma does not arise in Mexico alone; it is typical of situations of extreme violence and mass atrocity. The Irish case is another example, albeit of a different scale. After the period of extraordinary violence known as "The Troubles," Ireland worked together with England to form the International Commission for the Location of Victims' Remains, which operated under the jurisdiction of both countries. This commission used various legal measures to grant immunity to anyone who provided information on the whereabouts of missing persons who disappeared due to the paramilitary activities of the Irish Republican Army. Peake and Lynch 2016, 469.

8. OSF 2016, 12.

9. On the search for the disappeared in Mexico, see Gallagher 2022.

10. Marcial Pérez 2018.

11. Saffón and Gómez Pinilla 2023.

12. Ironically and unintentionally, international accountability led to a shift toward clandestine repression methods, such as disappearances. The changes in the human rights framework that followed World War II, such as the strengthening of international organizations that monitor states' compliance with their human rights obligations and the increasing speed of the spread of information, led to a shift in the crimes committed and the ways in which state repression was exercised: they resulted in the use of disappearances and other less visible crimes. The decision to use or not to use forced disappearance depends not only on external factors, but also on the characteristics of the regime itself, such as how consolidated it is. For example, disappearances are most useful during the initial years of a military dictatorship. After that, the dictatorship is more entrenched, and disappearances lose their usefulness. Aguilar and Kovras 2019.

13. Hernández-Hernández 2017.

14. Ansolabehere, Frey, and Payne 2017.

15. For a few examples, see Pradilla 2021; Animal Político Editorial 2021.

16. Hernández-Hernández 2022.

17. On the imagery of drug violence as a "machine," see Reguillo 2021.

18. Chamberlin 2019.

19. Zavaleta 2018.

20. Barragán 2023.

21. Beyond Mexico, a good illustration of the role of sentence reductions in helping to locate clandestine graves and exhume victims' bodies is the case of Colombia. In the demobilization of Colombian paramilitary groups at the turn of the twenty-first century, the Colombian Congress passed Law 975/2005. According to this law, demobilized ex-combatants facing trial who confessed and admitted their participation in crimes could "apply" and reduce their sentences. The so-called applicants (*postulados*) were required to

confess in "free versions" (*versiones libres*) their level of involvement within the paramilitary organization, whether they violated human rights or humanitarian law and any other information of public interest, particularly information leading to the discovery of clandestine graves. Those who cooperated fully had their sentences considerably reduced. For the crimes they committed, the sentence in the ordinary Colombian justice system ranged from twenty to sixty years in prison, but in the alternative system they were reduced to between five and eight years. This reduction depended on the severity of the crime and other factors such as the accuracy of the confession, nonrecidivism of the accused, and their willingness to provide reparations for the harm they caused the victims. The Colombian case stands in sharp contrast to the Chilean case. After the end of Augusto Pinochet's dictatorship, the first democratically elected government (led by Patricio Aylwin) proposed a law offering perpetrators incentives to reveal the location of clandestine graves in exchange for anonymity and confidentiality in their statements; the information collected would then be given to visiting ministers who served as investigative judges. The proposal failed, however, and faced opposition from across the political spectrum, including human rights groups. One was the Agrupación de Familiares de Detenidos Desaparecidos, a search group that succeeded in bringing international attention to the human rights violations of the Pinochet regime and mobilized transnational support networks. These stakeholders concluded that the proposal would perpetuate the impunity of the military regime (García-Godos and Lid 2010, 504–7; Kovras 2017, 216).

22. In the president's words: "It can't be that we don't know what happened when more than 100 people participated. . . . We are offering protection, amnesty, [and] compensation to whoever give us information, because this is a state issue" (Páramo 2020).

23. Hernández Herrera 2020.

24. One exception might be the case of Arbolillo in Veracruz, one of the states with the highest number of missing persons. The 238 people found so far in Arbolillo, only nineteen have been fully identified by 2020 (CNB 2020). A search in that municipality led to the discovery of human remains. The government in turn attributed the discovery to the testimony of a protected witness. Yet the prosecutor's file on the graves does not corroborate this, and Solecito, an organization that searches for missing persons, argues that this is a fabricated story (Ferri 2020). In this case, sources show that there has been no witness cooperation: "no member of the Arbolillo fishermen's cooperative claims to have witnessed anything or to have lent their boats for anything, even though there is suspicion that some bodies could only have been transported in boats" (Zavaleta 2018). Despite the very probable existence of witnesses, some of them likely accomplices, the authorities do not seem to have sought the cooperation of any of them.

25. The term *verdad histórica* is a legal term of art, used in Mexican law to designate the conclusion of an investigation. It gained media notoriety after it was used by federal prosecutor Jesús Murillo Karam and became synonymous with the fabricated version of the event that ended up in the massacre of the Ayotzinapa students.

26. This was not the only instance in which the official investigation by the Attorney General's Office was based on falsehoods or confessions obtained through physical or psychological torture.

27. Milenio 2021.

28. There is of course the concern that Juan's testimony is deliberately misleading. For one, in his version of the events, his own participation in the massacre was nil, which is doubtful. It is also possible that his testimony might have been driven in part by his attempt to implicate some local officials in the crime out of resentment for having identified him as a perpetrator.

29. The prosecutor for the Ayotzinapa case, Omar Gómez Trejo, acknowledged that the testimony of "people who had participated in the events" was one of the pieces of evidence that led them to the Barranca de la Carnicería. Centro de Producción CEPROPIE 2021.

30. Villafaña 2013.

31. Zavaleta 2018b, 311.

32. Zavaleta 2018b, 319.

33. Zerega 2024.

34. Kovras 2017, 173. See also 169–74, 242–44.

35. Proportionality can be understood either in a cardinal or in an ordinal sense. Cardinal proportionality proposes that the severity of the punishment should be adjusted to the gravity of the crime; there should be an absolute measure of punishment. Ordinal proportionality proposes a hierarchy of punishment, with the more serious crimes aligned with the more serious punishment, and the less serious crimes with the less serious punishment. Those who theorize on punishment are usually more concerned about proportionality to avoid the application of excessively harsh punishment than they are about proportionality to avoid application of mild punishment. Undoubtedly, the former presupposes a more significant normative limitation; both, however, are, in the end, normatively significant.

36. Murphy 2020.

37. For a more theoretical analyisis of the conflict between the proportionate punishment principle and the forensic principle, see Espíndola 2022.

38. Conversely, retributivist theory, in the tradition of Immanuel Kant (1999, 353–604) or Michael S. Moore (1997), maintains that punishing criminals has intrinsic value: transgressors of the law deserve punishment that is plain and simple for the crime committed. Hybrid theories, such as that of Tadros (2011) are instrumentalist yet recognize the expressive value of the punishment.

39. Vázquez 2023.

40. CNDH 2020, 122.

41. Tucker 2012.

42. Nussbaum 2000. The importance of shame-avoidance for self-respect is already fully articulated in Kant (1999, 6–336).

43. For Rawls (1999, 386–91), self-respect has two aspects. "It includes a person's sense of his own value, his secure conviction that his conception of the good, his plan of life, is worth carrying out. And second, self-respect implies a confidence in one's ability, so far as it is within one's power, to fulfill one's intentions" (386).

44. Feinberg1970; Hampton 2007.

45. Darwall 2010.

46. Payne and Ansolabehere 2021, 17–36.

47. Arendt 1976.

48. Lomnitz 2020.

49. Olmos et al. 2018.

50. Ornelas 2018.

51. Blustein 2014, 258. See also 187–89, 254–60.

52. For a conception of self-respect as the ability to appreciate one's worth and as living without falling below a standard of conduct that one has imposed on oneself, see Dillon 1995; Moody-Adams 1995, 64–66; Hill 1995, 76–92; Boxill 1995, 93–106.

53. Middleton 2006.

54. Honneth 1995.

55. Boss 1999.

56. Hollander 2016, 300.

57. Garrido 2019, 146.

58. Turati 2012, 113. See also Human Rights Watch 2013, 46.

59. By way of an example beyond Mexico, consider the experience of the relative of a person missing at the hands of the Irish Republican Army during "The Troubles" in Northern Ireland: "One of the feelings I also had was embarrassment and maybe that's why I have never spoken about it to friends or wanted to speak about it, or to teachers. . . . You know I felt embarrassed about it a bit because I didn't know the whole story. And I thought . . . he must have done something . . . and you know it was embarrassing which is terrible because it doesn't matter what he did, he didn't deserve his life to be taken." This testimony is illuminating, given the experience of shame and humiliation resulting from the disappearances described by Peake and Lynch (2016, 466). Other testimonies are along the same lines: "At the time people avoided me and all I did was cry, I went round the streets . . . no one knew nothing and that's the way you were left not even knowing. We were shunned everywhere we went. . . . It was basically a waiting game for 21 years" (460). And another one: "So the neighbours didn't openly offer any sympathy, you know they just kind of shrugged their shoulders and nodded their heads as if to say well 'maybe he got you know what he deserved' because they didn't know what he was accused of doing and neither did we" (468).

60. Middleton 2006.

61. Nozick 1981.

62. Boelen and Prigerson 2012; Hollander 2016.

63. Beyond Mexico, these attitudes are illustrated in the case of a mother in Sri Lanka who, after nine years of searching for her daughter, missing in the aftermath of that country's civil war, has lost all hope and no longer believes it worthwhile to demand anything from the government. Regarding a protest in her town, and wearing prayer ropes on her wrists, the mother says: "I didn't go . . . the doctor said you are just getting mentally more upset. They [authorities] are not giving any answers" (Mashal 2018).

64. Antillón Najlis 2018, 481.

65. Antillón Najlis 2018, 295.

66. The case of Colombia is similar. The representative of the families of victims of a massacre executed by the FARC guerrilla group in Colombia expressed this idea in the wake of the recovery of the bodies of the victims, more than ten years after the massacre. For the victims, their representative said, the return by the authorities of the bodies represents "the certainty that their remains are buried, the possibility of lighting a candle for them, leaving flowers, and talking with them." This representative goes on to add, "songs and prayers so that the souls of our family members may find eternal rest and finally gain some peace because they are no longer in purgatory" (Manetto 2019).

67. Christopher 2003.

68. Uprimny and Güiza 2023.

69. Nino 1996; Aukerman 2002.

70. Uprinmy and Güiza 2023, 280.

71. Escalante 1992; Espíndola Mata 2004; Salmón 2026.

72. Miller 2017.

73. Natapoff 2009.

74. Lippke's (2011, 146–66) position is not entirely inimical to plea bargaining. It is an indictment of certain forms of it, and an endorsement of other kinds. It is very likely that a carefully crafted plea bargain, such as the one considered here, would not meet his objection.

Chapter 2

1. An earlier version of this chapter appeared as Espíndola 2023.

2. Walzer 1973; Shue 1978.

3. Waldron 2003.

4. Kleinig 2009.

5. Harfield 2012; Dunnighan and Norris 1998.

6. Natapoff 2009, 42–43, 131–34; Lippke 2011, 154.

7. Plea bargaining is a legal practice whereby authorities, typically prosecutors, seek to induce wrongdoers to confess a crime and cooperate with them, or to plead guilty without a trail or with an abridged version of one, in exchange for reduced punishment. Plea bargaining is a rather heterogeneous legal practice that varies according to the kind of reward offered, the moment at which it takes place within the criminal process (before a trial, during one), the types of crimes that may warrant it, its formality or lack thereof, and so on. It is also a practice that has attracted numerous criticisms, particularly in the criminal justice system of the United States, where it is frequently used, on account of its excessive use and its failure to be constrained through accountability controls.

8. Natapoff 2009; Lippke 2011.

9. Bellaby 2012.

10. Quinlan 2007b.

11. Macnish 2015.

12. By analogy, some scholars have developed principles to constrain the motives and the ways to conduct surveillance: *jus ad speculandum* and *jus in speculando*. In the remainder of the text, I subsume surveillance into intelligence.

13. Omand and Phythian, 2013.

14. Diderichsen and Rønn 2017.

15. *Jus ad intelligentiam* principles are just cause, right intention, a legitimate authority, and proportionality and necessity at this level. For a complete list see Bellaby (2012, 109) and Lazar (2016).

16. The following paragraphs draw heavily on Macnish (2015).

17. Bellaby 2012, 114; Hurka 2005, 38; Macnish 2015, 532; Uniacke 2011, 225.

18. Omand and Phythian 2013.

19. Lazar, 2012, 6–7.

20. Miller 2021.

21. Macnish 2015, 539.

22. Méndez 2009, 3.

23. Méndez 2013. More generally, see Lopez Benítez 2009.

24. Ahmed and Villegas 2019. The article describes a clandestine, makeshift system that uses sentence reductions and protected witnesses. It was devised by Alberto Capella, Morelos's police chief. It was used in the release of a young hitman in exchange for his testimony about the Guerreros Unidos and the alleged crimes of his fellow gang members. By October 2018, the program already had twelve protected witnesses being held alongside the local jail.

25. Article 35 of this law establishes that members of organized crime groups who provide "effective assistance" to investigate and prosecute other members, especially those "with administrative, managerial and supervisory functions," may receive a variety of criminal benefits, depending on the procedural stage in which they collaborate (whether or not there is already a preliminary investigation, if they collaborate during the criminal process, or if they have already been sentenced). The benefits may range from refraining from considering evidence related to their collaboration to eliminating two-thirds of their sentences.

26. This law was the first in a series of legal and constitutional amendments that created a separate legal order for the investigation, prosecution, and punishment of criminal offenses perpetrated by organized crime. This regime was commonly credited with undermining the rights of the accused, especially of violating due process through practices such as pretrail detention (*prisión preventiva*); imposing harsher criminal sanctions; and giving law enforcement agencies greater discretion. Many critics understood the use of witness collaborators in this light, claiming, for example, that it eroded the right of the accused to know the identity of his accusers, which could in turn affect her ability to prepare her defense, or that it was unconstitutional, insofar as secret and anonymous denunciations of crime are prohibited by the Mexican Constitution (López Benítez 2009). Thus, it must be kept in mind that in Mexico the history of *testigos colaboradores* is intertwined with the emergence of a regime of exception for combating organized crime.

27. Santos Villarreal 2010, 8.

28. Darcy 2019, 174.

29. Darcy 2019, 189.

30. Something similar happened with Operación Limpieza (started in 2008). Its objective was to purge the army of suspected ties to the Beltrán Leyva cartel. There were several witnesses whose testimonies were somewhat lacking in clarity, to say the least. See Ravelo 2009.

31. Fondevila 2013, 117–18.

32. Interview Former Member of Prosecutor's Office 2021.

33. Interview with Federal Judge 2021a.

34. Interview with Federal Judge 2021b.

35. The prosecutor for the Ayotzinapa case recently acknowledged that the testimony of "people who had participated in the events" had been crucial in redirecting the investigation. Centro de Producción CEPROPIE, 2021.

36. Espino 2019.

37. Garcia and Castillo 2019.

38. Garcia and Castillo 2019.

39. Rainsford 2019.

40. Admittedly, sometimes collaborators are unwilling to accept the protection they are offered. A former member of the prosecution's office explained to me that some collaborators would manage to leave unnoticed the security location they had been assigned to, particularly at night. Sometimes they would not return. It is unclear how extended this practice was. Interview Former Member of Prosecutor's Office 2021.

41. Green 2011.

42. As mentioned before, similar dynamics occur at the local level, and there is some evidence of an informal system of plea bargaining and witness protection in the state of Morelos, organized by the Local Commissioner of Public Security. The program began in 2017–18 with an agreement with a young *sicario* (hitman)—he would not be prosecuted in exchange for his testimony against the crimes of members of Guerreros Unidos, a local criminal organization. In October 2018, the program already had twelve such collaborators. A news report describes their conditions in the following way: "With no other place to put them, the authorities housed the young men right next door to the jail that held the cartel members they were testifying against. Every few weeks, the police ferried them to court to provide evidence in cases. The witnesses slept on thin mattresses on the floor, ate at a cracked plastic table and sat in chairs shorn of their backs. Large blue tubs overflowed with water used for bathing and flushing. There were small comforts—a television, a microwave and an electric keyboard on which the *sicario* taught himself to play the theme song to the movie *Titanic*. And every weekday, the makeshift wing of the prison turned into an evangelical revival. The Commissioner's precarious system collapsed when he was removed from the state and assigned to a different one. All collaborators escaped out of fear of being imprisoned" (Ahmed and Villegas 2019).

43. Incidentally, he had also been an informant for the DEA; it is not uncommon for informants to obey two masters, as it were.

44. Proceso 2011.

45. Lippke 2011, 154.

46. Lippke 2011, 154.

47. Teague 2019, 803.

48. I draw on OSJI (2016, 29), Aguayo et al. (2020, 91–103), and the articles of Ginger Thompson (2017a, 2017b, 2017c) to reconstruct the events.

49. Correa-Cabrera 2017.

50. Pérez Ricart 2020.

51. Natapoff 2009, 49.

52. Thompson 2017b.

53. Castillo García 2013.

54. Office of the Attorney General 2002.

55. On the distinction between selective and indiscriminate violence, see Kalyvas (2004, 111; 2018). Indiscriminate violence is not a good strategy to solidify territorial control in the long run. The Zetas, nonetheless, engaged in it.

56. Kalyvas 2006.

57. Dudai 2018.

58. Smulders et al. 2017.

59. Smulders et al. 2017.

60. Foot 1967.

Chapter 3

1. I endorse Tommie Shelby's (2022) response to abolitionist critics in the United States, particularly those coming from Black Critical Theory. Shelby argues that abolitionist criticism of punishment is really directed at the background conditions in which punishment takes place, at the institutions that administer it, and at the failure of society to allow prisoners to rejoin society, not at punishment itself. According to Shelby, incarceration has legitimate and socially necessary uses, such as incapacitating offenders who pose a threat to the rights of others. It is not inherently unjust because, depending on the circumstances, it can be worth its undeniable risks.

2. Melchor 2022.

3. Rehabilitation is the other goal of punishment. I do not discuss it here because there is near universal agreement that prisons do not rehabilitate.

4. Hart 1968.

5. These theories mirror actual justifications instantiated in penal systems, past and present, and they have had their heyday and demise. Retributivism, for example, was the prevailing justification of punishment in eighteenth-century Europe, positing "a retributivism of symbolic equivalence" according to which it was relatively uncontroversial that harsh penalties, usually performed in public, like maiming, branding, or whipping were equivalent to criminal offenses. Consequentialist theories then fell into disrepute to witness the revival of retributivism under the guise of the just desert movement, which promised to deliver less arbitrary sentences. We will not enter these historical details either. See Lacey and Pickard 2015.

6. Flanders 2021, 168.

7. His works *Los Muros de Agua* (1941) and *El Apando* (1969) describe his experiences, respectively, in the Islas Maria, a penal colony, and later in Palacio de Lecumberri, a federal prison.

8. In 1967, during the presidency of American playwright Arthur Miller, PEN made an appeal to Nigeria concerning playwright Wole Soyinka, who was facing execution.

9. Revueltas 2016, 229. The translation is mine.

10. Revueltas 2016, 242–43. The translation is mine.

11. The following summary comes from the foremost authority on the penitentiary system in Mexico. See Azaola 2021, 2022.

12. The Mexican penitentiary system is varied: state prisons—which themselves are internally varied—coexist with federal prisons, detainment centers for minors, and military prisons.

13. Bentham 1838–43.

14. Birkbeck 2011.

15. Macaulay 2019, 243. The concept also entails the illegality in the state's practice of detention. See also Lessing and Willis 2019.

16. Macaulay 2019, 246–47.

17. Macaulay 2019, 246–47. Bergman and Fondevila (2021) call this the fallacy of separation, which carries consequences beyond the inability to incapacitate or deter.

18. Lessing and Willis 2019. To some degree this trend is extant outside of Latin America. Carceral mafias or *prison gangs* in California. The *Mexican Mafia* governed most gangs (outside of prison) in southern California. See Skarbek 2011.

19. Bergman and Fondevila 2021.

20. Chaparro Hernández and Pérez Correa 2017, 16–20; Bergman and Fondevila 2021.

21. According to a survey of recently admitted offenders, in Mexico: 73.1% theft or robbery; 7.7% homicide; 4.6% drug related; 5.0% sexual crimes; 9.6% others (including kidnapping or extortion). See Bergman and Fondevila 2021, 45.

22. An important point discussed by Bergman and Fondevila is that there is a high turnover rate in Latin American prisons, including Mexico. For every given year, the number of people who have passed through prisons is larger than the of stock of prisoners. This high turnover has contributed to high criminality.

23. Intersecta and Animal Político 2025.

24. Infobae 2020b; Observatorio de Prisiones 2023.

25. Moore 2012.

26. Aguayo and Dayán 2018.

27. Hobbes 1994, 76.

28. It might be retorted against Hobbes (1994, 203) that people who wrong others do indeed forfeit that right, or that some form of punishment, like imprisonment, is not tantamount to violence. Containment need not be violent. Curtailment of rights, if according to the rule of law, need not be violent either.

29. Brettschneider 2020.

30. Birkbeck 2011, 319.

31. Birkbeck 2011, 315.

32. Birkbeck 2011, 316.

33. Before drafting *Democracy in America*, Alexis de Tocqueville co-wrote a report on the US penitentiary system with his colleague Gustave Beaumont. Tocqueville and Beaumont disagreed about many aspects of the US penitentiary system, but they agreed on the following: whatever its ills, the despotic cell system established common equality. See Avramenko and Gingerich 2014, 71.

34. Lovett 2010, 111.

35. At the Topo Chico detention center, the inmates who exercise self-government are controlled by criminal groups held in the men's area. CNDH 2015, 15–17.

36. Azaola and Hubert 2016, 93.

37. CNDH 2022.

38. Vrousalis 2013, 123.

39. Observatorio de Prisiones 2023.

40. Mexico City Penitentiary Centers Law 2021.

41. Gutierrez 2016, 32–33.

42. Gutierrez 2016, 27.

43. El Universal 2022.

44. Davis 2003, chap. 5.

45. CNDH 2015.

46. While here I focus as an illustration on sex workers who are women, a good number are not. This is true inside and outside of prison.

47. Gutierrez 2016.

48. Martínez Ahrens 2016.

49. Azaola and Hubert 2016, 92.

50. Azaola 2021, 27–28. The translation is mine.

51. Milenio Digital 2018.

52. Aguayo and Dayán 2018.

53. Aguayo and Dayán 2018, 14.

54. CNDH 2024.

55. CNDH 2024.

56. Guillen 2024; Leyva 2023.

57. Favril et al. 2020, 689, 689.

58. Part of a lucrative deal with the government for eight federal prisons to be administered privately. The deal was promoted by Genaro García Luna, today in a US prison, under Felipe Calderón's (2006–12) government.

59. Maza 2023.

60. Some of the same problems persist in privately run federal prisons, in which the custodians are public officials. México Evalúa 2016.

61. Lippke 1998.

62. I use the terms *communicative* and *expressivist* interchangeably, although some authors distinguish between the two.

63. Scanlon 1998, 274.

64. México Evalúa 2013, 10.

65. Feinberg 1970; Hampton 2007; Duff 2001.

66. Although Duff does not associate his theory with retributivism.

67. Duff 2001, 28.

68. Hampton 2007.

69. Expressivism is not without its critics. An objection is that it is not obvious why punishment more effectively communicates the public condemnation of wrongdoers and the affirmation of their moral status than alternative methods. Zachary Hoskins and Duff (2024), himself an advocate of a communicative theory of punishment, raises this issue: "Censure can . . . be communicated by 'hard treatment' punishments . . .—by imprisonment, by compulsory community service, by fines and the like, which are burdensome independently of their censorial meaning . . . but why should we choose such methods of communication, rather than methods that do not involve hard treatment?" Some authors argue that hard treatment in fact interferes with the communicative enterprise.

70. Duff 2001.

71. Duff 2021.

72. Hampton 1992, 1659.

73. Forst 2007.

74. INEGI 2021b.

75. Magaloni and Razu 2018.

76. INEGI 2021a.

77. Ironically, the military, along with the navy, remain trustworthy despite their well-documented involvement in abuse. INEGI 2024c.

78. Betts and Gruen 2021.

79. Garland 2001, 1.

80. INEGI 2024b, 33.

81. INEGI 2024b.

82. Walen 2020; Husak 2000; Cahill 2011.

83. Donelson 2022, 65.

84. Flanders 2021, 170.

85. Flanders 2021, 170.

86. México Evalúa 2012, 10.

Chapter 4

1. Hobbes 1994, 230.

2. Here I follow Benjamin Ewing's (2018) analysis of criminogenic disadvantage for the purposes of meting out punishment.

3. Guerrero Guitierrez 2022.

4. Osorio 2011; Vilalta 2013.

5. Guercke 2021.

6. Silva Forné et al. 2017.

7. While factors like posttraumatic stress disorder or compassion fatigue might be

considered in a separate inquiry, they do not absolve the moral gravity of such acts. Cases of military wrongdoing demand their own rigorous moral examination.

8. Nino 1996.

9. For a discussion of these issues, see Elster 2004c.

10. Austin 1956–57.

11. A classic rendition on the subject: Fletcher 1978.

12. "The coerced actor differs dramatically from other excused actors. He is a moral agent, capable of understanding his choices and acting on those choices. Unlike an insane or mistaken actor, he has the capacity not to break the law but, under the circumstances, he finds it preferable to break it. His disabilities, compared to other excused actors, are, at best, partial. Considering all that, it seems fair to blame the actor who saves his skin by throwing others to the wolves. . . . This is inconsistent with the theory of excuses—at least complete excuses. A complete excuse eliminates the defendant's responsibility for the wrongful act and, accordingly, eradicates his blameworthiness. . . . The blameworthiness of the coerced actor sets him apart from all excused actors and, conversely, reveals his family resemblance with justified actors, which suggests that duress is only a partial excuse and that it has a strong justificatory component" (Bergelson 2018).

13. Delgado 1985.

14. Delgado 1985, 64.

15. The rotten social background defense is open to several objections. One is that not all citizens who live in a socially rotten environment commit crimes, and that this excuse undermines the courage of those who choose to abide by the law and even provides an incentive to commit crimes. Another is that this defense erases the distinction between the offender's character and his or her circumstances. A third objection is that this defense can serve to release criminals who endanger society. These objections are relevant, however, only if the rotten-social-background condition is taken to excuse every single person who lives under such conditions, rather than excusing only those who can show that a specific deprivation, say, their emotional trauma, was a factor in committing a specific crime, and where a causal connection can be firmly established. These objections are also relevant where the rotten-social-background defense is fully exculpatory, rather than only partially. Delgado 1985, 64, 66–67.

16. Bergelson 2018.

17. Berman and Farrell 2011, 1027.

18. Kelly (2018, 3–4) reaches the conclusion that, as a consequence of this, "We should abandon efforts to justify state-imposed punishment as morally deserved" (46). Even if one does not endorse the idea that, in view of the power of exculpating conditions, we ought to refrain from justifying criminal sanctions on the basis of moral desert, we should at least recognize that excuses must bear more significantly on the mitigation of responsibility, and therefore on the severity of the punishment.

19. Morris 1968, 478.

20. Lippke 2003, 465–66; Wallace 1994; Watson 2004.

21. Lippke 2003, 466.

22. This is the background of classical theories about crime, such as those of Émile Durkheim and Robert K. Merton, which, broadly speaking, establish a relationship between criminal conduct and the collapse of communal bonds.

23. Mendoza Rockwell 2012.

24. García and González 2009.

25. Returning transnational migrants were the primary consumers in the past. García and Gonzalez found that drug users expanded to include nonmigrants, mainly adolescents and people in their twenties and thirties.

26. García and González 2009.

27. García and González 2009.

28. Borges (2013) on the Michoacán case; Mendoza Rockwell (2012) on the Sonora case.

29. Chomczyński et al. 2023, 362. See also Chomczyński and Guy 2021; Chomczyński et al. 2019.

30. Chomczyński et al. 2023, 363.

31. Chomczyński et al. 2023.

32. Chomczyński et al. 2023, 364.

33. OMSMCSP 2021.

34. From 1999 to 2019, there are 8,803 drug-related deaths in official records. This is a modest number, but the national general drug-related mortality rate rose from 0.35 to 0.47 per 100,000 inhabitants between 2015 and 2019, an annual increase of 10.04%. Ospina-Escobar and Dávila Cervantes 2024.

35. Lomnitz 2022, 80–81, 102–3.

36. Morse 2000, 46.

37. Morse 2000, 44.

38. Morse 2000, 45.

39. Morse 2000, 42.

40. Garcia and Anderson 2016; Garcia 2015, 463.

41. García 2015; García and Anderson 2016.

42. Lozano-Verduzco 2016, 242.

43. Lozano-Verduzco 2016, 244.

44. To cite another case, in the *anexo* "Mazatlán Una Oportunidad de Vida A.C" in Sinaloa, a score of anexados was recruited by one organization to battle a rival organization in a different state and city for a weekly salary of $2,000 pesos (Infobae 2020b).

45. Lomnitz 2019, 116–17.

46. SSP 2010; Castillo 2013.

47. Valdés Castellanos 2013, 402.

48. According to some sociological theories, gangs arise primarily because many young people experience a mismatch between their aspirations and their actual socioeconomic success. This provides an incentive to forgo socially accepted methods of achieving such aspirations and to instead resort to crime. Secondly, these young people understand their socioeconomic failure as being the result of unjust social structures. In

their view, this situation "cancels out their obligations to the established order," taking away their feelings of guilt for violating that order. Cloward and Ohlin 1960.

49. Grillo 2014.

50. Buchanan 2002.

51. Pauer-Studer and Velleman 2011.

52. Su 2011.

53. Su 2011, 189.

54. Sánchez Godoy 2009; Córdova 2011; Madrazo 2013.

55. Maldonado 2012, 14.

56. Sánchez Godoy 2009, 85.

57. Astorga 1997, 247; 2000.

58. Córdova 2011, 90, 127–42.

59. Valdés Castellanos 2013, 268–74.

60. Lomnitz 2019, 100.

61. Moffett 2016.

62. Card 2002, 225.

63. Gallegos 2017.

64. Aristegui Noticias 2021.

65. With only some exaggeration, this study draws a parallel between this and Hamas's use of social media to idealize martyrs: Womer and Bunker 2010.

66. Salazar 2022.

67. Wood 2017.

68. See, along these lines, Alfano et al. 2018 and Nguyen 2020.

69. León Olvera 2023.

70. León Olvera 2023.

71. Ake-Kob 2020.

72. ICG 2023.

73. ICG 2023, 5–11.

74. Giacomello 2013; 2014; 2020.

75. Giacomello 2013, 121; 2020.

76. Giacomello 2020.

77. Giacomello 2020.

78. The word *cabrón* or *cabrona* suggests ruthlessness, strength, even the willingness to use violence. ICG 2023, 4.

79. Campbell 2008.

80. In Mexico, investigations about children involved in drug trafficking are scarce, and most of the available sources on the subject are journalistic. Martínez 2012; Cisneros 2014.

81. Between 2019 and 2022, arrests of children, adolescents, and young people up to eighteen years old for homicide, injuries, and crimes against health increased by 16%, rising from 8,854 under Peña Nieto to 10,295, according to twenty-seven prosecutors' offices. Similarly, arrests for carrying weapons and explosives reserved for military use

saw significant increases. In 2019, 3,420 young people from minors to twenty-nine years old were arrested, 159% more than in 2015. During López Obrador's first three years, 4,450 minors were investigated for crimes against health and injuries, 61% more than in Peña Nieto's last three years. Between 2019 and 2021, 1,584 minors were convicted of drug dealing, a 200% increase compared to 2016–18. Youths aged eighteen to twenty-nine imprisoned for homicide, intentional injuries, extortion, and crimes against health increased by 63%, from 7,400 to 12,047, compared to the last three years of Peña Nieto's administration (Animal Político 2025).

82. Approximately 250,000 minors concentrated in several Mexican regions are believed to be at risk of recruitment by armed groups (Reinserta.org, 2024). See also ONC 2024.

83. ICG 2023.

84. Steinberg 2007.

85. Ryberg 2014.

86. Dawes 2013, 50–57.

87. Valdés Castellanos 2013, 268–74. In his classic work on the Reserve Battalion 83, the infamous police corps of ordinary civilians recruited in Germany to, unbeknownst to them at the time, conduct massive killing in Poland, Christopher Browning (1998, 159) discusses other variables that turned ordinary people into *génocidaires*: "wartime brutalization, racism, segmentation and routinization of the task, special selection of the perpetrators, careerism, obedience to orders, deference to authority, ideological indoctrination, and conformity."

88. García-Reyes 2020.

89. Campbell 2009, 2.

90. Claudio Lomnitz (2023, 75–98) shows that this practice has a genealogy of meanings and functions that takes place within the context of what he calls the aporia of organized crime: criminal organizations seek to radically separate themselves from society by transgressing its norms (moral ones) to control it and be recognized by it.

91. Lomnitz 2023, 84.

92. Lomnitz 2023, 84.

93. Tadros 2009; 2011.

94. I borrow the formulation, with the United States in mind, from Erin Kelly (2018, 175).

95. Lenta 2019b, 391.

96. Hobbes 1994, 203.

97. Hobbes 1994, 144.

98. This list of epistemic vices comes from Meyer et al. 2021.

99. Caruso 2021, 137, 141.

100. González Ocantos 2023, 168.

Chpater 5

1. Some observers are skeptical that amnesties can be convincingly based on mercy. See Lenta 2019a.

2. An amnesty, as is well known, is a form of legal oblivion that extinguishes criminal liability. The etymological root of the word amnesty is "oblivion." Through an amnesty, the state "forgets" the offender's crime and refrains from prosecuting or punishing them. Civil liability may still be a possibility, but criminal liability is foreclosed for good.

3. I use the terms interchangeably, although a more refined conceptual discussion will make distinctions between them.

4. For Aristotle, mercy complements "strict legal justice," which cannot attend to the peculiarities of each case; mercy is a plea for doing so, and for a more precise classification of offenses, so that such peculiarities are taken into account when imposing the appropriate punishment. Thus, for Aristotle, mercy is merely a supplement to justice. Subsequent authors have painted a picture in which justice and mercy have a more strained relationship.

5. Nussbaum 1999; Tasioulas 2003; Murphy and Hampton 1998.

6. Tasioulas 2003.

7. Most believe that in one way or another mercy is a departure from justice. Because of mercy, perpetrators receive a more lenient punishment than they deserve. Paraphrasing Jeffrie Murphy (Murphy and Hampton 1998), tempering justice tampers with it. Mercy's injustice goes deeper than decreasing just punishment, however. Some would argue that if a judge felt compassion for a criminal, and therefore declared a lighter sentence than was the criminal's due, s/he would be acting objectionably because as an institutional agent of the state s/he has a duty to impose just punishment. S/he must not allow his/her personal feelings to intrude on the obligations of criminal law. As an agent of the state, s/he has an antecedent obligation to obey the rules of justice. Tasioulas 2003, 102.

8. Tasioulas 2003, 119.

9. Tasioulas 2003, 120–21.

10. Tasioulas 2003, 109.

11. Sánchez Cordero 2018.

12. On the prospects and limitations of transitional justice as applied to the war on drugs, see Espíndola and Serrano 2023.

13. Sánchez Cordero 2018.

14. By the same token, discrimination that arises from belonging to a certain group might also be offset, partially or fully, by the advantages those same persons gain by belonging to other groups. Crenshaw 1989, 141.

15. DOF 2019.

16. DOF 2020.

17. Villavicencio Ayala 2019.

18. For a careful analysis of the 2020 amnesty in its first year, see Observatorio de Amnistías 2021 and Gómez Mena 2021.

19. Gómez Mena 2021; Observatorio de Amnistías 2021.

20. SEGOB 2023. See also Guillen 2024a.

21. Equis Justicia Para las Mujeres 2022.

22. Unsurprisingly, no amnesty was extended in relation to abortion. The "offense"

of abortion fell within the purview of local jurisdictions, while the amnesty targeted federal crimes. Thus, according to one estimate, in 2018, under a fifth (2,024) of all women in prison awaiting a sentence or with one condemning them (10,047) had committed a federal crime (Fernández Villagómez 2020). The criminalization of abortion was found to be unconstitutional by the nation's Supreme Court in September 2021.

23. The federal government issued a decree to offer "preliberation" to prisoners who remained in prison without a sentence; who had been tortured; or who are over seventy years old (DOF 2021). Similarly, in view of the COVID pandemic, federal and state governments promoted the anticipated liberation of a few thousand convicts in order to "depressurize" the penitentiary system, characterized as it is by problems of overcrowding and lack of hygiene, although critics complain this was a belated and insufficient response to the pandemic. CDHMAPJ 2021; MUCD 2021.

24. Offenses that warrant this kind of mandatory pretrial detention had been excluded from the amnesty, to begin with.

25. INEGI 2024c.

26. Intersecta and Animal Político 2025.

27. INEGI 2024b.

28. Escalante 2009.

29. More cynically, a ruling elite can self-amnesty as a condition for leaving power. Self-amnesties are not the subject here.

30. Such justifications go as far back as the Athenian amnesty of 403 BC, during which time leaders advised their own to "pull their punches" for the sake of peace. Elster 2004a.

31. Schmitt 1995. The first version of the text appeared in 1949. The text was published several times in different places with minor revisions and with different titles ("Amnestie—Urform des Rechts," "Amnestie ist die Kraft des Vergessens," "Das Ende des kalten Bürgerkrieges—Im Zirkel der tödlichen Rechthaberei").

32. Schmitt's argument for amnesties in the specific postwar scenario is objectionable among other reasons because it turns a blind eye to the atrocities the Nazi regime committed against civilians, particularly Jews. Schmitt railed above all against what he perceived to be victor's justice. On Schmitt's views on amnesty see Espíndola 2014.

33. Schmitt 2005.

34. Meyer 1985.

35. Subsequent amnesties followed a similar course. To name just one, three years after Cárdenas's amnesty, Manuel Ávila Camacho decreed another amnesty with the Cedillista Rebellion in mind. This rebellion was quickly halted, the amnesty being one resource among many to deactivate the *levantados*. From the beginning, Ávila Camacho offered a total amnesty, announcing that he would help the families of the rebels and "the individuals who, ignoring the truth" had taken up arms, and promised them "all the facilities and guarantees necessary to return to their honest and simple lives as humble farm laborers." In addition, concrete benefits were given to those who surrendered. See Falcón 1984, 266, and Gonzales Navarro 2003.

36. CDCEUM 1936.

37. Aviña 2016, 144.

38. The military was the main perpetrator of violence. It was vested with the de facto authority to decide which detainees would be presented to civil authorities, which ones would be illegally detained, and which ones would be executed. On the rural front, the military deployed novel counterinsurgency strategies borrowed from guerrilla combat methods in Vietnam, with names such as Operation Telaraña (Spiderweb) or Amistad (Friendship). These operations sought to sever the ties between *guerrilleros* and the communities that supported them. Entire villages suspected of sympathizing with insurgent organizations were forcibly displaced, lumped together, and put under military encirclement for better control. Repressive strategies also included the creation of paramilitary groups, such as the Brigadas Blancas (White Brigades), and death flights, similar to those that were carried out in South America. Overseeing, and sometimes conducting, repression was the infamous Dirección Federal de Seguridad, the regime's secret police. Sierra 2006, 361–404; Gamiño Muñoz 2017, 201; Sánchez Serrano 2012, 137–78, 152; Oikión Solano 2007, 76; FEMOSPP 2006; Castellanos 2016, 266.

39. The ruling clique recognized the convenience of supporting mild forms of political liberalization (but not quite full democratization) by authorizing political representation outside of the PRI (especially for the Communist [left-wing] and Sinarquista [right-wing] opposition), turning to proportional representation to increase the presence of opposition parties in Congress, and so on, in what came to be known as the Political Reform. Both internal pressure—the most representative example of this was via the social movement called the Committee for the Defense of Persecuted, Disappeared, and Political Exiles of Mexico—and international pressure from organizations such as Amnesty International held the government accountable for the human rights violations perpetrated during the 1970s. This last point was extensively covered by the magazine *Proceso*. See, for instance, Proceso 1978a, 22.

40. Viale 1978, 20.

41. Reyes Heroles 1979.

42. López 1982.

43. On this, see the available files of the Dirección Federal de Seguridad. AGN. DFS 11–196. L 8.

44. Enríquez Perea 2015.

45. Reyes Heroles 1979.

46. CDCEUM 1978.

47. CDCEUM 1978.

48. Castellanos 2016, 269.

49. Ramírez 2001a.

50. Rivera 1978.

51. Proceso 1978b, 27. This was true at the local level as well. "The impressive control of the prisons and the possible amnestied persons remained under the command of those who had committed excess violence in Guerrero . . .—that is to say—everything remained under the control of the perpetrators of the dirty war, who were now also the ones granting the pardons" (Sánchez Serrano 2012, 172). Rubén Figueroa understood the

amnesty in the following way: "It is a simple arrangement to try to eliminate an annoy-ing situation; that is, to try to forget . . . the Amnesty Law is to forget the past" (Ramirez 1978). Hernández 1978; see also Reveles 1978.

52. Hernández 1978.

53. Hirales 2004.

Conclusion

1. Barragán 2023.

References

Ackerly, Brooke, Luis Cabrera, Fonna Forman, Genevieve Fuji Johnson, Chris Tenove, and Antje Wiener. 2024. "Unearthing Grounded Normative Theory: Practices and Commitments of Empirical Research in Political Theory," *Critical Review of International Social and Political Philosophy* 27 (2): 156–82.

AGN, *Dirección Federal de Seguridad*, Serie 11–196, Legajo 8,.

Aguayo Quezada, Sergio, Delia Sánchez del Ángel, Manuel Pérez Aguirre, and Jacobo Dayán Askenazi. 2016. *En el Desamparo: Los Zetas, el Estado, la Sociedad y las víctimas de San Fernando, Tamaulipas (2010) y Allende, Coahuila (2011)*. El Colegio de México.

Aguayo Quezada, Sergio, Raúl Benítez Manaut, Juan Antonio Le Clercq, Gerardo Rodríguez Sánchez Lara, and Keyla Vargas. 2021. *Atlas de la seguridad y la defensa de México, 2020*. Instituto Belisario Domínguez del Senado de la República.

Aguayo, Sergio, and Jacobo Dayán. 2018. *El yugo zeta: Norte de Coahuila, 2010–2011*. El Colegio de México.

Aguayo, Sergio, Jacobo Dayán, and JG Ramos. 2020. *"Reconquistando" La Laguna: Los Zetas, el Estado y la sociedad organizada, 2007–2014*. El Colegio de México.

Aguilar, Paloma, and Iosif Kovras. 2019. "Explaining Disappearances as a Tool of Political Terror." *International Political Science Review* 40 (3): 437–52.

Ahmed, Azam, and Paulina Villegas. 2019. "He Was One of Mexico's Deadliest Assassins. Then He Turned on His Cartel." *New York Times*, December 14. www.nytimes.com/2019/12/14/world/americas/sicario-mexico-drug-cartels.html.

Ake-Kob, Alin. 2020, "Goffman and the Mafia: Shaping YouTube's Technological Affordances in the War on Drugs." *Tapuya: Latin American Science, Technology and Society* 3 (1): 493–511.

Alfano, Mark, Joseph Adam Carter, and Marc Cheong. 2018. "Technological Seduction and Self-Radicalization." *Journal of the American Philosophical Association* 4 (3): 298–322.

Animal Político. 2025. "México destruyendo el futuro." Updated February. https://panel.animalpolitico.com/mexico-destruyendo-el-futuro/.

Animal Politíco Editorial. 2021. "Guardia Nacional irrumpe en casa de buscadora de Guanajuato y golpea a menores, denuncia colectivo." *Animal Político*, September 3. www.animalpolitico.com/2021/09/guardia-nacional-buscadora-guanajuato/.

Ansolabehere, Karina, Barbara Frey, and Leigh Payne. 2017. *Observatorio sobre desaparición e impunidad: Informe sobre desapariciones en el estado de Nuevo León con información de CADHAC*. Observatorio sobre Desaparición e Impunidad. FLACSO.

Antillón Najlis, Ximena, ed. 2018. *Yo sólo quería que amaneciera: Impactos psicosociales del Caso Ayotzinapa*. Fundar.

Arendt, Hannah. 1976. *The Origins of Totalitarianism*. Harvest.

Aristegui Noticias. 2021. "Exhiben el modus operandi de los narcos para reclutar a menores a través de videojuegos." *Aristegui Noticias*, October 20. https://aristeguinoticias.com/2010/mexico/exhiben-el-modus-operandi-de-los-narcos-para-reclutar-a-menores-a-traves-de-videojuegos/.

Astorga, Luis. 1995. *Mitología del "narcotraficante."* Plaza y Valdes.

Astorga, Luis. 1997. "Los corridos de traficantes de drogas en México y Colombia." *Revista Mexicana de Sociología* 59 (4): 245–61.

Astorga, Luis. 2000. "La cocaína en el corrido." *Revista Mexicana de Sociología* 62 (2): 151–73.

Astorga, Luis. 2005. *El siglo de las drogas: El narcotráfico, del Porfiriato al nuevo milenio*. Plaza and Janes.

Astorga, Luis. 2007. *Seguridad, traficantes y militares: El poder y la sombra*. Tusquets.

Aukerman, Miriam. 2002. "Extraordinary Evil, Ordinary Crime: A Framework for Understanding Transitional Justice." *Harvard Human Rights Journal* 15: 39–97.

Austin, J. L. 1956–57. "A Plea for Excuses." *Proceeding from the Aristotelian Society* 57: 1–30.

Aviña, Alexander. 2016. "México's Long Dirty War." *NACLA Report on the Americas* 48 (2): 144–49. https://oxfordre.com/latinamericanhistory/view/10.1093/acrefore/97801
99366439.001.0001/acrefore-9780199366439-e-387.

Aviña, Alexander. 2017. "Guerrilla Movements and Armed Struggle in Cold War Mexico." *Oxford Research Encyclopedia of Latin American History*. July 27, accessed February 11, 2025.

Avramenko, Richard, and Robert Gingerich. 2014. "Democratic Dystopia: Tocqueville and the American Penitentiary System." *Polity* 46 (1): 56–80.

Azaola, Elena. 2021a. "Nuestras cárceles en América Latina." *Revista Crítica Penal y Poder* (21): 26–30.

Azaola, Elena. 2021b. "Las cárceles en México hoy." In *Atlas de la Seguridad y la Defensa de México, 2020*, edited by Sergio Aguayo Quezada, Raúl Benítez Manaut, Juan Antonio Le Clercq, Gerardo Rodríguez Sánchez Lara, and Keyla Vargas. Instituto Belisario Domínguez del Senado de la República.

Azaola, Elena. 2022. "El sistema penitenciario en México." In *Aportes de Sergio García Ramírez al derecho penal*, edited by María Elisa Franco Martín del Campo, Guillermo Raúl Zepeda Lecuona, and Pedro Salazar Ugarte. UNAM.

Azaola, Elena, Marcelo Bergman, and Ana Laura Magaloni. 2009. *Delincuencia, marginalidad y desempeño institucional: Resultados de la tercera encuesta a población en reclusión en el Distrito Federal y en el Estado de México*. CIDE.

Azaola, Elena, and Maïssa Hubert. 2016. *¿Quién controla las prisiones mexicanas?* Colectivo de Análisis de la Seguridad con Democracia.

Barragán, Almudena. 2023. "Las madres buscadoras que negocian con el narco para encontrar a sus desaparecidos en México." *El País*, July 11. https://elpais.com/mexico/2023-07-12/las-madres-buscadoras-que-negocian-con-el-narco-para-encontrar-a-sus-desaparecidos-en-mexico.html.

Baumann, Peter, and Monika Betzler, eds. 2004. *Practical Conflicts: New Philosophical Essays*. Cambridge University Press.

Bellaby, Ross. 2012. "What's the Harm? The Ethics of Intelligence Collection." *Intelligence and National Security* 27 (1): 93–117.

Bentham, Jeremy. 1838–43. *Works of Jeremy Bentham*. Vol. 1, *Principles of Penal Law*, edited by John Bowring. William Tait.

Bergelson, Vera. 2018. "Duress Is No Excuse." *Ohio State Journal of Criminal Law* 15 (2): 395–428.

Bergman, Marcelo, and Gustavo Fondevila. 2021. *Prisons and Crime in Latin America*. Cambridge University Press.

Berman, Mitchell, and Ian Farrell. 2011. "Provocation Manslaughter as Partial Justification and Partial Excuse." *William and Mary Law Review* 52 (4): 1027–109.

Betts, Reginald Dwayne, and Lori Gruen. 2021. "Are Prisons Permissible?" *Philosophical Topics* 49 (1): 81–97.

Birkbeck, Christopher. 2011. "Imprisonment and Internment: Comparing Penal Institutions North and South." *Punishment and Society* 13 (3): 307–32.

Blustein, Jeffrey M. 2014. *Forgiveness and Remembrance: Remembering Wrongdoing in Personal and Public Life*. Oxford University Press.

Boelen, Paul A., and Holly G. Prigerson. 2012. "Commentary on the Inclusion of Persistent Complex Bereavement-Related Disorder in DSM-5." *Death Studies* 36 (9): 771–94.

Borges, Tomás. 2013. "Cómo operan los Caballeros Templarios de Michoacán." *Los Angeles Press*, September 26. www.losangelespress.org/como-operan-los-caballeros-templarios-de-michoacan/#sthash.9H8zsJ.dpuf.

Boss, Pauline. 1999. *Ambiguous Loss: Learning to Live with Unresolved Grief*. Harvard University Press.

Bourgois, Philippe. 2001. "The Power of Violence in War and Peace: Post–Cold War Lessons from El Salvador." *Ethnography* 2 (1): 5–37. http://journals.sagepub.com/doi/pdf/10.1177/14661380122230803.

Bourgois, Philippe. 2002. "The Violence of Moral Binaries: Response to Leigh Binford." *Ethnography* 3 (2): 221–31.

Boxill, Bernard. 1995. "Self-Respect and Protest." In *Dignity, Character, and Self-Respect*, edited by Robin Dillon. Routledge.

Brettschneider, Corey. 2020. "A Democratic Theory of Punishment: The Trop Principle." *University of Toronto Law Journal* 70 (5): 141–62.

Browning, Christopher. 1998. *Ordinary Men: Reserve Police Battalion 101 and the Final Solution in Poland*. HarperPerennial.

Buchanan, Allan. 2002. "Social Moral Epistemology." *Social Philosophy and Policy* 19 (2): 126–52.

Buchanan, Allen. 2004. "Political Liberalism and Social Epistemology." *Philosophy and Public Affairs* 32 (2): 95–130.

Campbell, Howard. 2008. "Female Drug Smugglers on the U.S.-Mexico Border: Gender, Crime, and Empowerment." *Anthropological Quarterly* 81 (1): 233–67.

Campbell, Howard. 2009. *Drug War Zone: Frontline Dispatches from the Streets of El Paso and Juárez*. University of Texas Press.

Card, Claudia. 2002. *The Atrocity Paradigm: A Theory of Evil*. Oxford University Press.

Caruso, Gregg. 2021. *Rejecting Retributivism: Free Will, Punishment, and Criminal Justice*. Cambridge University Press.

Castellanos, Laura. 2016. *México Armado, 1943–1981*. Era.

Castillo, Gustavo. 2013. "Cárteles mexicanos importan células criminales de Centroamérica." *La Jornada*, December 10. www.jornada.com.mx/2013/12/10/politica/013n1pol.

Castillo, Gustavo, and A. Cruz. 2009. "Ejecutan a ex comandante de la PFP que fue informante del cártel de Sinaloa." *La Jornada*, December 2. www.jornada.com.mx/2009/12/02/politica/014n1pol.

Castillo Garcia, Gustavo. 2013. "Captura de *El Z-40*, con apoyo de un *dron* de EU, dicen funcionarios." *La Jornada*, July 19. www.jornada.com.mx/2013/07/19/politica/013n1pol.

CDCEUM (Cámara de Diputados del Congreso de los Estados Unidos Mexicanos). 1936. "Diario de los Debates de la Cámara de Diputados del Congreso de los Estados Unidos Mexicanos." XXXVI Legislature, December 31.

CDCEUM (Cámara de Diputados del Congreso de los Estados Unidos Mexicanos). 1978. "Diario de los Debates de la Cámara de Diputados del Congreso de los Estados Unidos Mexicanos." L Legislature, September 1.

CDHMAPJ (Centro de Derechos Humanos Miguel Agustín Pro Juárez). 2021."COVID y cárceles: Otra cara de la pandemia." *Centro de Derechos Humanos Miguel Agustín Pro Juárez*. January 26. https://centroprodh.org.mx/2021/01/26/covid-y-carceles-otra-cara-de-la-pandemia/.

Centro de Producción CEPROPIE. 2021. *Visita a la Barranca de la Carnicería, Iguala, Guerrero*. September. 26 mis, 34 sec. www.youtube.com/watch?v=FsdPO5OAkMU.

Chamberlin, Michael W. 2019. "Tres condiciones para acabar a fondo con la violencia." *Aristegui Noticias*, June 1. https://m.aristeguinoticias.com/0106/opinion/tres-condiciones-para-acabar-a-fondo-con-la-violencia-articulo/.

Chaparro Hernández, Sergio, and Catalina Pérez Correa. 2017. *Sobredosis carcelaria y política de drogas en América Latina*. Dejusticia.

Chomczyński, Piotr A., and Roger Guy. 2021. "'Our Biographies Are the Same': Juvenile Work in Mexican Drug Trafficking Organizations from the Perspective of a Collective Trajectory." *British Journal of Criminology* 61 (4): 946–64.

Chomczyński, Piotr A., Roger Guy, and Elena Azaola. 2023. "Beyond Money, Power, and Masculinity: Toward an Analytical Perspective on Recruitment to Mexican Drug Trafficking Organizations." *International Sociology* 38 (3): 353–71.

Chomczyński, Piotr A., Roger Guy, and Rodrigo Cortina-Cortés. 2019. "Front Business—Back Business: The Social Anatomy of Small-Time Drug Dealing in a Mexico City Neighborhood." *Journal of Contemporary Ethnography* 48 (6): 750–72.

Christopher, Russell. 2003. "The Prosecutor's Dilemma: Bargains and Punishments." *Fordham Law Review* (72): 93–168.

CIDE (Centro de Investigación y Docencia Económicas), and CNDH (Comisión Nacional de los Derechos Humanos). 2018. *Estudio para elaborar una propuesta de política pública en materia de justicia transicional.* CIDE; CNDH.

Cisneros, José Luis. 2014. "Niños y jóvenes sicarios: Una batalla cruzada por la pobreza." *El Cotidiano* (186): 7–18.

Cloward, Richard A., and Lloyd E. Ohlin. 1960. *Delinquency and Opportunity: A Theory of Delinquent Gangs.* Routledge.

CNBP (Comisión Nacional de Búsqueda y Personas). 2020. *Informe sobre fosas clandestinas y registro nacional de personas desaparecidas o no localizadas.* SEGOB.

CNDH (Comisión Nacional de los Derechos Humanos). 2001. *Informe especial sobre las quejas en materia de desapariciones forzadas ocurridas en la decada de los 70 y principios de los 80.* CNDH.

CNDH (Comisión Nacional de los Derechos Humanos). 2015. *Informe especial de la comisión nacional de los derechos humanos sobre las mujeres internas en los centros de reclusión de la república mexicana.* CNDH. www.cndh.org.mx/sites/default/files/doc /Informes/Especiales/2015_IE_MujeresInternas.pdf.

CNDH (Comisión Nacional de los Derechos Humanos). 2020. *Informe de actividades del 1 de enero al 31 de diciembre de 2019.* CNDH. http://informe.cndh.org.mx/uploads /principal/2019/IA_2019.pdf.

CNDH (Comisión Nacional de los Derechos Humanos). 2022. *Diagnóstico Nacional de Supervisión Penitenciaria.* CNDH. www.cndh.org.mx/documento/diagnostico -nacional-de-supervision-penitenciaria-2022.

CNDH (Comisión Nacional de los Derechos Humanos). 2024. *Comunicado DGDDH /003/2024.* CNDH.

Congreso de los Estados Unidos Mexicanos. 1996. Federal Law against Organized Crime.

Congreso de los Estados Unidos Mexicanos. 2012. Federal Law for the Protection of Persons Involved in Criminal Procedure.

Córdova, Nery. 2011. *La narcocultura: Simbología de la transgresión, el poder y la muerte: Sinaloa y la "leyenda negra."* Universidad Autónoma de Sinaloa.

Corradetti, Claudio, and Nir Eisikovitz, eds. 2014. *Theorizing Transitional Justice.* Ashgate.

Correa-Cabrera, Guadalupe. 2017. *Los Zetas Inc.: Criminal Corporations, Energy, and Civil War in Mexico*. University of Texas Press.

Cossío Díaz, José Ramón. 2019. "Personas desaparecidas y declaración especial de ausencia." *Proceso*, May 13. www.proceso.com.mx/583756/personas-desaparecidas-y-declaracion-especial-de-ausencia-2.

Crenshaw, Kimberlé. 1989. "Demarginalizing the Intersection of Race and Sex: A Black Feminist Critique of Antidiscrimination Doctrine, Feminist Theory, and Antiracist Politics." *University of Chicago Legal Forum* 1989 (1): 139–67.

Darcy, Shane. 2019. *To Serve the Enemy: Informers, Collaborators, and the Laws of Armed Conflict*. Oxford University Press.

Darwall, Stephen. 2010. "Justice and Retaliation." *Philosophical Papers* 39 (3): 315–41.

Davis, Angela. 2003. *Are Prisons Obsolete?* Seven Stories Press.

Dawes, James. 2013. *Evil Men*. Harvard University Press.

De Vecchi Gerli, María. 2023. "Continuidades y rupturas en la desaparición de personas en México: De la represión estatal a la "guerra contra el narcotráfico." In *Verdad, justicia y memoria*, edited by Juan Espíndola and Mónica Serrano. El Colegio de México.

Delgado, Richard. 1985. "'Rotten Social Background': Should the Criminal Law Recognize a Defense of Severe Environmental Deprivation?" *Law and Inequality* 3 (1): 9–90.

Diderichsen, Adam, and Kira Vrist Rønn. 2017. "Intelligence by Consent: On the Inadequacy of Just War Theory as a Framework for Intelligence Ethics." *Intelligence and National Security* 32 (4): 479–93.

Dillon, Robin S. 1995. *Dignity, Character, and Self-Respect*. Routledge.

DOF (Diario Oficial de la Federación). 1976. "Ley de Amnistía." *Congreso de la Unión*. May 20. http://dof.gob.mx/nota_detalle.php?codigo=4845287&fecha=20/05/1976.

DOF (Diario Oficial de la Federación). 1978. "Ley de Amnistía." *Congreso de la Unión*. September 28.

DOF (Diario Oficial de la Federación). 1994. "Ley de Amnistía." *Congreso de la Unión*, January 22. www.diputados.gob.mx/LeyesBiblio/pdf/19.pdf.

DOF (Diario Oficial de la Federación). 2019. "Plan Nacional de Desarrollo, 2019–2024." Presidencia de la República. July 12. www.dof.gob.mx/nota_detalle.php?codigo=5565599&fecha=12/07/2019.

DOF (Diario Oficial de la Federación). 2020. "Ley de Amnistía." *Congreso de la Unión*. April 22. www.diputados.gob.mx/LeyesBiblio/pdf/LAmn_220420.pdf.

DOF (Diario Oficial de la Federación). 2021. "Acuerdo por el que se instruyen a las instituciones que en el mismo se indican, a realizar acciones para gestionar, ante las autoridades competentes, las solicitudes de preliberación de personas sentenciadas, así como para identificar casos tanto de personas en prisión preventiva, como de aquellas que hayan sido víctimas de tortura, en términos de las disposiciones jurídicas aplicables." *Andrés Manuel López Obrador, Presidente de los Estados Unidos Mexicanos*. August 25. https://dof.gob.mx/nota_detalle.php?codigo=5627705&fecha=25/08/2021.

Donelson, Raff. 2022 "The Inherent Problem with Mass Incarceration." *Oklahoma Law Review* 75 (1): 51–67.

Dudai, Ron. 2018. "Underground Penality: The IRA's Punishment of Informers." *Punishment and Society* 20 (3): 375–95. https://doi.org/10.1177/1462474517701302.

Duff, R. A. 2001. *Punishment, Communication, and Community*. Oxford University Press.

Dunnighan, Clive, and Colin Norris. 1998. "Some Ethical Dilemmas in the Handling of Police Informers." *Public Money and Management* 18 (1): 21–25.

El Universal. 1994. "Los movimientos armados en México, 1917–1994." *El Universal, Compañía Periodística Nacional*.

El Universal. 2022. "Desde 'privados,' restaurantes y ferreterías: Destruyen 104 cuartos ilegales en penal de San Miguel, Puebla." *El Universal*. July 14. www.eluniversal.com .mx/estados/desde-privados-restaurantes-y-ferreterias-destruyen-104-cuartos-ilegales -en-penal-de-san-miguel-puebla/.

Elster, Jon. 2004a. *Closing the Books: Transitional Justice in Historical Perspective*. Cambridge University Press.

Elster, Jon. 2004b. "Moral Dilemmas of Transitional Justice." In *Practical Conflicts: New Philosophical Essays*, edited by Peter Baumann and Monika Betzler. Cambridge University Press.

Elster, Jon. 2004c. "Retribution." In *Retribution and Reparation in the Transition to Democracy*. Cambridge University Press.

Enríquez Perea, Alberto. 2015. *Jesús Reyes Heroles: A través de sus aforismos, sentencias y máximas políticas*. El Colegio de México.

Equis Justicia Para las Mujeres. 2022. "Obtiene amnistía una de las mujeres indígenas que acompañamos, tras casi dos años de lucha." *Justicias para las mujeres*. May 24.

Escalante, Fernando. 1992. *Ciudadanos imaginarios*. El Colegio de México.

Escalante, Fernando. 2009. *El homicidio en México entre 1990 y 2007: Aproximación estadística*. El Colegio de México.

Escalante, Fernando. 2012. *El crimen como realidad y como representación: Contribución para una historia del presente*. El Colegio de México.

Espíndola Mata, Juan. 2004. *El hombre que lo podía todo, todo, todo: Ensayo sobre el mito presidencial en México*. El Colegio de México.

Espíndola, Juan. 2014. "The Force of Forgetting or Forced Forgetting? Schmittian Amnesties and Transitional Justice." In *Theorizing Transitional Justice*, edited by Claudio Corradetti and Nir Eisikovitz. Ashgate.

Espíndola, Juan. 2022. "Bargaining for the Disappeared? Rewarding Perpetrators in Transitional Justice Contexts." *Journal of Social Philosophy* 53 (2): 143–289.

Espíndola, Juan. 2023. "Bargaining with Criminals: The Morality of Witness Collaboration in Mexico's 'War on Drugs.'" *Theoretical Criminology* 27 (1): 5–22.

Espíndola, Juan, and Leigh Payne, eds. 2022. *Collaboration in Authoritarian and Armed Conflict Settings*. Oxford University Press.

Espíndola, Juan, and Mónica Serrano, eds. 2023. *Verdad, justicia y memoria*. El Colegio de México.

Espino, Manuel. 2019a. "Ponen fin a seguridad de testigos protegidos." *El Universal*, July 30. www.eluniversal.com.mx/nacion/ponen-fin-seguridad-de-testigos-protegidos/.

Espino, Manuel. 2019b. "Testigos protegidos, programa de Calderón en el abandono." *El Universal*, July 22. www.eluniversal.com.mx/nacion/seguridad/testigos-protegidos -programa-de-calderon-en-el-abandono.

Esteve Díaz, Hugo. 1996. *Las armas de la utopía: La tercera ola de movimientos guerrilleros en México*. Instituto de Proposiciones Estratégicas.

Ewing, Benjamin. 2018. "Recent Work on Punishment and Criminogenic Disadvantage." *Law and Philosophy* 37 (1): 29–68.

Falcón, Romana. 1984. *Revolución y caciquismo San Luis Potosí, 1910–1938*. El Colegio de México.

Favril, Louis, Rongqin Yu, Keith Hawton, and Seena Fazel. 2020. "Risk Factors for Self-Harm in Prison: A Systematic Review and Meta-Analysis." *Lancet Psychiatry* 7 (8): 682–91.

Feinberg, Joel. 1970. *Doing and Deserving: Essays in the Theory of Responsibility*. Princeton University Press.

FEMOSPP (Fiscalía Especial para Movimientos Sociales y Políticos del Pasado). 2006. *Informe Histórico a la Sociedad Mexicana*. FEMOSPP. https://nsarchive2.gwu.edu/ NSAEBB/NSAEBB209/informe/intro.pdf.

Fernández Villagómez, Vianney. 2020. "Ley de amnistía: Victoria pírrica para las mujeres." Nexos, May 4. https://seguridad.nexos.com.mx/ley-de-amnistia-victoria-pirrica -para-las-mujeres/.

Ferri, Pablo. 2020. "Veracruz busca los huesos de la vergüenza." *El País*, February 11. https://elpais.com/internacional/2020/02/10/mexico/1581371156_200741.html.

Flanders. Chad. 2021. "What Is Wrong with Mass Incarceration?" In *The Routledge Handbook of the Philosophy and Science of Punishment*, edited by Farah Focquaert, Elizabeth Shaw, and Bruce N. Waller. Routledge.

Fletcher. George P. 1978. *Rethinking Criminal Law*. Little, Brown.

Focquaert, Farah, Elizabeth Shaw, and Bruce N. Waller. eds. 2021.*The Routledge Handbook of the Philosophy and Science of Punishment*. Routledge.

Fondevila, Gustavo. 2013. "Controlling the Madrinas: The Police Informer Management and Control System in Mexico." *Police Journal* 86 (2): 116–42. https://doi.org/ 10.1350/pojo.2013.86.2.62

Foot, Philippa. 1967. "The Problem of Abortion and the Doctrine of Double Effect." *Oxford Review* (5): 5–15.

Forst, Rainer. 2007. *Das Recht auf Rechtfertigung*. Suhrkamp.

Gallaguer, Janice. 2022. *Bootstrap Justice: The Search for Mexico's Disappeared*. Oxford University Press.

Gallegos, Zorayda. 2017. "El cártel de Jalisco reclutaba a sicarios a través de Facebook." *El País*, August 1. https://elpais.com/internacional/2017/08/01/mexico/1501540661_553909 .html.

Gamiño Muñoz, Rodolfo. 2017. "Fuerzas armadas, contrainsurgencia y desaparición forzada en Guerrero en la década de los sesenta y setenta." *Letras Históricas* (17): 185–207.

Garcia, Angela. 2015. "Serenity: Violence, Inequality, and Recovery on the Edge of Mexico City." *Medical Anthropology Quarterly* 29 (4): 455–72.

Garcia, Angela, and Brian Anderson. 2016 "Violence, Addiction, Recovery: An Anthropological Study of Mexico's Anexos," *Transcultural Psychiatry* 53 (4): 445–64.

Garcia, Denis A., and Gustavo Castillo. 2019. "Testigos protegidos, abandonados desde el sexenio de Peña Nieto." *La Jornada*, April 1. www.jornada.com.mx/2019/04/01/po litica/003n1pol.

García, Victor, and Laura González. 2009. "Labor Migration, Drug Trafficking Organizations, and Drug Use: Major Challenges for Transnational Communities in Mexico." *Urban Anthropology and Studies of Cultural Systems and World Economic Development* 38 (2–4): 303–44.

García-Godos, Jemima, and Knut Andreas O. Lid. 2010. "Transitional Justice and Victims' Rights before the End of a Conflict: The Unusual Case of Colombia." *Journal of Latin American Studies* 42 (3): 487–516. https://doi.org/10.1017/S0022216X10000891.

García-Reyes, Karina. 2020. "Cuatro dimensiones de la violencia del narcotráfico en México: ¿Cómo las conciben los perpetradores?" *CONfines: Revista de Relaciones Internacionales y Ciencia Política* 31 (16): 33–60.

Garland, David. 2001. *Mass Imprisonment: Its Social Causes and Consequences*. Sage.

Garrido, Susana Angélica. 2019. "Compartiendo el dolor: Acciones políticas de mujeres familiares de personas desaparecidas en Tijuana, México y Medellín, Colombia para reivindicar a las víctimas de desaparición." PhD diss., El Colegio de la Frontera Norte.

Giacomello, Corina. 2013. *Género, Drogas Y Prisión: Experiencias de Mujeres Privadas de Su Libertad en México*. Tirant lo Blanch.

Giacomello, Corina. 2014. How the Drug Trade Criminalizes Women Disproportionately." *NACLA Report on the Americas*, June 17. https://nacla.org/article/how-drug -trade-criminalizes-women-disproportionately.

Giacomello, Corina. 2020. "The Gendered Impacts of Drug Policy on Women: Case Studies from Mexico." *International Development Policy* 12: 206–45. https://doi.org/ 10.4000/poldev.3966.

Gobierno de Tamaulipas. 2016. Tamaulipas Penal Code.

Gómez Mena, Carolina. 2021. "Ley de Amnistía no ha llegado a indígenas ni a discapacitados: Activista." *La Jornada*, May 13. www.jornada.com.mx/2021/05/13/politica /010n3pol.

Gonzales Navarro, Moisés. 2003. *Cristeros y Agraristas en Jalisco*. El Colegio de México.

González Casanova, Pablo. 1970. "Declaraciones del Rector de la UNAM." *Gaceta UNAM* 1 (29): 1–3.

González Ocantos, Ezequiel. 2023 "Condiciones de posibilidad para la justicia transicional en México." In *Verdad, justicia y memoria*, edited by Juan Espíndola y Mónica Serrano. El Colegio de México.

Green, Stuart. 2011. "Just Deserts in Unjust Societies: A Case-Specific Approach." In *Philosophical Foundations of Criminal Law*, edited by Richard A. Duff and Stuart Green. Oxford University Press.

Green, Stuart, and R. A. Duff, eds. 2011. *Philosophical Foundations of Criminal Law*. Oxford University Press.

Greer, Steven. 1995. "Towards a Sociological Model of the Police Informant." *British Journal of Sociology* 46 (3): 509–27.

Grillo, Ioan. 2014. "Michoacán: Deportados en las filas de las autodefensas." *Letras Libres*, January 28. www.letraslibres.com/blogs/polifonia/michoacan-deportados-en -las-filas-de-las-autodefensas.

Guercke, Lena. 2021. "State Responsibility for a Failure to Prevent Violations of the Right to Life by Organised Criminal Groups: Disappearances in Mexico." *Human Rights Law Review* 21 (2): 329–57.

Guerrero Guitierrez, Eduardo. 2022. "Jalisco: Exterminio criminal, desapariciones y com-plicidad." *El Financiero*, June 27. www.elfinanciero.com.mx/opinion/eduardo-guerrero -gutierrez/2022/06/27/jalisco-exterminio-criminal-desapariciones-y-complicidad/.

Guillén, Alejandra, Mago Torres, and Marcela Turati. 2018."El país de las 2 mil fosas." *A dónde llevan a los desaparecidos*, November 12. https://adondevanlosdesaparecidos.org /2018/11/12/2-mil-fosas-en-mexico/.

Guillen, Beatriz. 2024a. "Cuatro años de la Ley de Amnistía en México: De corregir injusticias a la libertad a dedo de López Obrador. *El País*, June 22.

Guillen, Beatriz. 2024b. "Tragedia en la cárcel de mujeres: Así estalló la ola de suicidios en el Cefereso 16." *El País*, May 21. https://elpais.com/mexico/2024-05-22/tragedia-en -la-carcel-de-mujeres-asi-estallo-la-ola-de-suicidios-en-el-cefereso-16.html.

Gutierrez, Gabriela. 2016. *Sexo en las cárceles de la Ciudad de México*. El Salario del Miedo.

Hampton, Jean. 1992. "Correcting Harms versus Righting Wrongs: The Goal of Retri-bution." *UCLA Law Review* 39: 1659–702.

Hampton, Jean. 2007. "Righting Wrongs: The Goal of Retribution." In *The Intrinsic Worth of Persons: Contractarianism in Moral and Political Philosophy*, edited by Daniel Farnham. Cambridge University Press.

Harfield, Clive. 2012. "Police Informers and Professional Ethics." *Criminal Justice Ethics* 31 (2): 73–95.

Hart, H. L. A. 1968. *Essays in the Philosophy of Law*. Oxford University Press.

Hernández, Anabel. 2013."Testigos caros y a conveniencia del PRI." *Proceso* (1907): 1–81.

Hernández, Roberto. 1978. "La amnistía en manos de los encarcelados." *Proceso*, Sep-tember.

Hernández-Hernández, Óscar Misael. 2017. "¿Podemos hablar de migranticidio?," *Milenio*, November 25. www.milenio.com/opinion/varios-autores/corredor-fronteri zo/podemos-hablar-de-migranticidio.

Hernández-Hernández, Óscar Misael. 2022. "Manos de chango para fosas clandestinas." Blog of El Colegio de la Frontera, April 28. www.colef.mx/opinion/manos-de-chango -para-fosas-clandestinas/.

Hernández Herrera, Issa Cristina. 2020. "Collaborating with Organized Crime in the Search for Disappeared Persons? Formalizing a Humanitarian Alternative for Mexico." *International Review of the Red Cross* 102: 607–28.

Herrera, Luis. 2018. "La Amnistía Fantasma." *Reporte Índigo*, October 5. www.reporte

indigo.com/reporte/la-amnistia-fantasma-instituciones-justicia-jalisco-transparencia
-datos-indultos-1978/.

Herzog, Lisa, and Bernardo Zacka. 2017. "Fieldwork in Political Theory: Five Arguments
for an Ethnographic Sensibility." *British Journal of Political Science* 49 (2): 763–84.

Hill, Thomas E. 1995. "Servility and Self-Respect." In *Dignity, Character, and Self-
Respect*, edited by Robin Dillon. Routledge.

Hirales, Gustavo. 2004 ."Los avatares de una justicia pospuesta." *Nexos*, July 1. www
.nexos.com.mx/?p=11213.

Hobbes, Thomas. 1994. *Leviathan*. Edited by Edwin Curley. Hackett.

Hollander, Theo. 2016. "Ambiguous Loss and Complicated Grief: Understanding the
Grief of Parents of the Disappeared in Northern Uganda." *Journal of Family Theory
and Review* 8: 294–307.

Honneth, Axel. 1995. *The Struggle for Recognition: The Moral Grammar of Social Conflict*.
MIT Press.

Hope, Alejandro. 2013. "Violencia 2007–2011: La Tormenta Perfecta." Nexos, November. www.nexos.com.mx/?P=leerarticulo&Article=2204455.

Hope, Alejandro. 2020. "Muchos homicidios, pocos homicidas." *El Universal*, February
5. www.eluniversalqueretaro.mx/content/muchos-homicidios-pocos-homicidas.

Hoskins, Zachary, and Antony Duff. 2024. "Legal Punishment." *Stanford Encyclopedia
of Philosophy*. Edited by Edward N. Zalta and Uri Nodelman. https://plato.stanford
.edu/archives/spr2024/entries/legal-punishment/.

HRW (Human Rights Watch). 2013. *Los desaparecidos de México: El persistente costo de
una crisis ignorada*. HRW.

Hurka, Thomas. 2005. "Proportionality in the Morality of War." *Philosophy and Public
Affairs* 33 (1): 34–66.

ICG (International Crisis Group). 2023. "Partners in Crime: The Rise of Women in Mexico's Illegal Groups." *International Crisis Group*. www.crisisgroup.org/latin-america-car
ibbean/mexico/103-partners-crime-rise-women-mexicos-illegal-groups.

INEGI (Instituto Nacional de Estadística y Geografía). 2021a. *Encuesta Nacional de
Victimización y Percepción sobre Seguridad Pública (ENVIPE) Principales Resultados*.
INEGI. www.inegi.org.mx/contenidos/programas/envipe/2021/doc/envipe2021_pre
sentacion_nacional.pdf.

INEGI (Instituto Nacional de Estadística y Geografía). 2021b. *Encuesta Nacional de
Población Privada de la Libertad (ENPOL) Principales Resultados*. INEGI. www.inegi
.org.mx/contenidos/programas/enpol/2021/doc/enpol2021_presentacion_nacional
.pdf.

INEGI (Instituto Nacional de Estadística y Geografía). 2024a. *Censo Nacional de Sistema
Penitenciario Federal y Estatales: Presentación de resultados generales*. INEGI. www
.inegi.org.mx/contenidos/programas/cnspef/2023/doc/cnsipef_2023_resultados.pdf.

INEGI (Instituto Nacional de Estadística y Geografía). 2024b. *Censo Nacional de
Sistema Penitenciario Federal y Estatales*. INEGI. www.inegi.org.mx/contenidos/pro
gramas/cnspef/2023/doc/cnsipef_2023_resultados.pdf.

INEGI(Instituto Nacional de Estadística y Geografía). 2024c. *Encuesta nacional de calidad e impacto gubernamental (ENCIG)*. INEGI. www.inegi.org.mx/contenidos/saladeprensa/boletines/2024/EstSegPub/ENCIG_23.pdf.

Infobae. 2020a. "El Cártel de Sinaloa recluta jóvenes en centros de rehabilitación por 2,000 pesos semanales." *Infobae*, November 6. www.infobae.com/america/mexico/2020/11/06/el-cartel-de-sinaloa-recluta-jovenes-en-centros-de-rehabilitacion-por-2000-pesos-semanales/.

Infobae. 2020b. "Penal de Puente Grande: Al menos siete muertos y nueve heridos deja riña entre reclusos." *Infobae*, May 22. www.infobae.com/america/mexico/2020/05/22/penal-de-puente-grande-detonaciones-de-arma-de-fuego-provocan-movilizacion-de-policias/.

Intersecta and Animal Político. 2025. "Prisión preventiva: el arma que encarcela pobres e inocentes." Updated February. https://panel.animalpolitico.com/prision-preventiva-delitos-encarcela-pobres-inocentes/.

Interview Former Member of Prosecutor's Office. 2021. May 18.

Interview with Federal Judge. 2021a. February 23.

Interview with Federal Judge. 2021b. September 6.

Interview with Former Member of the Federal Prosecutor's Office. 2021. May 18.

Kalyvas, Stathis. 2004. "The Paradox of Terrorism in Civil War." *Journal of Ethics* 8 (1): 97–138.

Kalyvas, Stathis. 2006. *In the Logic of Violence in Civil War*. Cambridge University Press.

Kalyvas, Stathis. 2012. "Micro-Level Studies of Violence in Civil War: Refining and Extending the Control-Collaboration Model." *Terrorism and Political Violence* 24 (4): 658–68.

Kant, Immanuel. 1999. *The Metaphysics of Morals*. In *Practical Philosophy*, edited by Mary J. Gregor. Cambridge University Press.

Kelly, Erin. 2018. *The Limits of Blame*. Harvard University Press.

Kleinig, John. 2009. "The Ethical Perils of Knowledge Acquisition." *Criminal Justice Ethics* 28 (2): 201–22.

Kovras, Iosif. 2017. *Grassroots Activism and the Evolution of Transitional Justice: The Families of the Disappeared*. Cambridge University Press.

Lacey, Nicola, and Hanna Pickard. 2015. "The Chimera of Proportionality: Institutionalising Limits on Punishment in Contemporary Social and Political Systems." *Modern Law Review* 78 (2): 216–40.

Lazar, Seth. 2012. "Necessity in Self-Defense and War." *Philosophy and Public Affairs* 40 (1): 3–44.

Lazar, Seth. 2020. "War." *Stanford Encyclopedia of Philosophy*. Edited by Edward N. Zalta. https://plato.stanford.edu/archives/spr2020/entries/war/.

Lenta, Patrick. 2019a. "Amnesty and Mercy." *Criminal Law and Philosophy* 13 (4): 621–41.

Lenta, Patrick. 2019b. "Transitional Justice and Retributive Justice." *Ethical Theory and Moral Practice* 22 (2): 385–98.

León Olvera, Alejandra. 2023. "Repensar el narcomarketing en las representaciones identitarias del narcomundo transmitidas en TikTok." *Aisthesis Revista Chilena de Investigaciones Estéticas* (73): 49–70.

Lepora, Chiara, and Robert Goodin. 2013. *On Complicity and Compromise*. Oxford University Press.

Lessing, Benjamin, and Graham Denyer Willis. 2019. "Legitimacy in Criminal Governance: Managing a Drug Empire from Behind Bars." *American Political Science Review* 113 (2): 584–606.

Leyva, Salvador. 2023. "El cementerio de las vivas: Mujeres privadas de libertad en el CEFERESO." *Animal Político*, August 5. www.animalpolitico.com/analisis/invitades/cementerio-de-las-vivas-cefereso-16.

Lippke, Richard L. 1998. "Arguing against Inhumane and Degrading Punishment." *Criminal Justice Ethics* 17 (1): 29–41.

Lippke, Richard L. 2003. "Diminished Opportunities, Diminished Capacities: Social Deprivation and Punishment." *Social Theory and Practice* 29 (3): 459–85.

Lippke, Richard L. 2011. *The Ethics of Plea Bargaining*. Oxford University Press.

Lomnitz, Claudio. 2019. "The Ethos and Telos of Michoacán's Knights Templar." *Representations* 147 (1): 96–123. https://doi.org/10.1525/rep.2019.147.1.96.

Lomnitz, Claudio. 2020. "Gobierno y desaparición." *Nexos*, October 1. www.nexos.com.mx/?p=50316.

Lomnitz, Claudio. 2022. *El tejido social rasgado*. Era.

Lomnitz, Claudio. 2023. *Para una teología política del crimen organizado*. Era.

López Benítez, Lilia. 2009. *Protección de testigos en el derecho penal mexicano*. Editorial Porrúa.

López, Saúl. 1982. "Reciben 40 personas los beneficios de la ley de amnistía; 7 están en el extranjero." *El Universal*, February 2.

Lovett, Frank. 2010. *A General Theory of Domination and Justice*. Oxford University Press.

Lozano-Verduzco, Ignacio, Rodrigo Marín Navarrete, Martha Romero Mendoza, and Antonio Tena Suck. 2016. "Experiences of Power and Violence in Mexican Men Attending Mutual-Aid Residential Centers for Addiction Treatment." *American Journal of Men's Health* 10 (3): 237–49.

Macaulay, Fiona. 2019. *Prisoner Capture: Welfare, Lawfare, and Warfare in Latin America's Overcrowded Prisons*. Routledge.

Machiavelli, Niccolò. 1998. *The Prince*. Translated by Harvey Mansfield. University of Chicago Press.

Macnish, Kevin. 2015. "An Eye for an Eye: Proportionality and Surveillance." *Ethical Theory and Moral Practice* 18 (3): 529–48.

Madrazo, Alejandro. 2013. "¿Criminales y enemigos? El narcotraficante mexicano en el discurso oficial y en el narcocorrido." In *Violencia, legitimidad y orden público*, edited by Marcelo Alegre et al. Librária.

Magaloni, Ana Laura. 2009. "El Ministerio Público desde adentro: Rutinas y métodos de trabajo en las agencias del MP." CIDE.

Magaloni, Ana Laura. 2014. "La arbitrariedad como método de trabajo: La persecución criminal durante la administración de Felipe Calderón." In *De la detención a la prisión: La justicia penal a examen*, edited by Catalina Pérez Correa. CIDE.

Magaloni, Ana Laura, and Zaira Razu. 2018. "La tortura como método de investigación criminal: El impacto de la guerra contra las drogas en México." *Política y gobierno* 25 (2): 223–61.

Maldonado, Salvador. 2012. "Drogas, violencia y militarización en el México rural: El caso de Michoacán." *Revista Mexicana de Sociología* 74 (1): 5–39.

Mallinder, Louise, and Kieran McEvoy. 2012. "Amnesties in Transition: Punishment, Restoration, and the Governance of Mercy." *Journal of Law and Society* 39 (3): 410–40.

Marcial Pérez, David. 2018. "El insólito viaje de 273 cadáveres por Guadalajara." *El País*, September 24. https://elpais.com/internacional/2018/09/23/actualidad/1537727838_487244.html.

Martínez Ahrens, Jan. 2016. "49 presos muertos en un motín en una cárcel en el norte de México." *El País*, February 11. https://elpais.com/internacional/2016/02/11/actualidad/1455194786_558490.html?event_log=oklogin.

Martínez, París. 2012. "Esclavos del Narco: Los niños del hampa." *Animal Político*, October 30. https://animalpolitico.com/seguridad/esclavos-del-narco-los-ninos-del-hampa.

Mashal, Mujib. 2018. "After a War's End, a Long Struggle to Patch Invisible Wounds in Sri Lanka." *New York Times*, December 4. www.nytimes.com/2018/12/04/world/asia/sri-lanka-suicide-civil-war-mental-illness.html.

Maza, Alfredo. 2023. "El cementerio de las vivas: El turbio negocio del Cefereso 16 de Morelos." *Animal Político*, October 23. https://animalpolitico.com/sociedad/cefereso-16-morelos-femenil-cementerio-vivas.

Melchor, Fernanda. 2022. *This Is Not Miami*. Translated by Sophie Hughes. New Directions.

Méndez, Alfredo. 2009. "Ya ni se moleste en citar al testigo, señoría: Está muerto." *La Jornada*, December 13. www.jornada.com.mx/2009/12/13/politica/003n1pol.

Méndez, Alfredo. 2013. "Utilizó la PGR a 379 testigos protegidos." *La Jornada*, May 6. www.jornada.com.mx/2013/05/06/politica/017n1pol.

Méndez, Alfredo. 2016. "Da de baja PGR a 55 testigos protegidos." *La Jornada*, October 6. www.jornada.com.mx/2016/10/06/politica/006n1pol.

Mendoza Rockwell, Natalia. 2012. "Crónica de La Cartelización." *Nexos*, June 1. www.nexos.com.mx/?P=leerarticulo&Article=2102733.

Mexico City Penitentiary Centers Law. 2021.

México Evalúa. 2013. *La cárcel en México: ¿Para qué?*. México Evalúa. www.mexicoevalua.org/wp-content/uploads/2016/05/MEX-EVA_INDX-CARCEL-MEXICO_10142013.pdf.

México Evalúa. 2016. *Privatización del sistema penitenciario en México*. Documenta / Análisis y Acción para la Justicia Social A.C; Fundación para el Debido Proceso Instituto de Derechos Humanos Ignacio Ellacuría SJ; Universidad Iberoamericana

Puebla; Instituto de Justicia Procesal Penal A.C; Madres y hermanas de la Plaza Pasteur; México Evalúa. www.documenta.org.mx/wp-content/uploads/2020/04/Informe-Privatización-del-sistema-penitenciario-en-México.pdf.

Meyer, Jean. 1985. *La Cristiada: El conflicto entre La Iglesia y El Estado, 1926–1929.* Siglo XXI Editores.

Meyer, Marco, Mark Alfano, and Boudewijn de Bruin. 2021."The Development and Validation of the Epistemic Vice Scale." *Review of Philosophy and Psychology* 15: 1–28.

Middleton, David. 2006. "Three Kinds of Self-Respect." *Res Publica* 12 (1): 59–76.

Milenio. 2021. *Testigo del caso Ayotzinapa exhibe pagos a funcionarios y mandos militares.* YouTube video. July, 10 mins., 22 sec. www.youtube.com/watch?v=ZzszqXFsrfQ.

Milenio. 2018. "Absuelven a ex mandos del Topo Chico por el asesinato de 49 reos." *Milenio*, July 8. www.milenio.com/policia/absuelven-mandos-topo-chico-asesinato-49-reos.

Miller, Seumas. 2017. "Torture." *Stanford Encyclopedia of Philosophy.* https://plato.stanford.edu/archives/sum2017/entries/torture/.

Miller, Seumas. 2021. "Rethinking the Just Intelligence Theory of National Security Intelligence Collection and Analysis: The Principles of Discrimination, Necessity, Proportionality, and Reciprocity." *Social Epistemology* 35 (3): 211–31.

Moffett, Luke. 2016. "Reparations for 'Guilty Victims': Navigating Complex Identities of Victim-Perpetrators in Reparation Mechanisms." *International Journal of Transitional Justice* 10 (1): 146–67.

Moody-Adams, Michele M. 1995. "Value, Welfare, And Morality." *Philosophical Books* 36 (1): 64–66.

Moore, Gary. 2012. "Mexico's Massacre Era: Gruesome Killings, Porous Prisons." *World Affairs* 175 (3): 61–67.

Moore, Michael. 2010. *Placing Blame: A Theory of Criminal Law.* Oxford University Press.

Morris, Herbert. 1968. "Persons and Punishment." *The Monist* 52 (4): 475–501.

Morse, Stephen. 2000. "Hooked on Hype: Addiction and Responsibility." *Law and Philosophy* 19 (1): 3–47.

MUCD (México Unido Contra la Delincuencia). 2021. *Informe: Libertad ante pandemia por COVID-19 en los centros penitenciarios: Medidas de preliberación implementadas durante 2019 y 2020.* México Unido Contra la Delincuencia.

Murphy, Jeffrie, and Jean Hampton. 1998. *Forgiveness and Mercy.* Cambridge University Press.

Murphy, Colleen. 2020. "On Principled Compromise: When Does a Process of Transitional Justice Qualify as Just?" *Proceedings of the Aristotelian Society* 120 (1): 47–70.

Natapoff, Alexandra. 2009. *Snitching: Criminal Informants and the Erosion of American Justice.* New York University Press.

Nguyen, C. Thi. 2020. "Echo Chambers and Epistemic Bubbles." *Episteme* 17 (2): 141–61.

Nino, Carlos. 1996. *Radical Evil on Trial.* Yale University Press.

Nozick, Robert. 1981. *Philosophical Explanations*. Harvard University Press.

Nussbaum, Martha. 1999. *Sex And Social Justice*. Oxford University Press.

Nussbaum, Martha. 2000. *Women and Human Development: The Capabilities Approach*. Cambridge University Press.

Observatorio de Amnistías. 2021. *Ley de Amnistía: Un año de simulación; Primer Informe Anual*. Observatorio de Amnistías. https://equis.org.mx/wp-content/uploads/2021/04/Ley-de-Amnistia-Un-ano-de-simulacion.pdf.

Observatorio de Prisiones. 2023 . "Conoce tus derechos." Updated February. https://observatorio-de-prisiones.documenta.org.mx/tus-derechos.

Oikión Solano, Verónica. 2007. "El Estado mexicano frente a los levantamientos armados en Guerrero: El caso del Plan Telaraña." *Tzintzun* (45): 65–82.

Olmos, José Gil, et al. 2018. *Los Buscadores*. Ediciones Proceso.

Omand, David, and Mark Phythian. 2013. "Ethics and Intelligence: A Debate." *International Journal of Intelligence and Counterintelligence* 26 (1): 38–63.

OMSMCSP (Observatorio Mexicano de Salud Mental y Consumo de Sustancias Psicoactivas). 2021. *Informe sobre la Situación de la Salud Mental y el Consumo de Sustancias Psicoactivas en México*. CONADIC.

ONC (Observatorio Nacional Ciudadano). 2024. "Publicaciones." Updated July. https://publicaciones.onc.org.mx/public/uploads/doc-reclutamiento.pdf.

Ornelas, Víctor Hugo. 2018. "Familiares de desaparecidos instalan plantón en Instituto Forense de Jalisco." *Milenio*, September 21. www.milenio.com/policia/instalan-planton-en-ciencias-forenses.

OSJI (Open Society Justice Initiative). 2016. *Atrocidades innegables: Confrontando crímenes de lesa humanidad en México*. Open Society Foundations.

Osorio, Javier. 2011. "Dynamics and Structural Determinants of Drug Violence." Presented at the Conference on Mexican Security in Comparative Perspective. October 3–4.

Ospina-Escobar, Angélica, and Claudio Alberto Dávila Cervantes. 2024. "Trends in Drug Overdose Deaths in Mexico (1999–2019)." A National Descriptive Analysis and Interstate Comparison. *International Journal of Drug Policy* 129. https://doi.org/10.1016/j.drugpo.2024.104464.

Paoli, José Francisco. 1978. "Lejos de la conciliación nacional." *Proceso*, October.

Páramo, Arturo. 2020. "Insiste López Obrador en romper pacto de silencio." *Excélsior*, February 11. www.excelsior.com.mx/nacional/insiste-lopez-obrador-en-romper-pacto-de-silencio/1363444.

Pauer-Studer, Herlinde, and J. David Velleman. 2011. "Distortions of Normativity." *Ethical Theory and Moral Practice* 14 (3): 329–56.

Payne, Leigh A., and Karina Ansolabehere. "Conceptualising Post-Transition Disappearances." 2021. In *Disappearances in the Post-Transition Era in Latin America*, edited by Karina Ansolabehere, Barbara A. Frey, and Leigh A. Payne. Oxford University Press.

Peake, Sandra, and Orla Lynch. 2016. "Victims of Irish Republican Paramilitary Violence— The Case of 'The Disappeared.'" *Terrorism and Political Violence* 28 (3): 452–72.

Pérez Caballero, Jesús. 2021. "Lo notorio al revés: El halconeo y lo secreto en México."

Athenea Digital: Revista de pensamiento e investigación social 21 (1): e–2550. https://doi
.org/10.5565/rev/athenea.2550.

Pérez Ricart, Carlos. 2020. "Taking the War on Drugs Down South: The Drug Enforcement Administration in Mexico (1973–1980)." *Social History of Alcohol and Drugs* 34
(1): 82–113.

Pfaff, Tony, and Tiel Jeffrey R. 2004. "The Ethics of Espionage." *Journal of Military
Ethics* 3 (1): 1–15.

Ponce, Aldo. 2014. "Satisfacción judicial, procedimientos judiciales y delitos contra la
salud: Evidencia de los Centros Federales de Readaptación Social mexicanos." In *De
la detención a la prisión: La justicia penal a examen*, edited by Catalina Pérez Correa.
CIDE.

Pradilla, Alberto. 2021. "'Tengo mucho miedo': Hombres armados persiguen a buscadoras en Guanajuato ante ausencia de autoridades." *Animal Político*, July 26. www.ani
malpolitico.com/2021/07/tengo-mucho-miedo-hombres-armados-persiguen-a-busca
doras-en-guanajuato-ante-ausencia-de-autoridades/.

Prieto-Curiel, Rafael, Gian Maria Campedelli, and Alejandro Hope. 2023. "Reducing Cartel Recruitment Is the Only Way to Lower Violence in Mexico." *Science* 281
(6664): 1312–16.

Proceso. 1978a. "Amnistía Internacional investigará la tortura en México." July.

Proceso. 1978b. "En Nuevo León condenan antes de procesar." October.

Proceso. 2011. "Caso Bayardo: sentencian a sus escoltas." June 2. https://www.proceso
.com.mx/nacional/2011/6/2/caso-bayardo-sentencian-sus-escoltas-87732.html.

Quinlan, Michael. 2007a. "Just Intelligence: Prolegomena to an Ethical Theory." *Intelligence and National Security* 22 (1): 1–13. https://doi.org/10.1080/02684520701200715.

Quinlan, Michael. 2007b. "Organisational Restructuring/Downsizing, OHS Regulation and Worker Health and Wellbeing." *International Journal of Law and Psychiatry*
30 (4–5): 385–99.

Rainsford, Cat. 2019. "México deja en el limbo a sus testigos protegidos." *InSight Crime*,
August 7. https://insightcrime.org/es/noticias/mexico-deja-en-el-limbo-a-sus-testi
gos-protegidos/.

Ramírez, Ignacio. 1978. "El Gobernador Rubén Figueroa: Muertos, los desaparecidos
políticos." *Proceso*, December.

Ramírez, Ignacio. 2001. "Encubre PGR a militares." *El Universal*, July 1. https://archivo
.eluniversal.com.mx/primera/6661.html.

Ravelo, Ricardo. 2009. "Instrumentos sucios en la Operación Limpieza." *Proceso*, January 4. www.proceso.com.mx/85743/instrumentos-sucios-en-la-operacion-limpieza.

Rawls, John. 1999. *A Theory of Justice*. Belknap Press of Harvard University Press.

Reguillo, Rossana. 2021. *Necromáquina: Cuando morir no es suficiente*. NED ediciones.

Reinserta.org. 2024. "Niñas, niños y adolescentes reclutados por la delincuencia organizada." Reinserta.org. https://reinserta.org/wp-content/uploads/2023/10/ESTUDIO
-RECLUTADOS-POR-LA-DELINCUENCIA-ORGANIZADA.pdf.

Reveles, José. 1978. "Doble sentido de una amnistía: El gobierno olvida los delitos, el
pueblo olvida los atropellos." *Proceso*, August.

Revueltas, José. 1941. *Los Muros de Agua*. Era.

Revueltas, José. 1969. *El Apando*. Era.

Revueltas, José. 2016. *México 68: Juventud y Revolución*. Era.

Reyes Heroles, Jesús. 1979. *La reforma política y su repercusión en los estados*. Presented at the second gathering of the Republic, February 5. https://archivos.juridicas.unam.mx/www/bjv/libros/3/1224/3.pdf.

Rius Facius, Antonio. 1960. *Méjico Cristero*. Editorial Patria.

Rivera, Miguel Ángel. 1978. "Mónico Rentería: 'No hay garantías de que los liberados seguirán vivos.'" *Proceso* (104). October.

Robins, Simon. 2010. "Ambiguous Loss in a Non-Western Context: Families of the Disappeared in Post-Conflict Nepal." *Family Relations* 59 (3): 253–68.

Ryberg, Jesper. 2014. "Punishing Adolescents—On Immaturity and Diminished Responsibility." *Neuroethics* 7 (3): 327–36.

Saffón, María Paula, and Pablo Gómez Pinilla. 2023. "¿Por qué no ha pegado la justicia transicional en México? In *Verdad, justicia y memoria*, edited by Juan Espíndola and Mónica Serrano. El Colegio de México.

Salazar, Amílcar. 2022. "Gana 'narcoguerra' terreno en plataformas digitales de música." *Milenio*, April 16. www.milenio.com/policia/playlist-narco-carteles-expanden-spotify-apple-youtube.

Sánchez Cordero, Olga. 2018. "Sebastiana, Andrés Manuel y la Ley de Amnistía." *Milenio*, April 25. www.milenio.com/opinion/olga-sanchez-cordero/casos-causas/sebastiana-andres-manuel-ley-amnistia-1.

Sánchez Godoy, Jorge Alan. 2009. "Procesos de institucionalización de la narcocultura en Sinaloa." *Frontera Norte* 21 (41): 77–103.

Sánchez Serrano, Evangelina. "Terrorismo de Estado y la represión en Atoyac, Guerrero, durante la guerra sucia." 2012. In *Desaparición forzada y terrorismo de Estado en México*, edited by Andrea Radilla Martínez and Claudia E. G. Rangel Lozano. Plaza y Valdés.

Santos Villarreal, Gabriel. 2010. *Protección de testigos contra la delincuencia organizada*. Centro de Documentación, Información y Análisis. www.diputados.gob.mx/sedia/sia/spe/SPE-ISS-01-10.pdf.

Scanlon, Thomas. 1998. *What We Owe to Each Other*. Belknap Press of Harvard University Press.

Schmitt, Carl. 1995. *Staat, Großraum, Nomos: Arbeiten Aus Den Jahren 1916 Bis 1969*. Duncker and Humblot.

Schmitt, Carl. 2005. *Political Theology: Four Chapters on the Concept of Sovereignty*. University of Chicago Press.

SEGOB (Secretaría de Gobernación, Government of Mexico). 2023. "Beneficio de Amnistía." Updated February. https://justicia.segob.gob.mx/es/UASJ/Ley_de_Amnistia.

Shelby, Tommie. 2022. *The Idea of Prison Abolition*. Princeton University Press.

Shue, Henry. 1978. "Torture." *Philosophy and Public Affairs* 7 (2): 124–43.

Sierra, Jorge Luis. 2006. "Fuerzas armadas y contrainsurgencia (1965–1982)." In *Movimientos Armados en México, siglo XX*, edited by Verónica Oikión Solano and Marta

Eugenia García Ugarte. El Colegio de Michoacán; CIESAS; UNAM.

Silva Forné, Carlos. Catalina Pérez Correa, and Rodrigo Gutiérrez Rivas. 2017. "Índice de letalidad 2008–2014: Menos enfrentamientos, misma letalidad, más opacidad." *Perfiles Latinoamericanos* 25 (50): 331–59.

Skarbek, David. 2011. "Governance and Prison Gangs." *American Political Science Review* 105 (4): 702–16.

Skinner, Quentin. 1978. *The Foundations of Modern Political Thought:* Volume 1, *The Renaissance.* Cambridge University Press.

Smulders, Anna. Stephanie Corte, Sarah Gohary, and Moravia de la O. 2017. *Control . . . over the Entire State of Coahuila: An Analysis of Testimonies in Trials against Zeta Members in San Antonio, Austin, and Del Rio, Texas.* Human Rights Clinic, University of Texas School of Law.

SSP (Secretaría de Seguridad Pública). 2010. *Pandillas: Análisis de su presencia en territorio nacional.* SSP. www.ssp.gob.mx/portalWebApp/ShowBinary?nodeId=/BEA% 20Repository/1214175//archivo.

Steinberg, Lawrence. 2007. "Risk Taking in Adolescence: New Perspectives from Behavioral and Brain Sciences." *Current Directions in Psychological Science* 16 (2): 55–59.

Stratfor. 2008. "The Barrio Azteca Trial and the Prison Gang-Cartel Interface." *Stratfor Global Intelligence.* November 19. https://worldview.stratfor.com/article/barrio-azte ca-trial-and-prison-gang-cartel-interface.

Su, Yang. 2011. *Collective Killings in Rural China during the Cultural Revolution.* Cambridge University Press.

Superson, Anita. 2010. "The Deferential Wife Revisited: Agency and Moral Responsibility." *Hypatia* 25 (2): 253–75. https://doi-org.pbidi.unam.mx:2443/10.1111/j.1527-2001 .2010.01103.x.

Tadros, Victor. 2009. "Poverty and Criminal Responsibility." *Journal of Value Inquiry* 43 (3): 391–413.

Tadros, Victor. 2011. *The Ends of Harm: The Moral Foundations of Criminal Law.* Oxford University Press.

Tasioulas, John, 2003 "Mercy," *Proceedings of the Aristotelian Society* 103 (1): 101–32.

Teague, Aileen. 2019. "The United States, Mexico, and the Mutual Securitization of Drug Enforcement, 1969–1985." *Diplomatic History* 43 (5): 785–812. https://doi.org/ 10.1093/dh/dhz035.

Thompson, Ginger. 2013. "A Drug War Informer in No Man's Land." *New York Times,* April 28. www.nytimes.com/2013/04/29/us/us-mexico-dea-informant.html.

Thompson, Ginger. 2017a. "DEA Operation Played Hidden Role in the Disappearance of Five Innocent Mexicans." *ProPublica,* December 21. www.propublica.org/article /dea-operation-played-hidden-role-in-the-disappearance-of-five-innocent-mexicans.

Thompson, Ginger. 2017b. "How the U.S. Triggered a Massacre." *ProPublica,* June 12. www.propublica.org/article/allende-zetas-cartel-massacre-and-the-us-dea.

Thompson, Ginger. 2017c. "Who Holds the DEA Accountable When Its Missions Cost Lives?" *ProPublica,* June 12. www.propublica.org/article/who-holds-the-dea-account able-when-its-missions-cost-lives.

Tucker, Aviezer. 2012a. "Scarce Justice." *Politics, Philosophy, and Economics* 11 (1): 76–96.

Turati, Marcela. 2012b. "Tras las pistas de los desaparecidos." In *Entre las cenizas: Historias de vida en tiempos de muerte*, edited by Daniela Rea y Marcela Turati. Sur+ ediciones.

Tzuc, Efraín. 2023. "México rebasa las 5,600 fosas clandestinas." *A dónde van los desaparecidos*, October 9. https://adondevanlosdesaparecidos.org/2023/10/09/mexico-rebasa-las-5600-fosas-clandestinas/.

Uniacke, Suzanne. 2011. "Proportionality and Self-Defense." *Law and Philosophy* 30 (3): 253–72.

UNODC (United Nations Office on Drugs and Crime). 2016. *World Drug Report*. UNODC.

Uprimny, Rodrigo, and Diana Güiza. 2023. "Justicia transicional sin transición: Del caso colombiano al mexicano." In *Verdad, justicia y memoria*, edited by Juan Espíndola and Mónica Serrano. El Colegio de México.

Valdés Castellanos, Guillermo. 2013. *Historia del narcotráfico en México*. Aguilar.

Vázquez, Luis Daniel. 2023. "Violaciones a derechos humanos e impunidad en México: La historia de justicia transicional que no fue." In *Verdad, justicia y memoria*, edited by Juan Espíndola and Mónica Serrano. El Colegio de México.

Vela, David Seúl. 2019. "PGR va contra la Siedo 'por poner' a Edgar Bayardo." *La Razón*, December 3. www.razon.com.mx/ciudad/pgr-va-contra-la-siedo-por-poner-a-edgar-bayardo/.

Viale, Emilio. 1978. "Captores y fiscales, expectantes ante la amnistía." *Proceso*, September.

Vilalta, Carlos. 2012. "Los delitos contra la salud en México, 1997–2011." In *Las bases sociales del crimen organizado y la violencia en México*. Secretaría de Seguridad Pública.

Vilalta, Carlos. 2013. "Anomia institucional, espacialidad y temporalidad en las muertes asociadas a la lucha contra la delincuencia organizada en México." *Mexican Studies / Estudios Mexicanos* 29 (1): 280–319.

Villafaña, Laura. 2023. "Encontrar a su familiar desaparecido, la única justicia que aspiran las buscadoras." *Zona Franca*, August 30. https://zonafranca.mx/politica-sociedad/encontrar-a-su-familiar-desaparecido-la-unica-justicia-que-aspiran-las-buscadoras/.

Villavicencio Ayala, Silvia Lorena. 2019. "Iniciativa que expide la Ley de Amnistía contra la criminalización de los derechos reproductivos de las mujeres, a cargo de la Diputada Silvia Lorena Villavicencio Ayala, del grupo parlamentario de Morena." *Cámara de diputados*. September 24.

Vrist Rønn, Kira, and Kasper Lippert-Rasmussen. 2020. "Out of Proportion? On Surveillance and the Proportionality Requirement." *Ethical Theory and Moral Practice* 23: 181–99. https://doi.org/10.1007/s10677-019-10057-z.

Vrousalis, Nicholas. 2013. "Exploitation, Vulnerability, and Social Domination." *Philosophy and Public Affairs* 41 (2): 131–57.

Waldron, Jeremy. 2003. "Security and Liberty: The Image of Balance." *Journal of Political Philosophy* 11: 191–210.

Walen, Alec. 2023. "Retributive Justice." *Stanford Encyclopedia of Philosophy*. https://plato.stanford.edu/archives/win2023/entries/justice-retributive/.

Wallace, R. Jay. 1994. *Responsibility and the Moral Sentiments.* Harvard University Press.

Walzer, Michael. 1973. "Political Action: The Problem of Dirty Hands." *Philosophy and Public Affairs* 2 (2): 160–80.

Watson, Gary. 2004. *Agency and Answerability: Selected Essays.* Oxford University Press.

Womer, Sarah, and Robert J. Bunker. 2010. "Sureños Gangs and Mexican Cartel Use of Social Networking Sites." *Small Wars and Insurgencies* 21 (1): 81–94.

Wood, Mark A. 2017. "Antisocial Media and Algorithmic Deviancy Amplification: Analysing the Id of Facebook's Technological Unconscious." *Theoretical Criminology* 21 (2): 168–85.

Zavaleta, Noé. 2018a. "Yunes dosifica cifra de cadáveres hallados en Alvarado." *Proceso*, September 25. www.proceso.com.mx/552432/yunes-dosifica-cifra-de-cadaveres -hallados-en-alvarado.

Zavaleta, Noé. 2018b. "Don Fernando no se rinde." In Olmos et al., *Los Buscadores.*

Zavaleta, Noé. 2018c. "Forenses por necesidad." In Olmos et al., *Los Buscadores.*

Zazueta Aguilar, Humberto, Joaquín Torrez-Osorno, and Cristina Hardaga Fernández. 2009. *La guerra sucia en México y el papel del Poder Legislativo: Comparativo internacional.* Centro de Producción Editorial de la Cámara de Diputados del H. Congreso de la Unión.

Zepeda Gil, Raúl. 2018. "Seven Explanatory Approaches about the Increasing of Violence in Mexico." *Política y gobierno* 25 (1): 185–211.

Zerega, Georgina. 2024. "Activistas hallan un supuesto crematorio clandestino con restos óseos en Ciudad de México." *El País*, April 30. https://elpais.com/mexico/2024 -05-01/activistas-hallan-un-crematorio-clandestino-con-supuestos-restos-humanos -en-ciudad-de-mexico.html.

Index

addiction, 109–11, 174n34

Agrupación de Familiares de Detenidos Desaparecidos, 163n21

Aguayo, Sergio, 85

Allende case, 61–62, 64–65

ambiguous loss, 36, 38–39

amnesty: abortion and, 139, 177–78n22; Athenian amnesty and, 178n30; Cedillista Rebellion and, 178n35; compassion and, 133–35, 139, 141–42, 150; concerns of, 140, 150; contradiction of, 141–42; crimes of, 148; Cristero movement and, 145; definition of, 177n2; Dirty War and, 134–35, 146–47; guerrilla groups and, 146–51; Indigenous peoples and, 133–34, 141–42; legitimacy and, 147; mercy and, 176n1; motivations of, 143–44; political crimes and, 134; "preliberation" and, 178n23; prudential model of, 144–45; results of, 140–41; self-amnesty and, 178n29; target population of, 139–40; transitional justice and, 146; War on Drugs and, 135, 146–47; women and, 133–34

Amnesty International, 179n39

anexos, 111–12

Aquinas, Thomas, 150

Arendt, Hannah, 34

Aristotle, 136, 177n4

Astorga, Luis, 116

atrocity, 125–27

Austin, J. L., 102

Ávila Camacho, Manuel, 178n35

Aviña, Alexander, 146–47

Aylwin, Patricio, 163n21

Ayotzinapa students: collaborators and, 53, 168n35; El Chereje and, 30; El Güero Mugres and, 25; El Patrón and, 30; Enrique Peña Nieto and, 24–25; Gildardo N. and, 24–25, 56; Guerreros Unidos and, 24–25; investigation into, 25–26, 30; Jesús Murillo Karam and, 24–25; Omar Gómez Trejo, 164n29

Azaola, Elena, 83

Barrio Azteca, 113

Bayardo del Villar, Edgar Enrique, 57–59, 168n43

Beaumont, Gustave, 171n33
Bellaby, Ross, 50
Beltrán Leyva cartel, 168n30
Bentham, Jeremy, 72–73
Bergman, Marcelo, 75, 170n22
Birkbeck, 78
Blustein, Jeffrey, 36
Boss, Pauline, 36
Brettschneider, Corey, 77–78

Caballeros Templarios, 117, 126–27
Calderón, Felipe, and Felipe Calderón
    administration; children and, 124;
    collaborators and, 53; criminal or-
    ganizations and, 14; disappearances
    and, 18–9; drug trafficking and, 116;
    Genaro García Luna and, 171n58;
    Mexican prisons and, 96; Osiel Cárde-
    nas and, 57; retributivism and, 91
Calles, Plutarco Elías, 145–46
Capella, Alberto, 167n24
Card, Claudia, 118–19
Cárdenas, Lázaro, and Lázaro Cárdenas
    administration, 149
Cárdenas, Osiel, 57
Carter, Jimmy, and Jimmy Carter admin-
    istration, 60
Catholic Church, the, 145–46
Catholic Partido Acción Nacional (PAN).
    See PAN (Catholic Partido Acción
    National)
CEFERESO (Federal Centers for Social
    Readaptation), 85–89
CMP (Committee for Missing Persons),
    27
"Code of the Knights Templar of Micho-
    acán," 117
Colectivo de Familiares Unidos de Desa-
    parecidos de Jalisco, 35
Colinas de Santa Fe, 22–23
collaborators: Alberto Capella and,
    167n24; Allende case and, 61–62, 64–
    65; Andrés Manuel López Obrador,

and López Obrador administration
    and, 53; Ayotzinapa students and, 53,
    168n35; Bayardo and, 57–59; counter-
    narcotics strategy and, 55; DEA and,
    60–61; Enrique Peña Nieto and, 53;
    Felipe Calderón and, 53; Genaro García
    Luna and, 54; Guerreros Unidos and,
    168n42; human rights framework and,
    53–54; intelligence operations and, 52–
    53; Javier Herrera and, 54; legal ground-
    ing of, 53; moral permissibility of,
    47–49; penal benefits and, 56; principle
    of necessity and, 54–55; principle of
    proportionality and, 55–60; protection
    of, 57–58, 168n40; retaliation against,
    50; Richard Lippke and, 59; rights of,
    48–49; socioeconomic statuses of, 57–
    58; Venus and, 57–59; Vicente Fox and,
    53; Zetas and, 64
Colombian Congress, 162–63n21
Committee for Missing Persons (CMP).
    See CMP (Committee for Missing
    Persons)
Committee for the Defense of Persecuted,
    Disappeared, and Political Exiles of
    Mexico, 179n39
communicative theory of punishment,
    92, 171n62, 172n69. See also retributive
    theory of punishment
compassion, 133–37, 139, 141–42, 150
consequentialist theories of punishment,
    68, 72–73
COVID pandemic, 178n23
criminal gangs, 113–4, 174–75n48
criminal justice system: amnesty and,
    137–44, 145, 146–48; Andrés Manuel
    López Obrador, and López Obrador
    administration and, 137–38, 142;
    compassion and, 136–37; legitimacy
    and, 67, 69–70, 76, 78, 80, 90, 93–96;
    marginalized populations and, 137–38;
    military intervention and, 142; puni-
    tive character of, 137–38

criminal organizations: addiction and, 110; atrocity and, 125–26; autonomy and, 122–24; children and, 175–76nn81–82; collective trajectory and, 108; deceptive digital recruitment and, 119; dehumanization and, 126; deindividuation and, 125; drug use and, 106–7; exculpation and, 108; families and, 107; gender norms and, 122–23; group connectedness and, 108–9; intra-individuation and, 125–26; narcoculture and, 116; persuasive digital recruitment and, 119; recruiters of, 108; regionalization and, 106; self-defense and, 113, 123–24; social media and, 119–21; the state and, 128–29; traditional media and, 119–20; women and, 121–24; youth and, 107–8

Cristero movement, 145–46

Davis, Angela Y., 5, 82
Dayán, Jacobo, 85
DEA (Drug Enforcement Administration), 60–66, 168n43
Dirty War, 134–35, 146–48, 151, 179n38
disappearances: ambiguous loss and, 36, 38; Andrés Manuel López Obrador, and López Obrador administration and, 34; Claudio Lomnitz and, 34; Colectivo de Familiares Unidos de Desaparecidos de Jalisco and, 35; disenfranchised grief and, 37; Felipe Calderón, and Calderon administration, 18–19; Hannah Arendt and, 34; human rights framework and, 162n12; interpersonal level of, 33, 36–38; Jeffrey Blustein and, 36; *madres buscadoras* and, 26; Nuevo León and, 22; personal level of, 33, 38–39; political level of, 33–36; San Fernando, Tamaulipas and, 21; self-respect and, 36, 38; SEMEFOS and, 19, 34, 35; stigma of, 36–38

disenfranchised grief, 37
Domitila, 141
Donelson, Raff, 96
Drug Enforcement Administration (DEA). See DEA (Drug Enforcement Administration)
drug use, 106–7
Duff, Anthony, 92, 172n69
Durkheim, Émile, 174n22

El Chapo, 76, 113, 155
El Chereje, 30
El Güero Mugres, 25
El Mayo, 155
El Patrón, 30
El Ponchis, 124
Eldredge, John, 117–18
Escalante, Fernando, 43
ethnographic sensibility, 12
Ewing, Benjamin, 172n2
exculpation: addiction and, 109–11; children and, 124–25; coerced actor and, 173n12; criminal organizations and, 108; deceptive digital recruitment and, 119; definition of, 102; duress and, 102–3; Erin Kelly and, 104; fairness and, 104; forced recruitment and, 105; insanity and, 102; J. L. Austin and, 102; mitigation and, 103–4, 173n18; social background and, 103–5, 173n15; soft recruitment and, 105; women and, 121–24
expressivist theory of punishment, 91–93, 171n62, 172n69. See also retributive theory of punishment

Familia Michoacana, 117
FARC guerrilla group, 166n66
Federal Centers for Social Readaptation (CEFERESO), 16. See CEFERESO (Federal Centers for Social Readaptation)
Federal Law against Organized Crime, 23–24, 53, 167nn25–26

Federal Law for the Protection of Individuals Who Intervene in Criminal Proceedings, 53
Fondevila, Gustavo, 54–55, 75, 170n22
Foot, Philippa, 65
Ford, Gerald, and Gerald Ford administration, 60
Forensic Identification Mechanism, 20
Forensic Medical Services (SEMEFOS). *See* SEMEFOS (Forensic Medical Services)
forensic principle, 28–29, 31–34, 40
forensic truth: definition of, 18; immunity and, 27; instrumental reasons for, 29; Iosif Kovras and, 18; noninstrumental reasons for, 32; penal awards and, 40; process of, 21; proportionate punishment and, 18
Fox, Vicente, and Fox administration, 14, 53

García, Angela, 111
García Luna, Genaro, 54, 171n58
General Law of Enforced Disappearance of Persons, 24
Gildardo N., 24–25, 56
Gómez Trejo, Omar, 164n29
Grillo, Ioan, 114
Guerrero, Jhosivani, 25–26
Guerreros Unidos, 24–25, 30, 167n24, 168n42
guerrilla groups, 146–51
Gulf Cartel, 21
Guzmán, El Chapo. *See* El Chapo

halconeo/halcones, 1–3, 5, 161n1
Hampton, Jean, 93
Herrera, Javier, 54
Herzog, Lisa, 12
Hobbes, Thomas, 77, 87–88, 97–98, 129
Hollander, Theo, 37
Hoskins, Zachary, 172n69

human rights framework, 53–54, 162n12
hybrid theories of punishment, 91

Ibarra de la Piedra, Rosario, 151
institutionalization, 44
instrumentalist theories of punishment. *See* consequentialist theories of punishment
International Commission for the Location of Victims' Remains, 162n7
Irish Republican Army, 162n7, 165n59

Jalisco Nueva Generación, 99, 119–20, 126–27
Jimenez Lugo, Edgar. *See* El Ponchis
Juárez, Benito, 144–45
just intelligence theory, 50–52, 54–57
just war theory, 50
justification: children and, 124; coerced actor and, 173n12; criminal responsibility and, 118; definition of, 102; duress and, 103; J. L. Austin and, 102; mitigation and, 103–4, 173n18; moral responsibility and, 118; self-defense and, 102, 113; the state and, 128–29; women and, 121–24

Kant, Immanuel, 164n38
Kelly, Erin, 5, 104
Knights Templar, 111–12, 114, 117–18
Kovras, Iosif, 18

La Familia Michoacana, 111–12, 126–27
Law of Disappearance, 20
Lazar, Seth, 51
LC23S, 150–51
Lecumberri palace, 70–71
legitimacy: criminal justice system and, 67, 69–70, 76, 78, 80, 90, 93–96; Mexican prisons and, 69, 76, 78, 80, 95–96
Lerdo de Tejeda, Sebastián, 144–45
Levi, Primo, 118–19

Leviathan (Hobbes), 77, 97–98

Lippke, Richard, 45, 59, 166n74

Lomnitz, Claudio, 34, 112, 117, 127, 176n90

López Obrador, Andrés Manuel, and López Obrador administration: 2020 amnesty and, 133; children and, 124, 175–76n81; collaborators and, 53; criminal justice system and, 137–38, 142; disappearances and, 19, 24; military intervention and, 142; National Development Plan of 2019–24, 139; penal benefits and, 24; principled leniency and, 156

López Portillo, José, and José López Portillo administration, 147, 149–50

Los Artistas Asesinos, 113

Los Ciclones del Cartel del Golfo, 23

Los Mexicles, 113

Lovett, Frank, 79

Macaulay, Fiona, 74

Macnish, Kevin, 52

madres buscadoras, 22–23, 26

Malverde, Jesús, 120

Martínez, Robert, 61–62

mass incarceration, 5

Melchor, Fernanda, 67–68

Mendoza, Natalia, 1

mercy, 136–37, 176n1, 177n4, 177n7

Merton, Robert K., 174n22

Miller, Arthur, 70–71, 170n8

Moore, Michael S., 164n38

Moreno El Chayo, Nazario, 112

Murillo Karam, Jesús, 24–26, 163n24

Murphy, Colleen, 28

mutual respect, 32–34, 40–41

narcoculture, 116, 118–19, 129–30

narcomantas, 23

narcotraficantes, 161n8

National Center for Human Identification, 20

National Human Rights Commission, 30, 72, 79–80, 82, 86–87

National Movement for Our Disappeared, 20

National Registry of Data on Missing and Disappeared Persons, 19

National Search Commission, 19, 20

Nazi regime, 115

Nozick, Robert, 38

Nuevo León, 22

Nussbaum, Martha, 32

Obregón, Álvaro, 145–46

Operación Limpieza, 168n30

PAN (Catholic Partido Acción National), 149–50

Partido Auténtico de la Revolución Mexicana, 149–50

Partido de la Revolución Democrática (PRD). *See* PRD (Partido de la Revolución Democrática

Partido Popular Socialista (PPS). *See* PPS (Partido Popular Socialista)

Partido Revolucionario Institucional (PRI). *See* PRI (Partido Revolucionario Institucional)

Partido Socialista Unificado de México (PSUM). *See* PSUM (Partido Socialista Unificado de México)

PEN International, 70, 170n8

Peña Nieto, Enrique, and Peña Nieto administration, 24–25, 30, 53, 124, 175–76n81

penal benefits: Andrés Manuel López Obrador, and López Obrador administration and, 24; collaborators and, 56; Colleen Murphy and, 28; Federal Law against Organized Crime and, 23–24; General Law of Enforced Disappearance of Persons and, 24; institutionalization of, 44; moral

penal benefits (*cont.*)
  acceptability of, 44–45; mutual respect
  and, 41; perpetrator self-interest and,
  45; perverse incentives and, 44; political violence objection to, 40–43; prosecutorial flexibility and, 43; relatives of
  the disappeared and, 45–46; Richard
  Lippke and, 45, 166n74; self-respect
  and, 42, 45; severity of punishment
  and, 41–42; support for, 41–42
Penal Code of Tamaulipas, 2
Peniche Bolio, Francisco J., 150
Piedras Negras prison, 76, 83–85
Pinochet dictatorship, 163n21
Plan Colombia, 15
plea bargains, 49–50, 166n7
Portes Gil, Emilio, and Emilio Portes Gil
  administration, 145–46, 149
PPS (Partido Popular Socialista), 149–50
PRD (Partido de la Revolución Democratica. *See* Partido de la Revolución
  Democratica (PRD)
PRI (Partido Revolucionario Institucional), 15, 149–50
Primeiro Comando da Capital, 74–75
principle of discrimination, 50
principle of necessity, 50–51, 54–55, 62–
  63, 65–66
principle of proportionality, 50–53,
  55–66
principled leniency, 3, 5, 6
prisons, American, 73–74, 78
prisons, Latin American, 73–74, 78
prisons, Mexican: domination and, 79;
  exploitation and, 79, 80–83; Felipe
  Calderón and, 96; governance of, 74;
  internment and, 78–79; intimate visits
  and, 81; legitimacy and, 69, 76, 78,
  80, 95–96; mass incarceration and,
  95–96; reformation of, 154; statistics
  of, 72, 95, 170n21; systems of, 73–74,
  170n12; *Proceso*, 179n39; proportionate

punishment, 18, 29–32; proportionate punishment principle, 28–33, 40;
  PSUM (Partido Socialista Unificado
  de México), 151

Rawls, John, 32, 36, 164n43
Reclusorio Norte, 80
recruitment, 105
Reflections of the Familia, 117
Revueltas, José, 70–71, 73, 170n7
responsibility, criminal, 101–2, 118
responsibility, moral, 101–2, 106, 109, 118,
  172–73n7. *See also* exculpation; justification
Reta, Rosalío, Jr., 124
retributive theory of punishment, 68, 90–
  91, 93–95, 128. *See also* communicative
  theory of punishment; expressivist
  theory of punishment
Reyes Heroles, Jesús, 148–49
Rodríguez, Christian, 25–26

Salas Obregón, Ignacio, 150–51
San Fernando, Tamaulipas, 21
Sánchez Cordero, Olga, 138–39
Santa Martha Acatitla, 82
Scanlon, Thomas, 90–91
Schmitt, Carl, 143–44, 178n32
Sebastiana, 138–39
self-defense groups. *See* vigilante groups
self-respect, 32–33, 36–40, 42, 45
SEMEFOS (Forensic Medical Services),
  19, 34–35
Seneca, 136
Shelby, Thomas, 5
Shelby, Tommie, 169n1
sicarios, 5
Sinaloa cartel, 58, 126–27
Slim, Carlos, 88
social media, 119–21
social norms, 106, 174n22
Solecito, 163n24

Soyinka, Wole, 170n8
state, the: complicity of, 128; criminal organizations and, 128–29, 156; epistemic infirmity of, 129; justification and, 128; legal culpability and, 130; legal equality and, 128; "macrocriminality" and, 130–31; moral authority of, 129; moral dilemma of, 128; narcoculture and, 129–30; negotiations and, 156; political infirmity of, 128–29; welfarist infirmity of, 127–28
Su, Yang, 115

Tadros, 164n38
Tasioulas, John, 136
"testigo Juan." *See* Gildardo N.
testigos colaboradores. See collaborators
Tigre. *See* Bayardo del Villar, Edgar Enrique
Tocqueville, Alexis de, 171n33
Topo Chico prison, 83–84, 171n35
Treviño brothers, 61–62

Valverde, Jesús, 116
Vatican, the, 145–46
Vázquez, José, 61–62
Venus, 57–59
vigilante groups, 114
Vrousalis, Nicholas, 80

War on Drugs, 135, 146–47, 177n12
Wild at Heart, 117–18

Zacka, Bernado, 12
Zambada, Ismael El Mayo. *See* El Mayo
Zetas: Allende case and, 61–62; Apodaca prison riot and, 76; background of, 61; business activities of, 61; Caballeros Templarios and, 117; collaborators and, 64; crimes of, 21; Familia Michoacana and, 117; Gulf Cartel and, 21; Piedras Negras prison and, 76, 83–85; Topo Chico prison and, 83–84; Treviño brothers and, 61–62; Venus and, 57

THE CULTURAL LIVES OF LAW
Austin Sarat, Editor

The Cultural Lives of Law series brings insights and approaches from cultural studies to law and tries to secure for law a place in cultural analysis. Books in the series focus on the production, interpretation, consumption, and circulation of legal meanings. They take up the challenges posed as boundaries collapse between as well as within cultures, and as the circulation of legal meanings becomes more fluid. They also attend to the ways law's power in cultural production is renewed and resisted.

Jessica Lake, *Special Damage: The Slander of Women and the Gendered History of Defamation Law*
2026

Marie-Eve Loiselle, *Building Walls, Constructing Identities: Legal Discourse and the Creation of National Borders*
2025

Joseph Mello, *Pot for Profit: Cannabis Legalization, Racial Capitalism, and the Expansion of the Carceral State*
2024

Chloé Deambrogio, *Judging Insanity, Punishing Difference: A History of Mental Illness in the Criminal Court*
2024

Daniel LaChance and Paul Kaplan, *Crimesploitation: Crime, Punishment, and Pleasure on Reality Television*
2022

Nesam McMillan, *Imagining the International: Crime, Justice, and the Promise of Community*
2020

Jeffrey R. Dudas, *Raised Right: Fatherhood in Modern American Conservatism*
2017

Renée Ann Cramer, *Pregnant with the Stars: Watching and Wanting the Celebrity Baby Bump*
2015

Sora Y. Han, *Letters of the Law: Race and the Fantasy of Colorblindness*
2015

Marianne Constable, *Our Word Is Our Bond: How Legal Speech Acts*
2014

Joshua C. Wilson, *The Street Politics of Abortion:
Speech, Violence, and America's Culture Wars*
2013

Irus Braverman, *Zooland: The Institution of Captivity*
2012

Nora Gilbert, *Better Left Unsaid: Victorian Novels, Hays
Code Films, and the Benefits of Censorship*
2012

Edited by Winnifred Fallers Sullivan, Robert A. Yelle,
and Mateo Taussig-Rubbo, *After Secular Law*
2011

Keith J. Bybee, *All Judges Are Political—Except When They
Are Not: Acceptable Hypocrisies and the Rule of Law*
2010

Susan Sage Heinzelman, *Riding the Black Ram: Law, Literature, and Gender*
2010

David M. Engel and Jaruwan S. Engel, *Tort, Custom, and Karma:
Globalization and Legal Consciousness in Thailand*
2010

Ruth A. Miller, *Law in Crisis: The Ecstatic Subject of Natural Disaster*
2009

Ravit Reichman, *The Affective Life of Law: Legal
Modernism and the Literary Imagination*
2009

*For a complete listing of titles in this series, visit
the Stanford University Press website, www.sup.org.*

The authorized representative in the EU for product safety and compliance is:
Mare Nostrum Group
B.V Doelen 72
4831 GR Breda
The Netherlands

www.ingramcontent.com/pod-product-compliance
Lightning Source LLC
Chambersburg PA
CBHW030820270326
41928CB00007B/820